Climbing and Exploring Utah's
Mt. Timpanogos

Also Featuring History of Provo & American Fork Canyons, Sundance,
Heber Creeper, Timp Hike, Timp Cave, Airplane Crashes, Hiking Deaths, &
Rocky Mtn. Goats and Geology

Michael R. Kelsey

Kelsey Publishing
456 E. 100 N.
Provo, Utah, USA, 84606
Tele. 1-801-373-3327

First Edition May 1989
Copyright © 1989   Michael R. Kelsey   All Rights Reserved
Library of Congress Number 88-082306
ISBN 0-944510-00-0

Distributors for the Kelsey Publishing
Please write to one of these companies when ordering any of Michael R. Kelsey's guide books. A list of his titles is in the back of this book.

Primary Distributor All books available at this Distributor.
Wasatch Book Distribution, P.O. Box 1108, Salt Lake City, Utah, USA, 84110, Tele. 801-575-6735.

Some of Kelsey's books are carried by each of these companies:
Alpenbooks, P.O. Box 27344, Seattle, Washington, 98125, Tele. 206-672-9316
Bookpeople, 2929 Fifth Street, Berkeley, California, 94710, Tele. 227-1516
Canyon Country Publications, P. O. Box 963, Moab, Utah, 84532, Tele. 801-259-6700
Gordon's Books, 2323 Delgany, Denver, Colorado, 80216, Tele. 303-296-1830
Many Feathers, 2626 West, Indian School Road, Phoenix, Arizona, 85012, Tele. 602-266-1043
Nevada Publications, 4135 Badger Circle, Reno, Nevada, 89509, Tele. 702-747-0800
Northern Arizona News Co., 1709 East Street, Flagstaff, Arizona, 86001, 602-774-6171
Pacific Pipeline, 19215 66th Avenue S., Kent, Washington, 98032-1171, Tele. 206-872-5523
Quality Books(Library Distributor), 918 Sherwood Drive, Lake Bluff, Illinois, 60044, Tele.
Mountain 'n Air Books, 3704 1/2 Foothill Blvd., La Crescenta, California, 91214, Tele. 818-957-5338
Recreational Equipment, Inc.(R.E.I.), P.O. Box C-88126, Seattle, Washington, 98188, Tele. 800-426-4840(or check at any of their local stores).

For the UK and Europe, and the rest of the world contact:
CORDEE, 3a De Montfort Street, Leicester, England, UK, LE1 7HD, Tele. 0533-54379

Printed by Press Publishing, 1600 West, 800 North, Provo, Utah.

All fotos by the author, unless otherwise stated.
All maps, charts, and cross sections drawn by the author.

Front Cover
1. Rocky Mountain Goat on Timp's Summit Ridge.
2. B-25 airplane motor in the Timpanogos Basin.
3. Emerald Lake Shelter and Timp Glacier.
4. Looking west at the summit of Timp in winter.

Back Cover
5. Sundance Ski Resort with Timp's Second & Southeast Summits.
6. Flowers in the Flower Garden and the Timp Glacier behind.
7. Emerald Lake Shelter with summit behind.
8. On Razorback Ridge with summit to the upper right.
9. Near Emerald Lake, with summit in the background.
10. The North Slopes of North Peak, seen from Tibble Fork Reservoir.

Table of Contents

Acknowledgments

There were many people who helped to put this book together, but special thanks should go to the following. Many of these people were interviewed by telefone only. The man who led the author to numerous interesting stories or events on or around the mountain was Joe Hilton of Pleasant Grove. The author first met Joe near the head of Grove Creek Canyon where he was doing voluntary work on the trail.

After beginning with Joe Hilton, the author got help from Forest Service employee Steve Winslow of the Pleasant Grove Forest Service office. Steve read the entire rough draft, while Malissa Ashbridge read parts of it. Paul Skablund of the Provo Uinta National Forest Service office was also helpful. Scott Isaacson and Mike Hill of Timpanogos Cave National Monument read the section on Timpanogos Cave. Eldon Johnson knew more than anyone about the later mining years in upper American Fork Canyon.

Much of the history of the Sundance area was supplied by Justin Stewart. At the time this book goes to press, he was just finishing a book about the History of Sundance. He allowed the author to quote some passages before it was published. Raymond and S. Paul Stewart also contributed to the history of Timp Haven Ski Resort and Sundance. Brent Beck, Terry Minger and Shelley Weiss helped to get some of the later history of Sundance right.

Much of the history of Provo Canyon came by way of Carol Bartlett Hoover and husband Mark Hoover; also Bert Bullock, Wayne C. Close, Richard Taylor, Ruth Kartchner and Bertha Offret McKean. Ray Crandall and Dave Grow were interviewed concerning the history, building and development of the Bridal Veil Falls Resort and Skytram. Lowe Ashton helped to clarify some of the recent history of the Heber Creeper.

Wes Walker of Pleasant Grove gave information about the trenching or terracing of the mountain sides along the Wasatch Front and of the removal of the penstock of the Battle Creek Power Station. Grant Fugal knew the history of the new culinary pipeline down Battle Creek Canyon and the construction of the new Letter "G" east of Pleasant Grove. Ora Thorne contributed details on the building of the first Letter "G". At 94 years of age, Eleroy R. West has an excellent mind, and shared some of his experiences of 1921 and 1922, when he was involved in the building of the Timpooneke, Aspen Grove and Timp Cave Trails. Garrett Davis helped with the history of Mutual Dell.

Jim Walker and Don Devey, along with Joe and Robert Hilton, shared their knowledge about the B-25 crash. Arlo Shelley contributed information about various subjects and also proof-read the entire rough draft. Effie Adams and Reed Warnick helped solved the problem of when the "Glass House" was first constructed on the summit of Timp. Eva Proctor's good mind at age 87 remembered many details of the Battle Creek Power Station and her home at the top of the penstock. Robert Hilton also shared information about the same power station.

Jerry Scott and Chris Reed identified where they and others dynamited the *killer snow holes* along the Aspen Grove Trail following several deaths. The self-published diary of former Sheriff Mack Holley was extremely helpful in finding many of the accidents and tragedies on the mountain. Wayne Barnes had many details about the recent history of Olmsted Power Plant, and Vic Oldroyd and Dave Eagar filled in some gaps on recent events in Provo Canyon. Grant Jense supplied information on the Mt. Timpanogos Rocky Mountain Goat herd

The Author

The author experienced his earliest years of life in eastern Utah's Uinta Basin, namely around the town of Roosevelt. Then the family moved to Provo, where he attended Provo High School, and later Brigham Young University, where he earned a B.S. degree in Sociology. Shortly thereafter he discovered that was the wrong subject, so he attended the University of Utah, where he received his Masters of Science degree in Geography, finishing that in June, 1970.

It was then real life began, for on June 9, 1970, he put a pack on his back and started traveling for the first time. Since then he has seen 130 countries and island groups. All this wandering has resulted in several books written and published by himself: Climbers and Hikers Guide to the World's Mountains(Out of print--3rd Ed. due in 1990); Utah Mountaineering Guide, and the Best Canyon Hikes(2nd Ed.); China on Your Own and the Hiking Guide to China's Nine Sacred Mountains(3rd Ed.); Canyon Hiking Guide to the Colorado Plateau(2nd printing); Hiking Utah's San Rafael Swell; Hiking and Exploring Utah's Henry Mountains and Robbers Roost; Hiking and Exploring the Paria River; Hiking and Climbing in the Great Basin National Park(Wheeler Peak, Nevada), and Boater's Guide to Lake Powell--Featuring Hiking, Camping, Geology, History and Archaeology.

Metric Conversion Table

1 Centimeter = 0.39 Inch	1 Mile = 1.609 Kilometers	1 Pound = 453 Grams
1 Inch = 2.54 Centimeters	100 Miles = 161 Kilometers	1 Quart(US) = 0.946 Liter
1 Meter = 39.37 Inches	100 Kilometers = 62.1 Miles	1 Gallon(US) = 3.785 Liters
1 Foot = 0.3048 Meter	1 Liter = 1.056 Quarts(US)	1 Acre = 0.405 Hectare
1 Kilometer = 0.621 Mile	1 Kilogram = 2.205 Pounds	1 Hectare = 2.471 Acres

METERS TO FEET (Meters x 3.2808 = Feet)

100 m = 328 ft.	2500 m = 8202 ft.	5000 m = 16404 ft.	7500 m = 24606 ft.
500 m = 1640 ft.	3000 m = 9842 ft.	5500 m = 18044 ft.	8000 m = 26246 ft.
1000 m = 3281 ft.	3500 m = 11483 ft.	6000 m = 19686 ft.	8500 m = 27887 ft.
1500 m = 4921 ft.	4000 m = 13124 ft.	6500 m = 21325 ft.	9000 m = 29527 ft.
2000 m = 6562 ft.	4500 m = 14764 ft.	7000 m = 22966 ft.	

FEET TO METERS (Feet ÷ 3.2808 = Meters)

1000 ft. = 305 m	9000 ft. = 2743 m	16000 ft. = 4877 m	23000 ft. = 7010 m
2000 ft. = 610 m	10000 ft. = 3048 m	17000 ft. = 5182 m	24000 ft. = 7315 m
3000 ft. = 914 m	11000 ft. = 3353 m	18000 ft. = 5486 m	25000 ft. = 7620 m
4000 ft. = 1219 m	12000 ft. = 3658 m	19000 ft. = 5791 m	26000 ft. = 7925 m
5000 ft. = 1524 m	13000 ft. = 3962 m	20000 ft. = 6096 m	27000 ft. = 8230 m
6000 ft. = 1829 m	14000 ft. = 4268 m	21000 ft. = 6401 m	28000 ft. = 8535 m
7000 ft. = 2134 m	15000 ft. = 4572 m	22000 ft. = 6706 m	29000 ft. = 8839 m
8000 ft. = 2438 m			30000 ft. = 9144 m

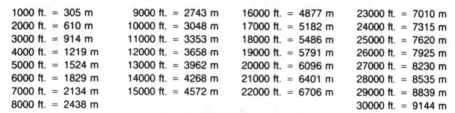

CENTIMETERS / INCHES

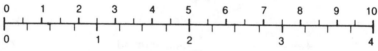

METERS / FEET

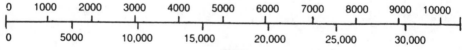

KILOMETERS / MILES

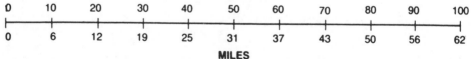

FAHRENHEIT / CENTIGRADE

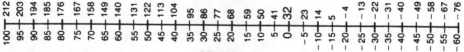

MAP SYMBOLS

Campsite	△	Route--No Trail	•.•
Timp Shelter or Summit Hut	▲	Peak & Prominent Ridge	✕
Community or Home	▢▫	Escarpment	
Forest Service Campground		Stream or Creek	
Visitor Center(NPS)		Waterfall or Dryfall	✕
Ranger Station		Dry Creek	
Lodge	⬆	Spring	o
Highway or Paved Road		Mine Adit or Prospect	↖↗
Dirt or Gravel Road		Lake or Pond	
Trailhead Parking	Ⓟ	Icefield or Glacier	
Trail		Timp Wilderness Area	
Pass	≍	Elevation in Meters	3573

ABBREVIATIONS

Canyon	C.	Peak	Pk.
Lake	L.	Campground	CG.
River	R.	Four Wheel Drive	4WD
Creek	Ck.	Spring	Sp.
Kilometer(s)	km(s)		

Part I--Introduction to Hiking and Climbing Mt. Timpanogos

Mt. Timpanogos is located in north central Utah, due north of Provo and southeast of Salt Lake City, in the Wasatch Mountains. Local people in Utah Valley call it **Timp** for short, which is the name most used in this book. Timp is the second highest mountain in the Wasatch Range at 3581 meters. Only Mt. Nebo to the south is higher.

The name Timpanogos comes to us from the diary kept by the Dominguez and Escalante Expedition, which came through Utah Valley in September of 1776. The expedition started in Santa Fe, New Mexico. The group was looking for a northern route to other Spanish colonies in California. During the last days of September, the expedition camped for several days in Utah Valley and along the lower Provo River, which they called the *Rio de San Antonio de Padua*. The Spaniards called the people living around Utah Lake the *Luguna Indians,* but the Indians in the area called themselves the *Timpanogotzis.* The Spaniards then called Utah Lake, *Lago Timpanogo,* and the mountain above, *La Sierra Blanca de Los Timpanois.* This is interpreted into English as *White Mountain of the Timpanogos Indians.* Since it was late September, the mountain must have had some fresh snow on the summit to have gotten this name.

Because Timpanogos is the highest and most dominant mountain surrounding Utah Valley, it has long been a landmark for local residents. Because of its physical setting, that of running northwest to southeast, it is the only mountain in Utah which has a glacier. For the most part it's not a true glacier-- just a large perpetual snow or ice field, but it does have some small bergschrunds. These are small crevasses which develop between the upper-most part of the ice and the mountain's headwall. However, these bergschrunds are insignificant and are normally incapable of swallowing hikers.

The mountain has about a dozen peaks or summits and 7 major upper basins or cirques. Running from northwest to southeast these basins are called: **Woolly Hole, Pica Cirque, Timpanogos Basin, Glacier Cirque, Hidden Lakes Cirque, Cascade Cirque,** and the **Big Provo Hole.** Each of these upper basins was formed by Pleistocene glaciation prior to about 10,000 years ago. Except for the last remaining snowfield in the Glacier Cirque, all are now covered with a lush green carpet of grasses and flowers(in most years there are small year-round icefields in the shaded areas of Cascade Cirque, the Timp Basin and in Pica Cirque). One of the major reasons for the popularity of this mountain are these high altitude mountain bowls.

Because of the beauty of the mountain there evolved in Utah Valley, a small group of outdoor people who went to the mountain during the summer season. Many of these enthusiasts were associated with Brigham Young University. As time went on, one of the coaches at the school by the name of Eugene Lusk Roberts, began taking groups up the mountain each summer. This tradition began in 1912 and immediately became known as the **Annual Timp Hike.**

History of the Annual Timp Hike

In was in the summer of 1912 when a group of 19 college students and teachers made it to the summit of Mt. Timpanogos. That was to be the first of 59 annual pilgrimages to the top of one of the prettiest mountains in the world. This hike was held at about the same time each year, always from mid to late July or in early August. The annual event lasted until 1970, when it was discontinued. The reason for its demise was because there were so many people on the mountain on one single day each year, it was creating an ecological nightmare.

The man who organized the first hike and later the annual event was Eugene Lusk Roberts, otherwise known as **Gene "Timp" Roberts.** Gene was born in Provo in 1880, and grew up exploring the mountains east of town. He later attended BYU, where he became a campus journalist for the college newspaper. Roberts participated in gymnastics and was the quarterback for the football team. He was a popular student and was elected president of his senior class in 1904.

To get through school he had to teach part-time to earn a living. He first taught at Franklin Elementary in Provo. Later he got married and was sent to Europe on a church mission where he had a chance to do some mountaineering in the Alps. Still later he worked at Yale University for one year in

A 1920's foto of Gene "Timp" Roberts and his wife on the glacier(BYU foto archives).

the Physical Education Department, but was then recruited by BYU to become the Director of Athletics, and to coach. Besides being Athletic Director, he coached football, basketball, track and gymnastics.

While living in Provo, he coached two world champion high jumpers, Alma Richards and Clinton Larson. Richards won the Olympic Gold Metal at the 1912 Stockholm Games, with a jump of 193 cms(6' 4"). In 1920, Gene organized the BYU Invitational Track Meet for high school students, a tradition continuing to this day.

After about 18 years at BYU, he was recruited by the University of Southern California. While there he became an Associate Professor in the school of Physical Education and Athletics. He retired in 1945 and returned to Provo, where he died on July 9, 1953 at the age of 73. Throughout the years, he was always known as **Timp Roberts.** There is one peak on the mountain which bears his name today. That's **Roberts Horn** just north of Emerald Lake.

Going back now to the **Annual Timp Hike.** On that first hike in 1912, the group of 19 hikers traveled to Provo Canyon in buggies and wagons, but they had to walk to what would later be known as Aspen Grove. The wagons slowly made it up the old sawmill drag road between Wildwood and Stewart's Flat(where Sundance is now located). They camped at the grove Friday night, and spent the entire next day reaching the summit of Timp. They stayed a second night at Aspen Grove and returned home Sunday.

In 1913, Roberts took another group of 56 hikers up the mountain which was the real beginning of the annual affair. In that year they had a camp fire program on Friday night attended by a total of 62 people. That Friday night event set the tone for the Timp Hike for years to come. As years went by there began some long time traditions such as having a large bonfire and fireworks. They later began giving out walking sticks, or *Timp Sticks,* to distinguished guests and to the oldest people attending the program.

Here's an excerpt from the July 24, 1913 Provo Post newspaper. *Sixty-two hikers, including B.Y.U. summer school students, teachers and prominent Provo citizens, bent on scaling Mt. Timpanogos, pitched camp last Friday evening at 7 o'clock in the quaking aspen grove up North Fork, just under the first of a series of beautiful waterfalls leading to the top of the big mountain. These mountain climbers had walked from Wildwood, a distance of four miles[actually about 8 kms], while their bedding and provisions were tugged along an almost impassable road in a heavy wagon drawn by six horses. For convenience of camping and cooking the company was organized into six divisions, each group having a captain......*

At 5 o'clock Saturday morning breakfast was spread and at 6 o'clock fifty-seven climbers were on the way up the mountain. The company kept all together in one long, zig-zagging and serpentine line, until at 11 o'clock all were seated safely on the banks of "Emerald Lake", devouring their lunch with unusual relish. After but an hour's rest the climb was made up the glaciers back to the saddle where the first glimpse of Utah Valley was had. From there many scaled the highest peaks, some of them nearly 12,000 feet[3581 meters] above sea level, and explored every point along the mountain's rugged back[56 made it to the top].

During the first 8 or 9 years of the event, the normal way of getting to the mountain was to first take the train from Provo to Wildwood. Most participants got on the train at the station nearest campus, which was the Smoot Station. It was located between 6th and 7th North and 200 West, about where the Storehouse Market is today. As stated above, at Wildwood, all tents, food and sleeping blankets were put into wagons drawn by horses. The hikers walked the 8 kms from Wildwood to Aspen Grove. The wagon teams and much of the camping and cooking arrangements were organized by Timp Roberts and BYU, since they were the guiding force behind those early hikes.

Much of the information about the annual hike comes from the newspaper of the day, the Provo Post, then the Provo Herald and a bit later, the Daily Herald. The article written after the trek in 1914, stated there were 152 hikers who made the summit, or at least to the Glacier Saddle, immediately above the glacier.

This scene is said to be from the first official Timp Hike back in 1912(BYU foto archives).

In 1915, there were about 250 people attending the Friday night pre-hike program, and most of them climbed the mountain the next day. That hike was marred by bad weather. At the summit it was reported that thunder and lightning occurred and some snow fell. Also, one young girl, Daphne Smith of Provo, broke her collarbone. She was sliding down the glacier when she struck a rock on top of the

A 1908? foto on the Timp Glacier showing what appears to be a crevasse(BYU foto archives).

This is the second metal flag to be erected on Timp, July 15, 1916(BYU foto archives).

snow. It was in 1915 when a group of men from Pleasant Grove climbed up the face of the mountain and installed a metal US flag on a flagpole for the first time.

In 1916, a total of 106 people showed up at the program and bonfire, and about 100 made it to the summit, which in those early days was called **Monument Peak.** It was so named because there was a small stone monument at the highest point. A February, 1916 foto by Alma Christiansen, shows the metal flag at the summit of Timp all but blown away, so on July 15, 1916, a second American flag was taken to the summit and reinstalled. This one didn't last very long either.

In 1917, newspaper accounts stated there were about 225 people on the mountain for the hike. The 1918 newspapers are missing. In 1919, the first year after the end of First World War, there were over 300 people attending the Friday night bonfire program and 172 made it to the top. Up to this point, most newspaper accounts called the starting point to the hike, *Quaking Asp grove,* but by about 1919, the official name was Aspen Grove.

For the 1920 annual hike, there was a slight change of scenery between Wildwood and Aspen Grove. The road built by Isaac Wadley and company from Pleasant Grove had been at least partially completed, and some cars for the first time made it all the way to the trailhead. The Provo paper had this to say, *About fifty cars reached Aspen Grove for the first time over the new road. The road is not what you would call a boulevard but is very creditable for a newly built mountain road. The grade is very steep in places but some of the finest cars in Provo were driven to the grove with little difficulty.* That year it rained a little and 36 hikers from the University of Utah joined in the pilgrimage.

In the beginning there wasn't much of a trail up the mountain beyond Aspen Grove. But there had been sheep grazing in the upper basins for nearly half a century prior to the beginning of the Annual Timp Hike. The route used in those early years had been along some of these sheep trails. The Chipmans and Becks of American Fork had sheep in the basins for many years.

According to an article by Timp Roberts in the annual booklet called *Timpanogos, Wonder Mountain* of 1922, he states: *perhaps the oldest routes to the top of Timpanogos are by way of the west face of the mountain. At least three distinct trails have been used, one by way of Dry Creek Canyon, the second through 'Pleasant Grove Canyon?, and the third through the gulches to the north and then upon the north Rim.* All the Timp Hikes however, have gone by way of the Aspen Grove side of the mountain.

According to Eleroy West of Pleasant Grove, who was born in 1895(and healthy as hell in 1989), the Forest Service sent a crew out in the summer of 1921 to build the Timpooneke Trail up the north side of the mountain. Eleroy started out as a cook and Jake Nelson was the crew foreman. Vivian West was the head forest ranger for the district. They worked on the Timpooneke Trail until

Cook tent for the men building the Aspen Grove Trail in 1921(BYU foto archives).

September 9, 1921, then they were forced off the mountain by a storm which put nearly half a meter of snow in the upper basins.

From there the crew went around the mountain to Aspen Grove in the North Fork drainage, and began to build the first real trail on that side of Timp. The same crew worked on the Aspen Grove Trail until about mid-November, then were forced off the mountain by cold and snowy weather. Just after Thanksgiving, the same Forest Service crew began work on a trail to the Timp Cave. They worked on that trail until about mid-winter, then snowslides from cliffs above forced their departure for a couple of months.

For the 1921 hike there were more changes. The new trail helped hikers greatly, but the newspaper accounts stated that the Forest Service needed to do more improvements. Apparently winter snows stopped the work before it was completed. It was reported that 1200 attended the pre-hike bonfire program, of which 200 were University of Utah students and faculty. That year for the first time, trucks were used to transport most of the hikers to the mountain, many of which were BYU students. About 650 people started up the trail, but only 593 reached the top. On that hike, an airplane from Salt Lake City buzzed the climbers on the summit. The year 1921 was the first time any kind of improved road was opened to regular traffic connecting American Fork Canyon and North Fork of Provo Canyon. It was gradually improved over the years to what we know today as the **Alpine Scenic Loop Road.**

No mention was made of the number of hikers who made it to the summit in 1922. This was the first year of existence for KSL radio station in Salt Lake City, and they broadcast the pre-hike program. This tradition lasted for many years.

Some changes took place during the 1923 hike. Newspaper accounts for the first time mentioned that Scott P. Stewart set up a little confectionery at his property next to Aspen Grove. This was partly because of the Timp Hike crowd, and partly for the summer school program(the Stewart cabin was destroyed by an huge avalanche in the winter of 1936). Also, a guy named Happy Hudson served

Work crew building the Aspen Grove Trail near the second waterfall(BYU foto archives).

meals at Aspen Grove to hikers at below city prices.

Prior to 1923, most hikers participating in the event made it a three day outing. Until that year, they apparently had another program of some kind on Saturday night, then would stay over and return to Provo and the valley on Sunday morning. But of course someone eventually complained about that and the hike organizers then had to make it into a two day affair. Some hikers however stayed at Aspen Grove Saturday night and attended church services at the summer school center.

A week after the annual hike of 1923, Timp Roberts organized another climb of the mountain. This one was billed as a *moonlight hike* up Timp. This had been held in 1918 and 1919, but the trail was so inadequate and dangerous it had been canceled. However, a group from the University of Utah did apparently continue that tradition for a year or two. With the new and safer trail, the all-night hike was tried again. It's not known how many more years this event took place.

In 1924, officials estimated 1500 people attended the bonfire program, and 300 reached the summit. The hike started at 6 a.m., and Bob Levitre of Provo reached the flagpole at 8:06 a.m. That was 2 hours and 6 minutes to the top, a record at the time and it stood for many years. This record was surpassed in 1967 by Mike Kelsey, who went up in 1 hour 30 minutes.

With the success of the Timp Hike, another mountain climb was started by Roberts. It was the Annual Autumn Leaf Hike up Timp. It apparently began in September of 1924, and was promoted as a hike which the regular student body could participate in(not just summer students). It was at a time when the mountain was in full fall color. This hike apparently didn't last long. In about this same period of time another annual hike was begun just east of campus. BYU students would hike up to the "Y" on the mountain, then go on up to Maple Flat, which is the big flat area just south of Y Mountain and on the face of Maple Mountain. This hike lasted for many years. Many of the hikes were moonlight hikes, which began at 10:30 p.m. on a night with a full moon.

In 1925, two thousand people attended the Timp Hike bonfire program, and 1000 headed up the mountain, but no mention is made in the newspaper of how many made it to the summit. One man from Australia was awarded a Timp(walking) Stick, for being the person who came the fartherest to make the climb.

In a pre-hike article in the Provo Herald, it stated this about the 1926 event. *The Theater of the Pines is ready for the Timpanogos Hike program. Two expert timbermen and seven workers in wood have been building log edged terraces upon the north-___? side of Guide's Peak this week, and they report that at least a thousand people can be seated in rustic fashion for the annual pre-hike program Friday night.* Lights were also installed along with a stage of some kind. About 3000 people attended the program and about 1000 set off to climb the mountain the next morning.

In another newspaper account after the 1926 hike, it stated in headlines, *Loop Road to be*

On the road to Aspen Grove in the 1920's(BYU foto archives).

Completed by 1927. It also stated that the county, state and Forest Service would all participate in building a two-way loop road early the next year(1927). This must have been an upgrading project, because there was a rough link over the Timp Divide for many years prior to that time.

In early July of 1927, they had some kind of a beauty contest to see who would light the bonfire the night before the big hike. The Herald stated, *Miss Aline Coleman of Provo has been chosen to light the ceremonial bonfire for the Sixteenth Annual Timpanogos Hike. She will be accompanied by sixteen dancing nymphs in the performance of this official duty.* Later reports stated 5000 people were at the pre-hike program and many were on the mountain the next day.

The year 1928 brought on a couple of firsts for the event. Buses were first used to transport hikers who otherwise didn't have their own cars. Also, in the Sunday Herald for July 22, 1928, it states, *the new glass observatory on the summit of Utah's wonder mountain is ready for inspection. Rangers believe it will attract many people to the summit who otherwise might not go that far this year.*

In doing research for this book, the author talked to a number of people who thought the **Summit Hut** was first built in the early 1920's, and that it was built in stages. But according to research done by Ralph Iorio who worked at the Timpanogos Cave National Monument from 1959 to 1961, it was built in 1928, as the Daily Herald indicates. He states in an unpublished document called *The History of Timpanogos Cave National Monument*(available at the monument visitor center) that, *On only one occasion money from guide fees[from Timp Cave] was spent for development outside of the canyon. In 1928, a sum of $1,000 was donated to the Forest Service for the construction of a metal observation tower and shelter on the peak of Mt. Timpanogos.*

Despite the differing opinions as to the date of construction, it appears that George Richards was the wrangler in charge of taking supplies up the mountain. He had a number of horses, mules and donkeys at a base camp which was at Mutual Dell. Supplies for the construction of the hut were taken up on his pack animals. He also hired out his pack animals to visitors going up the mountain. Viv West, was the ranger in charge, and it's been stated by several people in Utah County that LeRoy Thorne, Jake Nelson, Lee Warburton and Amber Boulter helped build the shelter. Because they installed glass in the hut, it became known at the time as the **Glass House.** When the sun would shine just right, people in the valley could see it reflecting. The glass didn't stay long however, as the high winds broke it out after only a year or two.

Dancing on the summit of Timp in the early 1920's(BYU foto archives).

Eldon Johnson of Pleasant Grove remembers that he was staying at Mutual Dell about the time he graduated from high school in 1928. He states that the Summit Hut or Glass House at that time had 15 or 20 small metal arrows or indicators mounted on an inside railing, each of which was pointed to and set on some landmark in the valley or along the horizon in all directions. He also stated that someone had originally mounted a telescope in the middle of the observatory, but it wasn't long before someone must have grabbed it for a souvenir.

The hut is fastened down securely with cables and bolts. It does give some protection from the wind, but sometimes it's better just to climb down over the cliffs a ways on the east side. Some years later, a bright red and white marker was placed on top of the Summit Hut and used as a USGS triangulation station for survey work.

In 1929, there were an estimated 5000 people at the pre-hike program at Aspen Grove. Before the hike, the road was improved to the point where it could handle two-way traffic. About 300 hikers made it to the summit that year. The year 1930 brought 6000 enthusiasts to Aspen Grove for the program in the Theater of the Pines. It was also the first year commemorative **Timp Badges** were given out to those who made it to the summit. They had 500 badges made, and they ran out early. Names of those who made it were written down, and later 252 more badges were mailed out to those hikers. The total number at the top that year was 752.

In 1931, newspaper accounts stated 10,000 people showed up at Aspen Grove on Friday night, but that was just an estimate. For this 20th Annual Hike they made up 1000 badges, and 225 Timp Sticks(for walking), some of which were sold to help pay for the expenses of the event. It appears that was the first year Mrs. John C. Stewart(wife of one of the original homesteaders of the North Fork), began selling hot coffee and sandwiches at Emerald Lake. The supplies must have been taken up on horseback. This practice last for several years. That year 902 badges were handed out at the summit.

The next year, 1932, they made up another 1000 badges, but 1460 hikers made it to the summit, a record which lasted for many years. The crowd at the pre-hike program was estimated at 10,000-12,000, very likely overestimated.

There were several firsts for the hike in 1933. The road from the Provo Canyon Highway to Aspen Grove was graded and oiled for the first time(but not quite the same as paved). The amphitheater was enlarged, and seating capacity doubled. Here's an interesting quote from the July 23, 1933 Sunday Herald: *Notwithstanding the seating capacity of the gigantic amphitheater had been more than doubled, many were digging out seats half a mile up in nigger heaven.* About 12,000 showed up for the 1933 pre-hike program, which featured loudspeakers for the first time. An estimated 2000 hikers started off to the mountain, many right after the program, but there was some bad weather for that hike. However, 1277 hikers reached the top to become members of the Timp Summit Club.

By 1934, the Provo Canyon road was totally paved except for a couple of hundred meters. This improved transportation system brought about 7500 spectators to Aspen Grove under threatening skies for the Friday night program. That program featured for the first time, a short play depicting the Legend of Timp, which had been written by Timp Roberts years earlier. In that summer the Forest Service had piped water to different locations at Aspen Grove, and had improved sanitation facilities. Only 558 badges were handed out, because the top was obscured by clouds. The glacier that year was the smallest in the memory of old timers, due to severe drought conditions.

The CCC crews helped to renovate the Theater of the Pines in 1935, and because of that work, the program was staged in the middle of a grassy area with bleacher seats. Weather was a little bad that year too, and only 5000 people showed up at Aspen Grove. No figures were given as to the number of summiteers.

Sometime during the late winter of 1936, a huge snowslide began roaring down the east face of Roberts Horn, and didn't stop until it reached the present-day trailhead parking lot at the beginning of the Aspen Grove Trail. According to Timp Haven Ski Resort founder Raymond R. Stewart, the slide stopped about 60 meters short of the cabin owned by Scott P. and Myrtle Stewart, but the winds generated by the huge avalanche destroyed the cabin anyway.

By 1936, there were so many people on the mountain, the Forest Service made and set up portable toilets somewhere in the area of Emerald Lake. The pre-hike newspaper accounts began urging people to not cut trail and that girls should not hike in high-heeled shoes. There were another 5000 people at Aspen Grove on Friday night, but camping conditions had changed because a big winter snowslide had taken out and re-arranged some of the trees. The 25th anniversary hike was a good one, with 987 hikers making it to the top. Mrs. John C. Stewart continued to sell food at Emerald Lake.

The hike in 1937 brought more new firsts for the hike. Horses were not allowed on the Aspen Grove Trail, and the road up to the grove was fully paved for the first time. The slightly rainy weather didn't stop 8000 folks from attending the Friday night program or 954 hikers from getting their badges

This is the old cabin belonging to Scott P. and Myrtle M. Stewart at Aspen Grove. A 1933 foto with Ray Stewart left, and brother Hank Stewart. The cabin was destroyed by an avalanche in the winter of 1936(Ray Stewart foto).

on top. In previous years, there had been a few minor injuries but nothing serious. In 1937, the hike had its **first fatality.** A hiker from Ohio, Wendell Pfouts, age 53, died of a heart attack. He had been to the summit and was on his way down near the glacier, when he passed out on the trail. Read more details on this in the chapter, *Tragedies on Mt. Timpanogos.*

Here's a grisly footnote to the Timp Hike, which took place on July 17, 1937. A **Western Air Express plane** carrying mail crashed in the area of the Lake Hardy northeast of Alpine on **December 15, 1936,** with 7 people on board. Only two bodies were found at the time. With the melting snow of summer, a third body was found on July 16, while a fourth was found on the 17th. Others were recovered later as the snow melted.

Four days before the scheduled hike in 1938, a heavy cloudburst hit Provo Canyon on July 13. Heavy flooding occurred in Lost Creek and Snowslide Canyons(on the northeast end of Cascade Peak and just below Vivian Park) which brought tons of rock, dirt and trees down onto the highway and into the river. The Snowslide Canyon debris temporarily blocked the Provo River, sending water into most of the cabins at Vivian Park. The hike had been scheduled for July 16, but was postponed one week because the road was blocked. When the hike did take place, they came up with the figure of 5372 visitors at the Friday night pre-hike program. No figures were given as to how many got to the summit.

In 1939 the newspaper accounts mention that 74 hikers went to the summit of Timp the weekend before the annual hike to test the snow conditions. There were again 5000 people attending the pre-hike program and the next day about 1200 hikers reached the top, despite temperatures in Provo reaching 41.6 C(107 F). On this hike one woman was injured. The Sunday Herald for July 16, 1939 states: *Mrs. Leslie McPhie of Heber City today was "resting easy" in a Heber hospital following an accident at the glacier near Emerald Lake, which left her with a fractured pelvis and a probable back injury. The Heber woman was injured Saturday morning when she hit a soft pocket of snow while sliding down the glacier.*

For the first time in Timp Hike history, some short wave radios were taken to the summit in 1940. Contact was made between people on top and others in Provo. There were more than 1000 cars counted at Aspen Grove Friday night for the pre-hike program, and more than 1000 hikers were off to the summit. No figures were given as to how many reached the top and won their badges.

In 1941, another 5000 people attended the bonfire program at the Theater of the Pines before the hike. A first for the 1941 Annual Timp Hike, was a Timpanogos Summer Ski Classic. At 8:30 am on the glacier, there was some kind of summer skiing, where Alf Engen was the honored guest. At 10:00 am, they organized a contest called the Sitdown Slide Race. This involved racing down the glacier in the sitting position. This apparently didn't go off as well as the organizers had hoped, because it was never heard of again.

Because the war was on in 1942, they organized the hikers to build a large stone cairn near Emerald Lake to remember the fighting men overseas. Everyone brought one stone and added it to the pile. The war, plus bad weather on Friday night and Saturday, kept the number of hikers way down from previous years. Only 334 hikers made the summit in 1942. In that year they attempted to stop or slow down the number of people making the hike at night, by not giving out Timp Badges until 7:30 am Saturday morning. Several people who arrived at the summit in the middle of the night nearly froze to death waiting to get their badges. The year 1942 was the first year they had no Friday night pre-hike program. This would last through the war years and resume again in 1946.

It must be understood that during the early and mid-1940's, World War II was raging in Europe and the Pacific. Everyone had ration books and gasoline was both scarce and rationed, which prevented many people from traveling very far from home. Also, most of the healthy young men were in combat. These were the primary reasons the number of hikers was way down during that period of time. The newspapers during the 1910's, 1920's and 1930's, carried the Annual Timp Hike on the front page and in big headlines. Beginning about the time the USA entered the war, the front page was almost exclusively devoted to war stories. The Timp Hike was then relegated to back pages. Americans were preoccupied with other things in the 1940's.

In 1943, 340 hikers made the summit, and in 1944, only about 500 hikers started up the mountain. About 250 made it to the top that year. Because the crowds were much smaller and likely better mannered, the hike committee attempted to keep people together along the trail so they could all hear short lectures along the way by BYU professors. The subjects covered were geology, botany and zoology. The year 1945 was another war year, and only about 700 people reached the summit of Timp. The paper had very little to say about it that year.

For the first time in 5 years, they had a Friday night pre-hike program in the Theater of the Pines in the summer of 1946. The last time they did that was in 1941. In 1946, they made up 1500 Timp badges, and Don Brimhall, a large football player for BYU, carried them up and distributed them to hikers who reached the top. This year they again had some ski races down the glacier--both downhill and slalom. There were about 5000 spectators at the pre-hike program, and about 1200 badges were handed out by 3 p.m. Saturday.

The hike in 1947 was held early, on July 13, perhaps the earliest of any Timp Hike. Because of the early start there was lots of snow around. Newspaper accounts stated that an estimated 10,000 people attended the pre-hike program. They had another ski demonstration of some kind on the glacier, after which an estimated 1200 hikers made it to the Summit Hut for badges. They had made up 1500 badges that year.

A 1949 foto of the ski racing on the Timp Glacier. Skiing on the glacier took place during the Annual Timp Hikes of 1941, 1946, 1947, 1948 and 1949(Ray Stewart foto).

At the pre-hike program in 1948, they had as many of the members of the 1912 hike in attendance as they could find. There were 19 hikers who made the summit that first year. In this year the hike organizers were informed that the region had been re-surveyed, and the altitude of Mt. Timpanogos had been changed. It was revised down from 3660 meters(12008 ft) to 3581 meters(11750 ft). They also rewarded Alfred Pace of Provo a Timp Stick for having the most badges. He started the hike in 1930, the first year they began handing out badges.

It was a cold hike in 1948, the coldest any of the hike veterans could remember. There were clouds and fog from about 3000 meters on up, and hikers who made the summit were soaked by condensation. Only 845 hikers reached the top that year.

The winter preceding the 1949 hike was one of heavy snows, so the hike was delayed until July 30. By this year there were about 30,000 members of the Timp Summit Club. Someone estimated that 5000 people went to Aspen Grove for the fireside program. That year they made up only 1200 badges, but 1430 climbers had reached the summit by 12:30 p.m. Those who didn't get badges had one mailed to them later. In 1949, they again had a big ski meet called the Glacier Cup Race. About 30 of the top skiers in the area were invited to participate. This was the last year ski racing was held on the glacier.

For the 1950 hike, they began a foto contest for the first time. It had two categories; human interest and scenery on Timp. The first place prize was $5. For this year, there were 1009 badges given away, but there were an estimated 150 other hikers who reached the hut after the summit crew left the top. In 1951, they had bad weather with rain off and on all day long. Still about 1200 reached the top.

For 1952, there were 52 citizens of American Fork who put on a play at the pre-hike program about the Legend of Timp. This had been done in years past, but was the first time recently. This was the last year Eugene Timp Roberts gave out Timp Sticks at the Friday night program, because he died before the next Timp Hike took place. They gave out 1200 badges, but had a list of about 100 who they mailed badges to at a later date.

Timp Roberts was honored on the 1953 Timp Summit Club Badges. About 1400 were given out at the top that year. Two hikers came up with minor injures on the glacier and had to be helped off the mountain. The Denver & Rio Grande Western Railroad sent a film crew up the mountain to record the event.

In 1954, there were several firsts. Most importantly, Vera Mecham of Provo, was killed by a falling rock on the glacier, the hike's first accidental fatality. Read more on this in the chapter *Tragedies on Mt. Timpanogos*. In the years after 1954, more emphases was placed on safety. Timp Hike organizers also asked for donations to be made for the construction of the Timp or Emerald Lake Shelter. About 1400 hikers reached the top that year.

The National Geographic Society had a fotographer on the 1955 hike, where 1350 badges were given out. However, they estimated about 1500 to 1600 made it up, because some got there both very early in the morning and later in the afternoon, and didn't get badges. For the 1956 hike, the Forest Service built a new trail between Emerald Lake and the Timp Saddle for the first time. This allowed hikers to go up an easier route than up the glacier. The hike committee tried to keep people off the glacier that year, because there was so little snow and so many rocks showing at the icefield's surface. After 1956, the normal way up was to use the trail to the Timp Saddle, then return via the glacier. There were 1432 who made the top that year.

At the pre-hike program in 1957, Alfred Pace of Provo, would get another Timp Stick for having the largest family in attendance--9 altogether. He also had a Timp Badge for every year since they began giving them out starting in 1930. There were 1297 badges handed out in 1957. In September of that year, the Emerald Lake Shelter was first begun with donated materials.

The hike in 1958 was a record-setting year. A total of 2200 made it to the top. Four hikers had minor injuries as well, all from sliding down the glacier. At the pre-hike program, they honored 8 of the original 19 members of the first official Timp Hike which was in 1912. Before the 1959 hike, someone wrote a letter to the Daily Herald, stating that she had hiked with Gene Roberts to the top of Timp in 1908 on a three day climb. Apparently there were other climbs before 1912, but it wasn't an organized effort until that year. In 1959, a total of 1767 badges were handed out by 3 p.m. Saturday.

The construction for the **Timp Shelter,** sometimes known as the **Emerald Lake Shelter,** was actually begun in September of 1957, several years before it was dedicated in 1960. It was during the later years of the Annual Timp Hike that the number of hikers increased at alarming rates. During that period of time, in the 1950's and 1960's, there developed the need for a shelter of some kind on the mountain.

One reason for a shelter was to have sanitation facilities at an important resting place along the way to the summit. Up to that time there was no place available for mother nature to run her course, except behind some trees, and there aren't any trees above Emerald Lake. A second reason was a need for an emergency shelter for hikers caught out in bad weather or for those who might be injured.

- Majestic Mount Timpanogos, monarch of the Wasatch Range, reaches 12,008 feet above sea level.

- Pack horses carry skiing equipment to Timpanogos Glacier where mid-summer ski meet is held.

- Diagram of the race down the glacier. Race starts with an almost vertical drop.

- Hugh Cummings and Susie Harris receive trophies after winning Glacier Cup Race 1948.

ENTRY BLANK
Timpanogos GLACIER CUP Race

● In consideration of the acceptance of this entry for the annual Mid-Summer ski meet, I do hereby relieve the Timpanogos Mountain Club, The Deseret News, and The Provo Chamber of Commerce from any and all liabilities which I may suffer and any and all injuries which may be sustained by me through competing in this affair. I furthermore agree to do my part in cooperating with the race officials to run off this affair in the best manner possible.

Signed _____

Address _____

City _____ State _____

Ski Club _____

Classification Card No. _____

Parents signature (if under 21)_____

I do hereby certify that the above contestant is eligible to compete in Class A or Open meets and that he is fully qualified and certified as represented on this entry blank.

Signed _____
                                    Club Secretary

Please inclose a snapshot of yourself and a few facts that you feel would be suitable for publication before the race.

● This entry must be mailed together with $2.00 (entry fee) to Timpanogos Ski Race Committee, Miller's Ski Shop, Provo, Utah, before July 20, or it will not be considered.

An entry form for the Timp Glacier Cup Ski Race. A 1949 event on the Timp Glacier(Ray Stewart).

The Emerald Lake or Timp Shelter was finished in 1960 and still standing.

A third reason for a shelter was the need for a kind of base camp or communications headquarters during the Timp Hike, where first aid and medical equipment could be stored.

The design for this structure was prepared by Reginald C. Pragnell of the Forest Service in 1954. James Jacobs, then supervisor of the Uinta National Forest with a committee consisting of enthusiastic mountain men from the Provo area, began making plans for the building of the Timp Shelter. The actual construction however, started under the direction of supervisor Clarence Thornock in September of 1957. Some supplies such as cement, sand, lumber, and other building materials were hauled up on pack horses. Parts of the disassembled massive steel roof were toted up the trail on a two wheeled in-tandem vehicle furnished by the Forest Service. Most of the structure was finished by late summer of 1959, but the dedication ceremonies were held on Saturday, July 16, 1960, during the 49th Annual Timpanogos Hike.

The building is about 6 x 6.75 meters, and 4.5 meters high. The walls are made of cement and stone and very massive. The roof is of 12-gauge steel, and strong enough to withstand the heavy snows of winter. The windows at either end are heavy plate glass reinforced with wire. It has a rock and stone foundation, and on the west end are two toilets with an enclosed cement septic tank. They are no longer usable today, but a portable toilet is hauled in by helicopter each summer. Inside the shelter is a fireplace, plus a stone and cement sitting area extending around the perimeter of the room.

The shelter cost approximately $12,000, of which $9000 was contributed by cooperating organizations and expended for labor and hire of pack horses. The Forest Service contributed materials equivalent to $3000. Inside the shelter and just above the fireplace is a plaque crediting the cooperating agencies who helped build it. It states: *TIMPANOGOS SHELTER, erected 1959, Utah County, Forest Service, Provo City, Provo Chamber Commerce, and Brigham Young University*(from a Forest Service handout).

In 1960, there were another 1800 hikers at the summit, but also about 15 people were injured. Most of them were minor accidents which came by sliding down the glacier. Two victims had to be carried off the mountain.

Early reports said 1900 hikers got to the top, but later that figure went up to 2100 for the 1961 hike. This was the 50th anniversary year, and some of those on the original Timp Hike were at the pre-hike ceremonies. In 1962, the final tally stated that 1975 reached the summit. There were an estimated 7000 people attending the Friday night program that year.

At first the total number of hikers on top for 1963, was set at 2488, but was later revised to 2525. Two hikers that year had to be carried off the mountain with broken bones. The next year(1964) another tragedy occurred. Nine year old Paul K. Neilson of Orem fell and rolled about 100 meters down from the summit on the east side, and eventually died of injuries. He was the third fatality in Timp Hike history, the second resulting from an accident. Read the details on this boy's death under the chapter *Tragedies on Mt.Timpanogos*. In 1964, a total of 2400 hikers reached the Summit Hut.

The 1965 hike was postponed a week because of heavy snows on the mountain, and because the road in American Fork Canyon had been damaged by heavy July rains. There were no serious injuries and revised figures stated that 2325 people became summit club members. The 1966 hike started off with a bang. There were 43 law enforcement officers at the pre-hike program and 12 young men were arrested for drunkenness, one being taken to jail. In the last years of the annual hike, rowdiness was a big problem for the hike organizers, and perhaps one reason for the eventual cancelation of the annual event.

By 1967, more work had been done on the Timpooneke Trail, the foto contest had a $50 first prize, and 2361 hikers got their summit badges. An estimated 5000 hikers got to Emerald Lake, about half of which made it all the way. One Canadian girl was hurt sliding down the glacier and had to be taken out by helicopter. Mike Kelsey made it to the summit in 1 hour and 30 minutes, and come down in 45 minutes.

Another new record was set in 1968 with 2736 hikers making it to the top. It was also one of the safest in years. The Aspen Grove Trail was also rebuilt, making it much longer, but less steep. The 1969 hike saw an estimated 8000 people on the mountain, most of whom got only as far as Emerald Lake, with 2685 people reaching the summit.

The 1970 Annual Timp Hike was a huge success and a disaster at the same time. In that year there were two pageants, one on Thursday night in the old BYU football stadium, the other at Aspen Grove Friday night. Newspaper accounts stated that an estimated 7000 people set off to climb the mountain, but no one knew exactly how many actually made it to the summit. The best estimates were around 3500. In that year the Timp Badges were lost in the mail from Salt Lake City. Those living in Utah were able to stop by the BYU campus and pick up their badges, while out-of-staters got their badges through the mail(their addresses were recorded at the summit).

The disaster part of the 1970 hike was that it was so successful, and there were so many people on the mountain in one single day, that it about ruined the mountain. Shortly after the hike, the Timp Hike Committee, which was made up of about 20-25 people from the Forest Service, BYU and various community organizations, got together and decided to discontinue the event. It had been under consideration for two or three years prior to 1970, but it wasn't until that year that the decision was finally made.

The primary reason for the decision to end this long tradition was that the mountain simply could not withstand thousands of hikers stomping around on one single day. If the numbers of hikers were reduced and spread out over a two or three month period, then it was thought the mountain could survive. The committee did however vote to continue making summit badges for 1971, which hikers could pick up at the Provo Chamber of Commerce after they had gone to the top. This policy was changed the next year however, when no badges were made and no public statements were made in the local newspapers. Thus ended The Annual Timp Hike after 59 consecutive years.

Alfred Pace of Provo, showing all 42 of his Timp Hike badges collected from 1930 through 1971. This is the only complete set of badges in existence.

Mt. Timpanogos Wilderness Area

On July 21, 1961, Regional Forester Floyd Iverson of the U. S. Forest Service Intermountain Region designated 4460 hectares(10,750 acres) of this magnificent mountain as the *Mt. Timpanogos Scenic Area*. But in recent years and with the greater interest in outdoor recreation, Timp was made into an official wilderness area. The **Mt. Timpanogos Wilderness Area** encompasses 4460 hectares of land in the Uinta National Forest. It was established by the Utah Wilderness Act of 1984 and Public Law 428 of the 98th Congress. The Timpooneke and Aspen Grove Trails have National Trail designation. The map shows the approximate boundaries.

Trailheads and Access Roads

In this book are 12 different places where you can start hiking to various parts of the mountain. Nine of these would be called trailheads, because the route involved is a trail. The other 3 locations might be called car-parks, because there are no real trails above.

The normal route to the top of Timp is via the **Aspen Grove Trail** on the east side of the mountain. This trail takes you to the summit, as well as to Emerald Lake, the Second Summit, The Shoulder, East Peak, the Timp Glacier and Roberts Horn. To get there, drive up Provo Canyon to the small summer home community of Wildwood and turn north on the Alpine Scenic Loop Road toward Sundance. About 8 kms above Wildwood is Aspen Grove. The second trailhead is at **Sundance,** also on the eastern side of the mountain. By using the trail running west from Sundance, you can gain access to Stewart Falls, the Big Provo Hole and Cascade Cirque.

The next two beginning points are in **Provo Canyon.** One of these is about half a km to the west or down-canyon from Vivian Park, and in the area of Frazier Park. This **Southeast Ridge Route** runs up an open ridge to the top of Arrowhead Peak and to the South Peaks of Timp. The other car-park can be at Bridal Veil Falls, or just to the west. This is where you park if you want to get up on the **South Ridge.** This route takes you to the South Peaks, a circle of summits surrounding Big Provo Hole--and for really fit hikers, to the summit of Timp.

There are three starting points on the southwest face of Timp. The first is at the mouth of **Dry Canyon.** To get there make your way to 20th North in Orem, which is the same road as 200 South

Ready for a winter climb. The Aspen Grove Trailhead in March 1970.

MT. TIMPANOGOS WILDERNESS AREA

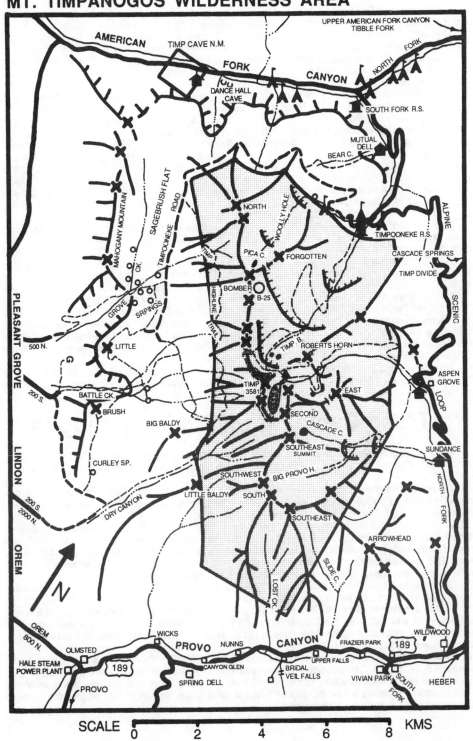

SCALE

0   2   4   6   8   KMS

Street in Lindon. This is the boundary between the two cities. Drive east until you come to the dirt road at the mouth of Dry Canyon, then look for side roads heading in the direction of the trailhead. You can reach any of the highest summits, as well as Big Baldy from this trailhead.

The next trailhead on the southwest face is at the mouth of **Battle Creek Canyon.** To get there, head for Pleasant Grove. Find 200 South Street, which is also called Battle Creek Drive, and follow it east until it ends at the Kiwanis Park right at the mouth of the canyon. This is where the old Battle Creek Power Station used to be. Use this trail to gain access to Little Mountain, Big Baldy, the old Pleasant Grove Water Tunnel and the summit.

The last trailhead leading to the summit ridge from the west side is at the mouth of **Grove Creek Canyon.** From the middle part of Pleasant Grove, drive north until you find 500 North Street, some times known as Grove Creek Drive. Drive east on this street until you're in the mouth of Grove Creek Canyon. This is a good place to start to climb North or Bomber Peaks.

On the American Fork Canyon side, there are 5 starting points for hiking. To get into American Fork Canyon, exit the freeway at Pleasant Grove, American Fork or the first exit south of the Point of the Mountain. Then follow the signs to Timpanogos Cave National Monument. About 5 kms up the canyon is the visitor center and trailhead to the **Timp Cave.** The road in American Fork Canyon, which also goes over the Timp Divide and down to Aspen Grove, Sundance, then to the Provo Canyon Highway, is called the **Alpine Scenic Loop Road.** It used to be designated State Highway 80, but recently it was re-numbered "92".

If you continue up American Fork(AF) Canyon and into the right or South Fork, you will soon come to the **Mutual Dell Summer Camp.** You can park there at the trailhead to Bear Canyon and hike up to the Timpooneke Road.

If you continue up along the Alpine Loop, you will come to the little paved side-road on the right or west, which leads into the Timpooneke Campground. Just follow the signs. About half a km from the Alpine Loop Road, will be the **Timpooneke Trailhead,** which is at the bottom of the Timpooneke Trail. From this point you can reach all or most of the peaks on the northern half of the mountain.

From the Timpooneke Trailhead, drive west along what is known as the Timpooneke Road. This road skirts the north end of Timp and allows road access to the intermediate bench on the southwest side of the mountain. If you drive this road about one km past the Timpooneke Trailhead, you will be at the end of the **Upper Timpooneke Campground.** There is no trail up from there, but you can easily route-find up to the North Peak, and Woolly Hole and Pica Cirque.

The last starting point is for the climb up Roberts Ridge to Roberts Horn. It's right at the top or highest point of the Alpine Scenic Loop Road. At the **Timp Divide** is a parking place, and it can be used by those who want to try a little known route up Roberts Ridge.

No Trace Camping on Mt. Timpanogos

The following is a set of guidelines to hiking and camping in or around the Mt. Timpanogos Wilderness. It comes from an information sheet handed out by the Uinta National Forest.

Our wilderness areas are receiving increased use yearly. This increased pressure is having a negative effect on our efforts to maintain a quality *wilderness experience* for you and your children. Please help us by following these guidelines.

1. Mt. Timpanogos is limited to foot and horse travel only. Horses are not allowed on the Aspen Grove Trail, but are allowed on all other trails on the mountain, including the Timpooneke Trail. **All motorized and mechanical equipment(including mountain bikes) are prohibited by law.** This includes the three canyons east of Orem, Lindon and Pleasant Grove, which is not in the official wilderness area, but which is still an administrative vehicle closure area.

2. **Group size should be limited to 10 people** or less. This helps maintain an enjoyable experience for others and lessens trail damage.

3. **Toilets are provided** on Mt. Timpanogos just as you enter the Hidden Lakes Cirque, at Emerald Lake, and as you first enter the Timp Basin along the Timpooneke Trail. If these toilets cannot be used, the best method of waste disposal is to dig a *cat hole* 20 cms(8 in.) deep at least 60 meters from streams, springs and lakes.

4. **Backpacking stoves are now required** for cooking. **Open fires are no longer permitted in the Mt. Timpanogos Wilderness** due to scarce or non-existent firewood.

5. **Please avoid short-cutting** of switchbacks on the trail. Short cuts cause erosion problems hard to repair. Violators will be cited. Boy Scout or other group leaders should discuss this problem before beginning their hike up the mountain.

6. **No Trace Camping means leaving your campsite clean.** Please pack out all your garbage including cans and aluminum foil.

Please let other people know your plans for using the wilderness. Dress properly and always use common sense. In the past we spoke of mans ability to survive in the wilderness. Today we speak of wilderness survival as the lands ability to survive man.

Water on Mt. Timpanogos

Not long after the Mormons arrived in Utah Valley, they began using Mt. Timpanogos for grazing sheep and cattle. The period of time when the most livestock was on the mountain was during the 1880's and 1890's, but heavy usage extended well into the 20th century. In time the numbers were slowly reduced because of overgrazing and erosion. Today there are but two small allotment areas on the mountain which are still grazed and the number of sheep are now down to 1200 in each allotment. These two areas are northwest, north and northeast of the main Timpanogos Massif, and are all outside the wilderness area. Grazing is mentioned here only to remind people that although some believe the streams on Timp are polluted today, it's very likely they are extremely clean when compared to what it once was.

There was likely a lot more water-born diseases in the water in those *good old days* than today, because of the heavy grazing. Today there is increased awareness of the various *bugs* because of all the warnings from the various government agencies. However, there are several simple ways you can play it safe and get around these problems. One is to take a bottle of water with you from home. The author does this on all hikes, because he's never sure where lunch will be eaten. Another thing to remember, try to take water directly from a spring source if you can. If you can't, then get as close to the spring as possible. The further from the spring, the better the chances are of picking up contaminated water. However, since there is no longer any livestock grazing in the areas where you'll be hiking, chances are good you will never pick up anything.

The stream which may pose the biggest health hazard is the creek below Emerald Lake(officially called the North Fork of Provo River). This is because of the heavy concentration of hikers, but even so, most hikers on the mountain eventually drink from it and there is no record of anyone dying because of it. In researching history of the Annual Timp Hike in old newspapers, never did the Timp Hike Committee ever warn hikers not to drink the water. So remember, just use a little common sense and you'll never have any problems.

Hiking Equipment

Day Hikes

For those who haven't hiked much here is a list of items or equipment you will need when climbing Mt. Timpanogos during a day-trip in the summer. Most people prefer a pair of hiking or climbing boots, but if you're going to be staying on one of the two main trails, most people can get by with a pair of simple **running-type shoes.** If you try the running shoes, make sure the soles are fairly thick, so sharp rocks won't bruise the bottoms of your feet. On the other hand, if you're planning to climb some of the less-used ridge routes which have no trails, then the best choice of footwear is a pair of rigid boots of some kind. The new light weight nylon-leather hiking boots are pretty good, but they aren't as rugged as **leather boots.**

In the warmer summer months, which will be from about July 1 until early September, you can usually get by wearing a pair of **shorts** or cut-offs. But that's only if it is really warm weather. Remember, at the top it'll be much cooler than at the bottom of the mountain. It's probably best to take a pair of **long pants** in your day-pack just in case. Also, a **T shirt** is usually best, at least for much of the climb, but as you near the summit, a **long sleeved shirt** will be required. If the temperature is 38 C(100 F) in the valley, then the temperature on Timp's Summit will be in the neighborhood of 18 C(64 F). If there is a breeze, and there usually is, it will be chilly. For use in an emergency, a **light jacket** or a **hooded sweat shirt** should also be taken in your day-pack.

A small **day-pack** is perhaps the most important piece of equipment. They come in all sizes, but it should be large enough for a pair of long pants, a light jacket, a lunch and water bottle. If the temperature isn't really hot in the valley, better take a pair of **gloves** as well. At or near the summit, these can come in handy even on a warm summer day.

For those with light colored skin, a **cap** or **hat** of some kind is necessary. At higher altitudes and with the presence of sun and snow, your face and neck will be *fried well-done* by the end of your hike.

To protect the face and neck from sunburn, the author uses an adjustable baseball cap with a curtain sewn on around the sides and back. This is much better in windy conditions than a large cowboy-type hat. Also, a **handkerchief** can come in handy to tie around your face. This will protect the nose from sunburn, as will a **sun lotion.** If you spend much time on the glacier, you will have to have some kind of protection, or you'll arrive home in *lobster-red* condition.

Everyone should have a **lunch** of some kind and a **one liter bottle of water.** Here are some other items you may or may not want either in your pockets or day-pack. A tube of **chapstick** or lip ointment, **compass, pocket knife, map** of the mountain, **toilet paper,** a **camera**--plus extra lenses and film, and some may want a light weight walking stick and small note book and pen.

If you plan on going up in early summer, say in June, you may want a couple of other things. Because there will be lots of snow at that time, an ice ax would be handy, as well as crampons, but of the two, crampons would be less important.

If you're doing a day-hike in winter, here are some things you will need in addition to what is mentioned above. An **ice ax** and **crampons, heavy boots** and either **gaiters** or **expedition overboots.** A pair of **sunglasses** or **ski goggles** is very necessary, as are a good pair of **gloves or mittens.** The author prefers a light weight pair of knit gloves, which can be worn under a heavy pair of mittens. A **bandana** worn around the face and neck is also important in winter for sunburn protection. Also, another heavy **long sleeved shirt,** perhaps a **sweater or sweat shirt with hood,** and a **heavy parka with hood.**

Overnight Hikes

Besides what is already discussed above for day hikes, here are some things you'll need for overnight camping or climbs. A tent, sleeping bag, foam sleeping pad(Therm-a-Rest is best), small backpackers stove, several cigarette lighters or matches to light stove and candles, large water jug(3.78 liters or one gallon) for use around camp, a one liter water bottle, canister with odds and ends such as bandaids, patching kit for sleeping pad, wire, pens, needle and thread, etc. Also, candles, small flashlight, sun screen lotion, reading book, tooth brush and paste and raincoat if the weather looks threatening.

Here's a simple list of food items you might be interested in. You can add to this list. Food for breakfast might include oatmeal or cream of wheat cereal, coffee or chocolate drink, powdered milk and sugar. Lunch might be cookies, candy bars or chocolate, an orange or apple(fruit that doesn't squash--like bananas), and sometimes a powdered fruit drink. A supper list might include Ramen instant noodles, soups, macaroni, instant mashed potatoes and canned tuna fish, or sardines, Vienna sausages, corned beef, cheese or peanuts. Also, more fruit like apples or oranges, raisins or other dried fruit, carrots, instant puddings, crackers, cookies, bread, butter, peanut butter. In addition, a plastic eating bowl and cup, spoon, knife, can opener, small cooking pot, salt and pepper, and extra fuel for the stove. All of these items can be purchased at any grocery store.

Climbing Seasons

While most people prefer to climb Timpanogos in the warm season of July, August and September, the mountain can be climbed during any mouth of the year. Each month or season has it's own special attractions, even during the dead of winter. Of course each season will require special clothing or equipment to climb the mountain. In this book there are about 9 different seasons discussed, each requiring different clothing, equipment or strategy.

The most popular time for hiking Timp is in the **summer season.** This is from about early to mid-July through early or mid-September. This is the warmest season and the time when the mountain is mostly free of snow and the trails are usually dry. You will find the meadows in the high cirque basins a green carpet of grass and multi-colored flowers. In July and early August you will find the flowers blooming in these high basins. Each year is different, but by late August and into September, the mountain loses all or most of its snow banks except the glacier and about three other tiny icefields and it becomes dry. After the snowbanks melt, the higher altitude creeks and streams stop flowing, requiring hikers to carry water or other drinks to destinations high on the mountain.

It's in this summer season you can hike in a pair or shorts or cut-offs(beware of sunburned legs!) and usually a T shirt. However, it's wise to take a pair of long pants and a long sleeved shirt in your day-pack, as it can be chilly on the summit ridge. There is often a good breeze blowing on top. At times a light-weight pair of gloves and jacket can come in handy as well.

Early fall is another pleasant season on Timp, but the weather can change and each year is different. This period is from about mid-September until late October. This is the most colorful season on the mountain, especially around the lower elevations where the oak brush and aspen trees wear fall colors. The first week of October is when many people drive the Alpine Scenic Loop to see and fotograph the fall colors.

If you're hiking at this time, you'll need to wear long pants, a long sleeved shirt, a sweat shirt with a hood, a lightweight jacket and definitely some gloves or mittens. If you begin hiking early in the morning, you will likely need to wear all of these clothing items, but when the day warms up, part will be stowed in your pack. When you reach the summit it will be getting cold, but if the region is covered by a high pressure system, it can be very pleasant. In some years, early winter snows come and make hiking in October the same as in winter, but normally this can be a pleasant time to climb the mountain.

Late fall is a kind of in-between season on the mountain. It runs from about late October until mid-November. There is normally snow around, at least on the higher slopes, but it usually isn't deep enough to use skis or snowshoes. For this reason, it can be a bit unpleasant. In places you may need snowshoes, but in other places they will be useless. Temperatures at night will be getting cold and winter-type clothes will often be needed, especially in the morning hours. By this time all the leaves will be on the ground. The Alpine Scenic Loop Road is sometimes open for awhile, but late in this period, it's normally closed. The Utah Department of Transportation will close the gates along this road at Aspen Grove and just above Mutual Dell.

The next season will be called **early winter.** This is a short season, lasting from about mid-November until the first of December. This is another transition time. You will have snow that is usually deep enough to use skis or snowshoes in most places, but in other places it usually isn't that deep yet. Winter climbing during this period of time can be enjoyable because there is usually little danger from avalanches and you can often times get by without skis or snowshoes, depending on the route used. You will have to dress for winter conditions, because from late November until late February, are the coldest 90 days in Utah. It's also a period of time with long nights and short days.

The next season is the **dead of winter** or just plain **winter.** This is from about December 1 until the end of February. For about a 3 month period of time you will encounter the coldest weather of the year and usually lots of deep powdery-type snow. You will need either skis or snowshoes on almost all routes. On some routes(especially the South Ridge) you can use crampons to good advantage.

During this period of time you may have limited access, but throughout the year the Alpine Scenic Loop Road will be open up to Aspen Grove in the North Fork drainage, and to Mutual Dell on the American Fork Canyon side. You will still be able to drive up to the mouth of Battle Creek, Grove Creek and Dry Creek Canyons regardless of the time of year.

The winter season is one of the most avalanche prone times on Mt. Timpanogos and special care should be taken. For those who don't fully understand avalanches or how to predict their danger, it is wise to telefone the **Utah Avalanche Forecast Center,** at 374-9770(or 364-1581 in Salt Lake, or 621-2362 in the Ogden area) for their very good daily updated information. Even experienced climbers should take note of this service. Under each hiking section of this book, avalanche areas are discussed in more detail.

During this period of time, one disadvantage will be the long cold nights and very short days. This limits the amount of climb-time available and lengthens the time one must sit in a tent. If you're out doing a two-day climb, take plenty of candles and perhaps some reading material.

If you're interested in winter climbing, the best time to do it would be in **late winter,** which is in the month of March. At this time of year you will have lots of snow, in fact the deepest of the season, but it will usually be packed down and hard, and you can often climb with crampons and without snowshoes or skis. This is especially true late in the month, and extending into April. But with all that deep snow, avalanches are a big concern on some routes, especially during the mid-day hours or when the warm serges of air come in from the southwest. The biggest snowslides of the year often come during this time period in Provo Canyon, some times blocking the highway at Bridal Veil Falls and at the mouth of Snowslide Canyon. A good time to climb is right after one of these warm spells, after the big slides have come down and when colder weather returns to freeze the snow solid.

Another advantage for climbing in late winter will be lots of daylight hours, at least compared to what you have in December. On March 21 you will have the same length of days and nights as you find on September 21. This gives you much more time to make a one day climb to the summit, something that's very near impossible during the dead of winter.

Another nice thing about climbing or hiking in March, is that you don't have the extremely cold temperatures common in the middle of winter. Things are warming up and some snow is melting in the mid-day hours, but it's cold enough at night to make the snow rock hard in the morning hours. This means you'll have to take and use winter clothes, but it's much more tolerable temperature wise. For winter climbs, the author prefers the month of March.

The next season might be called **early spring.** This will be the month of April. Things are definitely warming up and in the valleys things are starting to turn green. Up high, it's still winter and the snow is deep, but it's very crusty and hard in the morning hours. In the afternoons snow is slushy and wet. The lower altitude snow leaves and access is a little easier. If you do most of your climbing in the morning hours, you can get by without skis or snowshoes at this time. An ice ax and crampons are needed on steep slopes during this period of time.

In the morning hours, you'll still have to wear some warm clothes, but much lighter clothes than in winter. At mid-day, you can usually strip down into a T shirt, if it's a sunny day with no wind. The days are becoming long and the nights are short. Climbing during April could also be classified as winter climbing, but without the extreme temperatures. With all the hard snow, it's easy to reach the summit of Timp in one day for most healthy climbers. By this season avalanche danger is usually low, except right after a big storm.

The next period might be called **late spring.** This would be in the month of May. Up high, you will still have winter conditions, but the lower slopes of the mountain will be cleared of snow, and leaves are starting to come out. Climbing at this time will be on dry trails at lower elevations, wet trails further up the mountain, and on winter-type snows higher on the mountain.

The temperatures are becoming warm and pleasant, although up on the highest peaks, you may still see some ridge cornices and total snow cover. You won't need snowshoes, because the morning snow will be hard, and the afternoon snow will be wet but firm. If you're camping during this period, there will be lots of daylight hours and climb-time. You can easily get up the mountain to the top and into the upper basins which will still have continuous snow cover. Camping during this time would be a mixed bag; about half way between winter and summer camping. An ice ax and crampons can come in handy at this time.

One danger you will encounter in late spring along the Aspen Grove and Timpooneke Trails, will be the **hidden snow caves** or **snow bridges.** They are usually situated right over the stream where water pours over a cliff. During winter time, these creeks either dry up or are reduced to a trickle. The snow and avalanches cover them completely, then when water does begin to flow around the first part of May, it creates large caves beneath. If you walk over some of these areas the roof can collapses sending you down 10, 15, or possibly 20 meters to the creek bed below. The result will be death in many cases. During the late spring--early summer period in 1980 and 1982, a total of **4 hikers were killed** falling through snow bridges along the Aspen Grove Trail. Read about all these accidents in the chapter *Tragedies on Mt. Timpanogos.*

Early summer is the last time period on the mountain. This is from about the first of June until about early July. During this time the sun is high and warm, the snows are melting fast high on the mountain, the lower slopes are green, and lots of people want to head for the hills. It can be a good time to climb Timp, but you'll have to expect wet trails, especially up high. The upper basins are generally snow covered, but snow is melting fast, and some green comes as soon as the snow leaves. The snow is always hard and easy to walk on, especially in the mornings, but very wet in the afternoons. There will be some places you could use an ice ax and crampons, especially in areas where winter avalanches normally occur.

This is another time of year for the **deadly hidden snow caves or bridges,** especially if the winter snowpack is extra heavy. Read more on this under the late spring period to get more details on this danger. Each year now the Forest Service goes up the mountain erecting signs in the danger areas trying to avert the same kind of tragedies which occurred in the 1980 and 1982 seasons. Please watch for these signs and stay away from these deadly areas near the waterfalls.

Camping on the mountain can be pleasant at this time, because there shouldn't be so many people around. However, the upper basins are still normally snow-bound so you will have to look for a place for a tent. The ground at this time would be wet in many places, otherwise it can be a good time to camp.

One minor disadvantage to camping in late June and July would be you may run into a few mosquitos. Typically in mountain areas you will see some of these insects around(especially at night) just after the snow melts and when there's plenty of wet ground and boggy places. When the high basins dry out later in summer, there should be no mosquitos.

Snowmobiling

Mt. Timpanogos is so steep and rugged, there is no chance whatsoever to use snowmobiles on the mountain itself. Besides, the steeper parts are part of America's wilderness system and all motorized vehicles are prohibited. But on the north and east sides of the mountain there are several roads which can be used during winter with snowmobiles.

The Forest Service and State Parks and Recreation Department have in recent years, opened a groomed snowmobile trail to the north and east of Timp. It begins(or ends) at the parking lot at Tibble Fork Reservoir in the North Fork of American Fork Canyon. The trail heads northeast along the road to Dutchman Flat, then runs east up to Pole Line Pass, and down the other side. After a ways it turns south toward Cascade Springs, and from there west to the Timp Divide and along the Alpine Scenic Loop route down to Mutual Dell. The state keeps the road open as far as Tibble Fork Reservoir and to Mutual Dell throughout the winter months, but the Wasatch Mountain State Park crews groom the trail just described. You can also reach this area by snowmobile from the Heber Valley side via the Wasatch State Park.

You can also drive to Aspen Grove throughout the winter months and snowmobile up the Alpine Scenic Loop Road from there. Both the state and BYU keep the road open from the Sundance area to Aspen Grove. However, BYU keeps its own parking lots cleared of snow and for that they charge $2 a day for parking. Those parking lots are crowded on Saturdays, otherwise there is plenty of room for all. There is no grooming of the Alpine Loop Road above Aspen Grove.

Another area where snowmobiles are allowed to go is along the Timpooneke Road. Drive to and unload at or near Mutual Dell, then head up to the Timpooneke Campground, and from there along the summertime Timpooneke Road. Stay on the road however, because along the southwest face of the mountain it's a wilderness area above the road, and an administrative vehicle closure area below the road. This includes Battle Creek and Grove Creek Canyons.

For those who aren't as familiar as others about snowmobiling, here are some common-sense safety tips from a Forest Service pamphlet.

1. Know your snowmobile and keep it well maintained.
2. Never travel alone; let others know your destination and route. A party of 3 people and at least two machines are strongly recommended.
3. Do not attempt a long trip that may be beyond your capability.
4. Carry emergency supplies--flares, snowshoes, first aid kit, simple tools, map, ax, extra fuel, and rations.
5. Check and know the weather forecast before any trip to avoid bad weather conditions.
6. Look for trail markers and follow them. They will keep you on safe and interesting trails.
7. **Go prepared** for any foreseeable emergency.

Typical winter scene. The southwest face of Timp as seen from north Provo.

Hiking Maps of Mt. Timpanogos

There are several good maps suitable for hiking or climbing Mt. Timpanogos to choose from. Some are the topographic series put out by the USGS, and one is by the Forest Service.

One of the best maps around is from the USGS called **Orem**. It's a topo map(showing contour lines) at 1:62,500 scale, or as some prefer to call it, a 15 minute quadrangle. This one map covers the entire mountain and all access roads. This might be the best all-around map you can buy, but it does have a flaw--it's dated 1948. However, all the important roads and trails on or near the mountain are shown on this map, because there has been very little change in recent years. Basically, only the Timpooneke Road is not shown on this map, but the trails presently on the mountain are shown. The USGS could update this one at any time.

Another map that's rather good is the **Wasatch Hiking Map--Provo Area**. It's a topo map at 1:24,000 scale, or 7.5 minutes. This one is put out by the University of Utah Press and Geography Department and is made of a good quality waterproof paper which is more-or-less fold-resistant. It is dated 1984, so it's as up to date as any map around. It has a minor error or two in the placement of trails, but they are not serious problems. Perhaps the biggest problem with this map is that it does not show the access roads or the beginning of the the routes to the southwest and south sides of the mountain. This is a major disadvantage if you're planning to climb up the southwest face or the south ridge. It does however, show the two normal routes up the mountain from Aspen Grove and Timpooneke, as well as most of the newer campgrounds in the canyons along the Alpine Scenic Loop Road.

The Wasatch Hiking Map--Provo Area is based on the USGS topographic series at 1:24,000 scale. You can also buy the USGS maps at 1:24,000 scale. The only disadvantage to these is that although they have all been updated to the late 1960's or 1970's, you must buy 4 different maps to cover the entire mountain. You can cut and tape these together easily, but you end up with a large bulky map. These are very detailed maps however, with all the important features and trailheads shown. The maps are titled: **Aspen Grove, Bridal Veil Falls, Orem,** and **Timpanogos Cave.** The **Aspen Grove** and **Timp Cave** maps cover most of the mountain including the two normal routes.

In this same 1:24,000 scale USGS series there are also geology maps available. This series is commonly called the *Geologic Quadrangle Maps of the United States*. The four maps covering Timp all date from the 1960's. You will have to buy these in a USGS outlet or order them special. Their names and numbers are: **Aspen Grove(Map GQ-239), Bridal Veil Falls(Map GQ-998), Orem(Map GQ-241),** and **Timpanogos Cave(Map GQ-132).** Each map has a geologic explanation of the rocks included in that particular mapped area.

One last USGS map you can buy is called **Provo**. It is part of the *metric series* and is at 1:100,000 scale. It came out in 1986 so it's very up to date as far as recently built roads in new sub-divisions is concerned. However, although it shows the two main trails up the mountain, it is not nearly as detailed as the 1:24,000 and 1:62,500 scale maps of the mountain. It does show all the access roads and all the mountains around Utah Valley to as far south as Loafer Mountain, but it's not recommended as a hiking map.

The best place to buy any or all USGS maps is at the Federal Building in Salt Lake City. They are open from 8 to 5, Monday through Friday. This is the place to go if you can make it there. In Utah County you can buy USGS maps at Utah Office Supply, 69 East Center Street, and at the Uinta National Forest office at 100 North and 100 West in Provo. In Orem, you can buy USGS maps at Hansen Mountaineering, 757 North, State Street.

One last map you can use is one put out by the Forest Service titled **Uinta National Forest**. It is apparently at 1:125,000 scale. This map shows all the Uinta National Forest and all the normal Forest Service trails on Mt. Timpanogos, as well as the campgrounds and picnic sites in the region. It also shows Forest Service boundaries and private land in different colors. Because it does not show contour lines and is at a rather small scale, it's not recommended as a hiking map. However, it's a good map to have around. Forest Service maps can be purchased at ranger stations or offices of the Uinta National Forest in Pleasant Grove, Provo, Spanish Fork and Heber, or at other regional Forest Service office along the Wasatch Front. The Timpanogos Cave National Monument visitor center also sells this Forest Service map.

USGS TOPOGRAPHIC MAPS OF MT. TIMPANOGOS

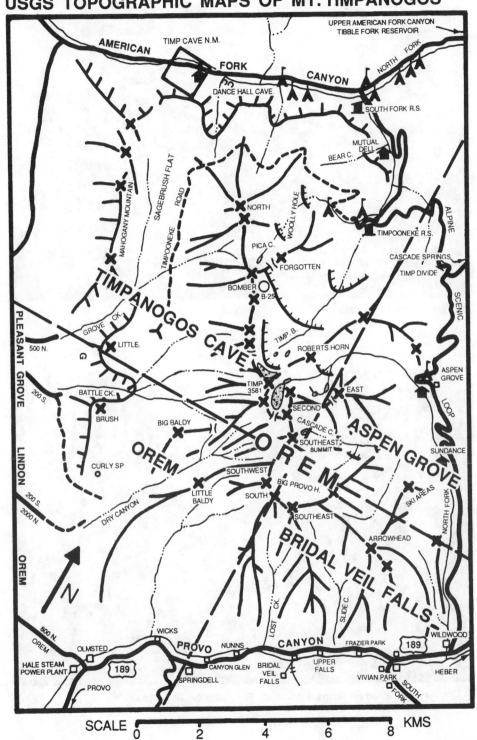

The Timp Summit Hut in 1988.

An October scene along the Alpine Scenic Loop Road near the Timp Divide.

REFERENCE MAP OF HIKES

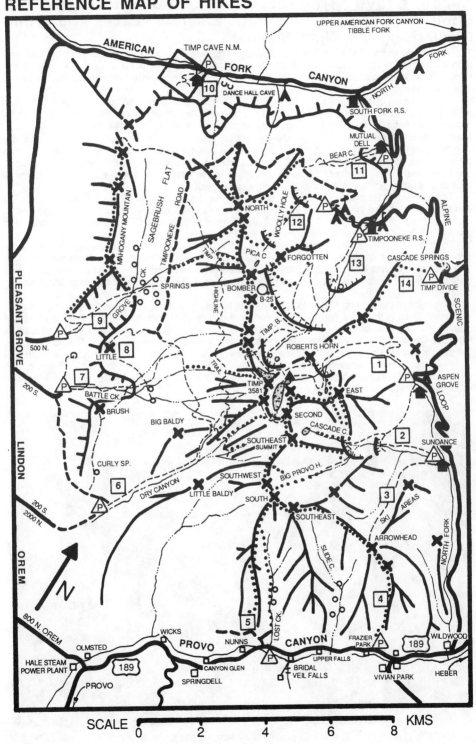

SCALE 0 2 4 6 8 KMS

33

Aspen Grove Trail--East Peak, Roberts Horn, The Shoulder, Second Summit, Emerald Lake, the Timp Glacier and the Timp Summit

Trailhead Location To reach the Aspen Grove Trailhead, drive up Provo Canyon to Wildwood, then turn north toward Sundance and the Aspen Grove Family Camp. When you arrive at Aspen Grove, park in the upper Theater-in-the-Pines Picnic Area parking lot where the Aspen Grove Trailhead is located.

The trail from Aspen Grove to the summit of Mt. Timpanogos is the route of the original Timp Hike which started in 1912, and is the most popular and most used route on the mountain. It's also the easiest route to East Peak, The Shoulder, the Second Summit and to Roberts Horn.

Route Description From the trailhead parking lot walk up the trail to the west. Very near the beginning of the trail will be a couple of signs. One gives the distances to various places on the mountain, the other advises the public that horses are not allowed on this trail. Horses are allowed on the Timpooneke Trail however. Although water is found at many locations along the trail, it might be best to fill a water bottle at the picnic site before starting out.

The first part of the trail is almost level and very wide. It's also paved for the first km, up to the first two waterfalls. Along the way, you will cross over a dry creek bed on a newly constructed bridge, pass a sign commemorating E. L. "Timp" Roberts(founder of the Annual Timp Hike), and another sign marking the boundary of the Mt. Timpanogos Wilderness Area.

This first part of the trail was paved because of the heavy foot traffic, but many people have since complained about it. In the future, the Forest Service will allow it to deteriorate. Since the pavement was laid, the area has been made into an official wilderness area and is supposed to be as natural as possible. Another complaint was from people with bad knees, who said it hurts the joints when walking downhill.

When you get to the first two waterfalls, the trail begins its winding course to the upper basins and the summit. It's in this area you will find a very real danger in May or June in years which have had heavy amounts of snowfall. In the area of these first waterfalls, as well as all the waterfalls in Primrose Cirque, there develops each year some holes or caverns under the snow. They are made by the stream flowing under the snow. Slowly but surely, the top part of these caverns become thin as melting occurs from underneath, and if you walk over the top, you can crash through and fall from 10 to 20 meters. Such falls through these snow holes at this first set of waterfalls **killed 3 hikers in 1980 and 1982.**

A 1980 foto showing the Sheriff's Department blowing up the snow bridge at the lower *Killer Snow Hole*(Chris Reed foto).

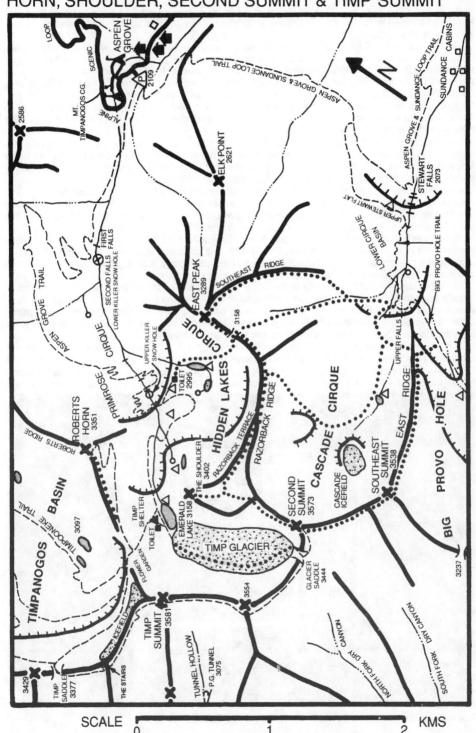

SCALE 0 1 2 KMS

Three hikers fell into the same hole, called here and on the map the **Lower Killer Snow Hole.** It's located about a km above the Aspen Grove Trailhead and at the second waterfall. Each spring and summer, the Forest Service goes up the trail and either puts up warning signs or blows them up. Please pay attention to this situation and stay on the trail as it winds up the snow fields in the late spring or early summer.

In the second km of the hike, there should always be some kind of running water crossing the trail in several places. This should be good water, as the springs are very near. After several switchbacks, the trail then heads southwest toward the upper part of Primrose Cirque. As you near the upper part of this lower cirque, you will have Roberts Horn and Roberts Ridge on your right, or to the northwest. In this area you will pass several snowslides if you're there in early or mid-summer. Further along, the trail begins some short zig zags or switchbacks. Please stay on the main trail, because taking short-cuts will create erosional problems on this very heavily used trail. It can also result in rocks falling down on other hikers.

Just below the rim of the upper basin and where the stream begins to cascade over several cliffs is another danger area during the late spring or early summer season. This is called the **Upper Killer Snow Hole** on the map. It's where a 14 year-old boy from Orem fell through a thin snow bridge above a waterfall and was killed. Avoid all of these waterfalls when there's lots of snow around.

After more zig zagging, the trail finally reaches the rim of the upper basin. At about that point, you will see a small sign pointing out a second trail leading to a toilet on the left. About 250 meters along this trail will be a toilet under some pine trees. In 1988, it was a portable type, brought there with the aid of a helicopter. In the future, another type may be placed there permanently.

From the trail leading to the toilet, the Aspen Grove Trail circles around into **Hidden Lakes Cirque.** At one point the trail passes directly above a good spring, then a little further along, it crosses a small stream, which originates from still another spring not far above. Finally, the trail heads west toward Emerald Lake and the Timp or Emerald Lake Shelter.

All along the way, and especially in the upper basins, please stay on the trail. This is the most heavily used route on the mountain, so it's important that everyone help to maintain the pristine and scenic values of the mountain. Once in the upper basins, the flowers and meadows are a main attraction, so please don't wade through the meadows. Usually you can get whatever fotos you want from the main trail, without messing up the scene for others who will follow.

The **Timp Shelter** is a rock building measuring about 6 x 7 meters inside. It has several windows, a front door(which has long been destroyed), and a fireplace. The floor is cement and the roof is made of corrugated steel. Built onto the west end are toilets, but they aren't being used any more. Instead, the Forest Service brings in a portable toilet by helicopter each summer, and places it

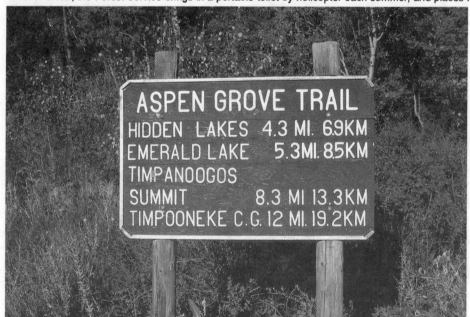

The trailhead sign at the beginning of the Aspen Grove Trail in 1988.

One of about a dozen waterfalls along the Aspen Grove Trail.

Along the trail in Primrose Cirque. The Second Summit and The Shoulder are above and in the background.

just behind the shelter. Please use the toilets if you can, to protect the water quality on the mountain. Many people stop at the shelter or the nearby Emerald Lake for lunch. This ice-water lake sits at the bottom of the **Timp Glacier,** and is fed by small rills coming off the icefield(actually this is closer to being a **perpetual snowfield** than a real glacier, because it hardly moves). The scene from this lake is one of the best anywhere in the world.

From the shelter, one route heads south and up the glacier, while another trail goes west toward what is usually called the Timp Saddle. You can take either of these routes to reach the summit, but the normal way up is to take the trail to the west, then loop around the summit and slide down the glacier and back to the shelter. Sometimes after a heavy winter snowpack, the top part of the glacier can be very steep, so it's often best to come down the glacier, instead of trying to go up. This route description will follow the normal route taken by most hikers.

From the shelter, head west along the main trail as it passes through what the author calls the **Flower Garden.** This is probably the most colorful meadow on the mountain, and the trail runs right through the middle. Please stay on the trail. These flowers are usually in full bloom in mid-July and last for about a month--but each year is different. For example, in the hot and dry summer of 1988, they were blooming in late June, and lasted through July. In most years the blossoms last until mid-August or there-abouts.

After passing through the Flower Garden, you will come to the edge of the Timpanogos Basin. At that point you will turn west and in early and mid-summer, will walk along the lower part of a snowfield which has accumulated at the base of the north face of the main peak. Part of this small **icefield** stays year-round, but it's often covered by rocks in late summer or early fall.

Further along, the trail gradually veers to the right or northwest and becomes steeper as it nears the top of the main northwest--southeast summit ridge. As you walk along this section of the trail, have a watchful eye out for Rocky Mountain goats, which are often seen in the cliffs and crags of the north face of the Timp Summit. Also, just before you arrive at the pass, look north on the same bench you're on, and you may see nanny goats and their kids grazing in meadows. Once you reach the ridge-top at the **Timp Saddle,** you will have your first panorama view down into Utah Valley.

From the pass the trail continues south, then zig zags up a steep rocky gully or couloir called the **Stairs.** Above the Stairs, the trail runs along at or near the ridge line. After several short switchbacks, you'll arrive at the highest peak of **Mt. Timpanogos.**

On top is a small tin shelter or **Summit Hut.** A few years after it was first built, it had glass in the windows, but that has long since been blown out. Read more on this hut under The Annual Timp Hike in the introduction of this book. It does give some shelter, but not much. The wind is usually blowing and it's rather chilly at the summit, even in summer. During the warmest season, you can normally get by

The *flower garden* foreground, the Timp Glacier in the background.

without mittens or gloves or a jacket, but often times a long sleeved shirt and long pants will make the summit stay a bit more enjoyable. You can also get down on the sunny eastern side of the peak out of the wind. From there you can enjoy a fine view of the Timp Glacier and Emerald Lake far below.

From the summit, most people take the alternate route down to the Timp Shelter via the glacier. To use this route, walk south from the Summit Hut along the summit ridge. It's a good trail and you'll have a view of all western Utah on your right hand side as you walk along. About one km from the summit, you'll make a descent to what is known as the **Glacier Saddle.** This is the low point at the head of the icefield and between the main summit and what the author is calling in this book, the **Second Summit.** It's only about 8 meters lower than the main peak. From the Glacier Saddle, you can walk up the southwest ridge of the Second Summit along a hiker-made trail. From that point, you will have some different views of the glacier, the main summit and down into Cascade Cirque.

Going down the glacier in early summer(June and early July) can be a bit scary. Right at the top of the Glacier Saddle it's often times very steep. If you slide down in the normal sitting position, it'll be a fast ride--perhaps too fast for some. However, by the the end of July, normally enough snow has melted from the top of the icefield to make it a fun and safe slide down the top part. Most of the time it's safe, but be alert for small shallow depressions in the snow and for rocks. People are injured sliding down the glacier every year.

Some people take plastic garbage can liners to make it an even faster ride. However, some people end up leaving these sacks on the glacier, which doesn't add to the pristine values of the mountain. If you find this kind of garbage on the mountain, why not put it in your pack and dispose of it properly?

On the lower part of the glacier, you can walk down on either side, but the normal way is along the west side. When early fall rolls around, all of the previous winter snow has melted, and what is left is a rock-covered sheet of ice. During the heat of the summer, you'll see small rills of water running down the middle of the western half of the icefield.

Other Peaks and Climbs Another interesting, fun and easy climb is to the top of **East Peak.** When you arrive at the edge of the Hidden Lakes Cirque, take the trail signposted for the toilet on the left. Walk along this good trail past the toilet and campsites and toward Hidden Lake. This is the largest of the two small ponds in the basin. From the east side of the lake, walk southeast toward the obvious pass between the East Peak and the east end of Razorback Ridge. As you go up towards East Pass marked 3158 meters, veer to the right and you'll find it easier to walk up this steep slope in the trees rather than up the middle of the talus slope.

When you reach East Pass, turn left and ridge-walk northeast to the summit of East Peak, which is 3289 meters in elevation. From this eastern-most summit of Mt. Timpanogos, you will have some

The Timp Shelter at Emerald Lake. The summit of Timpanogos in the background.

From the top of Timp looking northwest and down at the trail, the summit ridge and the North Peak.

The Summit Hut seen from the east side of the ridge.

excellent views of Hidden Lakes and Cascade Cirques, as well as the Southeast Summit, Second Summit, The Shoulder, the main summit of Timp, and Roberts Horn. One can even see the North Peak. Getting up to the top of East Peak is easy and safe along the normal route just described.

Here is one of the more exciting hikes on the mountain. From East Pass, turn right and head up the rocky ridge toward the east end of **Razorback Ridge.** This first part is steep and you may have to climb on all-fours in a place or two, but anyone can make it. Just don't roll rocks down on other members of your group.

When you arrive on top of the eastern end of Razorback, you will find an almost level and flat-topped ridge. It's much different than it appears as you look at it from below. Walk west along the top until you reach some jagged pinnacles and a buttress. At that point the climb on this ridge becomes impossible to all except experienced rock climbers.

When you reach the first buttress, walk down the steep slope to the right or north, and get down onto the first little bench or terrace just below the top of Razorback Ridge. The author is calling this **Razorback Terrace.** It's a steep talus slope all along the way to The Shoulder. As you walk along this bench, you will find one or two trails made by either deer or mountain goats. The author never felt in any danger, but it's recommended you not take a group of Boy Scouts along this part of the route, because of the huge dropoff.

After walking about 500 meters along this north-facing slope, you'll come to an area where some snowbanks seem to stay almost the entire summer. If there is snow on the ground, then you will see a small trickle of water or two cascading down-slope. At the first convenient point, head up the steep eastern slope of **The Shoulder.** When you reach the top you'll be on a relatively flat portion of this buttress. Veer to the right or northwest, and walk to the highest and northern-most point of The Shoulder. From there, you'll have some excellent views of the Timp Summit, the glacier and all points north, east and west. You will also be looking straight down on Emerald Lake.

From The Shoulder, walk south and up the north ridge of the **Second Summit.** It's an easy climb even along the steepest part. Once on top of the ridge, then simply ridge-walk south to the peak. From this second highest point on Mt. Timpanogos, you will again have fine views in all directions. From this peak, walk down the rocky slope to the southwest. After a ways, you'll find a minor hiker-made trail leading down to the Glacier Saddle, then to the glacier and on down to Emerald Lake; or on to the highest summit of Timpanogos.

Once you reach Emerald Lake and the Timp Shelter, you will have still another alternate hike to choose from. This is to **Roberts Horn,** located just north of the lake and shelter. This peak is named after the man who originally started the Annual Timp Hike back in 1912, E. L. "Timp" Roberts.

From the summit you look directly down on the end of the glacier and Emerald Lake.

From the top of Roberts Horn one can see the glacier, left and the Timp Summit in the middle.

The Shoulder and Second Summit in the background with the glacier to the right.

From the east end of Razorback Ridge looking west. From the left, Second Summit, Timp Summit and The Shoulder.

Along the Razorback Terrace with The Shoulder in the background on the right.

From the top of The Shoulder looking southeast at Razorback Ridge and Terrace.

From near the top of Second Summit, looking down on Razorback Ridge and the East Peak.

From near the top of Second Summit, looking at the upper face of Cascade Cirque.

From the top of Second Summit, looking northwest along the ridge at the Timp Summit.

This is the normal route to the summit of Roberts Horn. First, take the trail west toward the Timp Saddle, but stop as you reach the lip of Timpanogos Basin. From that point walk in a northeast direction and toward the southwest ridge of the Horn. You may see a trail-of-sorts as you begin. A little further along, you will see an obvious man-made trail near the ridge line, which runs out on the south face of the peak. From the lake you can see this old trail zig zagging up the slope.

At that point, you have two choices. You can walk up this old trail to the summit, or you can get on the ridge. The trail hasn't been used much in recent years, but you can still find and follow it easily. The ridge route is very easy walking and since it's rocky, it seems that even if a lot of people use it, erosion won't take place. The ridge route will be easier and faster.

Distance and Time Needed The distance from Aspen Grove to Emerald Lake is 8.5 kms. From Emerald Lake to the summit via the trail passing over the Timp Saddle is about 4.8 kms. This makes the one way distance to the top 13.3 kms. The distance from the summit to Emerald Lake via the glacier is just slightly shorter, but not much.

The record time for this hike was made in the summer of 1967. That was 1 hour and 30 minutes to the summit, and 45 minutes down, for a round-trip hike of 2 hours and 15 minutes. However, most hikers prefer to take more time and enjoy the mountain. Strong hikers can reach the top of Timp in about 4 hours, then will need another 2 or 3 hours for the descent. For other hikers, it might take 5 or 6 hours for the ascent, and 3 or 4 for the trip down. In other words, for most hikers, it'll be an all day affair during the summer season with an early morning start.

From the Aspen Grove Trail(at the edge of Hidden Lakes Cirque) to the top of East Peak is only about one km. Normally this can be hiked in less than an hour by almost anyone. If you decide to climb to the top of the Second Summit via Razorback Ridge and The Shoulder, it will take about the same length of time as if you were climbing to the Timp Summit. In other words, it will be an all day hike to the top of the Second Summit and back. However, only the very strongest hikers should try this alternate route to the Second Summit and include the main peak of Timp on the same day-hike. To do both summits in one day via Razorback Ridge would be a very long and tiresome climb.

If you decide to climb Roberts Horn when you reach Emerald Lake, it should take less than an hour to reach the top. This will be a good alternate hike for those people who haven't the energy to reach the highest summit.

Main Attractions This is probably the most scenic route to the top of Utah's best mountain. Emerald Lake, the Timp Glacier, some of the most colorful meadows and a chance to view Rocky Mountain goats can be seen on this hike. The views from East Peak, The Shoulder, the Second Summit and from Roberts Horn are all worth the effort of climbing to these points.

Elevations Aspen Grove Trailhead, 2109 meters; East Peak, 3289; The Shoulder, 3402; Emerald

The Timp or Emerald Lake Shelter, with Roberts Horn in the background.

Lake, 3158; Roberts Horn, 3351; Timp Saddle, 3377; Timp Summit, 3581; and the Second Summit, 3573 meters.

Water From the first two waterfalls on up to Emerald Lake, you will pass by a number of small streams and springs, especially if it's early or mid-summer. In late summer and in the fall, many of the smaller streams dry up. When most of the snowbanks on the mountain are gone, so are most of the small streams.

As far as drinking the water on this route is concerned, the official Forest Service policy is that it is safest to take water with you in a water bottle, or if you have to drink mountain water take it directly from a spring. The water coming off the glacier can be polluted by so much human traffic, therefore, the water in Emerald Lake and the stream running down to Aspen Grove may also be polluted. With so many people on the mountain in July, August and September, this could definitely be a possibility.

In recent years, the author has for the most part, avoided drinking the water from the creek running down the mountain from the lake, but not always. It's likely you won't get sick by drinking it, but if you can drink from one of the little streams crossing the trail or from one of the springs in the upper basin. If you feel the need, you can find water at the picnic site or campground near the trailhead at Aspen Grove. Normally however, there are lots of places along the trail to get good safe water, unless you're hiking late in the season.

If you're out on the Razorback Ridge and The Shoulder, and there are still snowbanks on the upper slopes, then you will always have some running water on or near The Shoulder which will be safe to drink.

Boots or Shoes Running shoes work well, at least if you stay on the trail. More serious hikers however, often use a pair of the new light weight hiking boots with lug soles. If you climb the Razorback Ridge to The Shoulder and on to the Second Summit, a more rugged hiking boot would be best. If it's early in the season with lots of snow around, boots or shoes with a lug sole would make it easier and safer. If you're hiking in July, August, September or October, there will be no need for an ice ax or crampons.

Campsites For the most part, hiking this route on Timp is just a day hike, but camping is permitted. There are several fine campsites in the vicinity of the toilet in Hidden Lakes Cirque. You could also bed down inside the Timp Shelter, but it has no door. Or you could pitch a tent somewhere around Emerald Lake. A better place would be near the spring and small pond east of Emerald Lake.

If you're camping, please use a previously used campsite and leave the ground as little scarred as possible. This is a heavily used area, and a lot of tents and campsites won't add to it's beauty. Boy Scouts, be sure and pack out all your garbage.

Winter Climbing One good thing about winter climbing on this route is the paved road from Provo

Looking west at the east face of Roberts Horn from Aspen Grove.

Canyon to Aspen Grove is kept open on a year-round basis. So access should always be easy. The BYU Aspen Grove Family Camp is also kept open year-round. In winter time they open their lodge for various activities and rent out snowshoes and skis on Saturdays.

With the many people in the Aspen Grove area during winter, you can expect the lower end of the Aspen Grove Trail to be well groomed. The most used part goes up to about the first waterfalls, then most people stop. From that point on you may be on your own, or with a little luck, will be able to follow someone else's tracks. From the lower falls, forget the trail and just head straight up the canyon, but stay on the right or north side of the Primrose Cirque. This is the area where the sun always shines, therefore the snow will always be harder and crusted and easier to walk on.

When you get near the upper end of the Primrose Cirque, you must beware of the danger of avalanches coming down from the east face of Roberts Horn. If it's been 4 or 5 days or longer since the last storm, then there should be little danger from any big avalanches. But if you're there right after a storm--watch out! The author was in that area once only a day after a light snow storm and had two minor avalanches come down at him. They ended up being rather harmless, but it was scary none-the-less. Walking along the base of Roberts Horn is one of the worst places on the mountain for avalanches. For the best and latest information on avalanches, call the Utah Avalanche Forecast Center at 374-9770, 364-1581 or 621-2362.

In this same area, another big problem you will almost always face is deep powder snow. The reason for the powder is that in the upper part of Primrose Cirque, you'll be on a north facing slope. The sun doesn't shine on it, so there's little or no crusted snow. This, plus the steepness, means the walking will be difficult, and you'll almost always have to have snowshoes or skis to make it up. If you're there in early winter with a light snow cover, then it should be easy walking. If you climb near the end of March or April, the snow will be crusted over so you can walk on top of it.

Once you get into the upper basin, travel is almost on a flat track all the way to the Timp Shelter. From there the easiest route to the summit would likely be up the glacier. If you're doing this climb early in the season, perhaps around Thanksgiving time, then you can likely make it without snowshoes or skis. But if you're there from about the first of December until late March, you'll always need them.

If you decide to climb East Peak from Hidden Lakes Cirque, use the same route as in summer to East Pass. Although you'll be climbing a north facing route, the author found the snow very hard right in the gully. This must have been caused by some minor avalanches compacting the snow. From the pass you can easily climb up the hard crusted snow of the ridge to the summit. You could also try climbing the west face of East Peak. It's steep all the way, but snow conditions would likely be good.

The east face of Roberts Horn. Notice the avalanche cones at the bottom of the foto. The Aspen Grove Trail runs along the bottom of this face.

The route along and over Razorback Ridge to The Shoulder is not recommended in winter. The problem area would be the very steep Razorback Terrace, which is on a north facing slope. The danger is you might start an avalanche and be carried over the rim and into the basin below. One slip and you're a gonner on this route!

For winter climbing on the Aspen Grove Trail, it's recommended you go during the last two weeks of March or in early April. At that time you'll have hard crusted snow, warmer more comfortable weather, and much more daylight than in the dead of winter. Otherwise, you will still need the same cold weather clothing and camping gear.

If the snow conditions are right--with a good hard crust, then a strong climber can climb the main peak of Timp in one long day, but camping one night on the mountain will insure the summit. The Timp Shelter has no door, so it will likely be best to forget sleeping inside this drafty icebox which will be half-filled with snow. You'd be better off to pitch a tent outside, and use the shelter in an emergency situation only. In winter, Emerald Lake is just a big sink hole with no water or ice, so you have to melt snow for water. Take extra fuel for that.

Rock Climbing to the Timp Summit Ridge

Arriving days before this book went to the printers was a letter from rock climber Joel Bown of Park City. In it he described how he and several other climbers scaled the northwest ridge or corner of the main summit of Timpanogos. Part of his letter went like this.

One climb we made on Timp was up the north east corner of the main peak directly above Emerald Lake. This corner is almost a perfect right angle connecting the east face and the north face. The bottom third or so is nearly vertical, the remainder is considerably less steep.

Dave George and I think this climb was done on about May 10, 1970. George Lowe and Jock Glidden joined us to make a foursome. We hiked up from Aspen Grove late in the evening and bivvyed in the small hut near Emerald Lake. We started this climb at first light on what we all agreed was the worst rock any of us had ever seen. George had spent the previous summer in the Canadian Rockies and said nothing there was as rotten as Timp.

Our decision to climb early in the year and early in the day is the only reason we succeeded in climbing the route. Only because the rock was frozen in place would it remain long enough for us to climb it. Each of the 4 or 5 pitches in the vertical band was about 5.7 in difficulty. Not being killed by the rock fall from the leader or his rope was the major concern of all of us. Descent would have been almost impossible due to the lack of reliable rappel anchors.

Once we reached the top of the vertical band, the remainder of the climb was reasonable. Steep firm snow extended almost all the way to the summit. We descended using the summer hiking route and did one of the best glissades any of us had ever done back down to Aspen Grove.

This route is definitely not recommended for anyone who values his skin. A year or two later while hiking up Timp in the late spring, I witnessed an enormous rock fall near this route in which about a two hundred foot[60 meter] wide section of the vertical band peeled off and crashed onto the snow field below. It is entirely possible that the entire route could fall off while someone is climbing on it.

For obvious reasons, any climb directly from the Emerald Lake area to the summit is for experienced and well equipped rock climbers only. The rest of us will sleep better at night if we plan to go up one of the normal routes.

The Timp Shelter at Emerald Lake and the summit of Timpanogos in the background to the west.

A scene from the top of East Peak. Second Summit left, Timp Summit in background.

From the summit of East Peak. Razorback Ridge, then Southeast and Second Summits beyond. Hidden Lake Cirque is in the lower right.

The upper east face of Southeast Summit, as seen from the East Peak with a telefoto lens.

From the summit of East Peak looking at Big Provo Hole, the East Ridge of the Southeast Summit and the Cascade Cirque.

The east face of the summit ridge and the Summit Hut, as seen from Emerald Lake (210mm telefoto lens).

Looking north along the summit ridge of Timp. Summit Hut in the upper left hand corner.

At the Summit Hut looking south in March 1970.

Stewart Falls Trail--Stewart Falls, East Peak, Second and Southeast Summits, South Peaks and the Cascade & Big Provo Hole Cirques

Trailhead Location There are two trailheads you can choose from to reach the eastern peaks and southern cirques of Mt. Timpanogos. One is at the Sundance Ski Resort, the other at Aspen Grove. You can start at either place and make a loop-hike via Stewart Falls, then go on to the other trailhead. The author calls this trail the *Aspen Grove & Sundance Loop Trail* on the map. Drive up Provo Canyon and turn north at Wildwood onto the Alpine Scenic Loop Road. Sundance is about 4 kms from the main canyon highway, while Aspen Grove is another 4 kms above Sundance.

If you decide to start at Sundance, park at the main parking lot at the bottom of the ski lifts. You can also start hiking at Aspen Grove. When you arrive there, park in the same parking lot as if you were heading up the Aspen Grove Trail. This is at the Theater-in-the-Pines Picnic Area.

Route Description No matter which trailhead you begin at, your first destination is **Stewart Falls** at the eastern base of the mountain, due east of Sundance. On many maps it's called **Stewarts Cascade,** but it seems to be better known as Stewart Falls. The distance from each trailhead to the falls is about the same, approximately 2 1/2 or 3 kms.

If you begin at Sundance, make sure you park in the main parking lot. From there begin walking west past the front of the building with the Tree Room Restaurant and small store. Just beyond this building, turn left and walk across a wooden bridge to the grassy area at the bottom of the Mandan Lift. From there walk up the maintenance road to the southwest. About a 100 meters past the bottom of the lift, you will see a sign pointing out the nature trail to the right. Follow this trail through the pines. After another 300 meters or so, you will cross a paved road and the small stream which comes down from Stewart Falls.

From this crossing, follow the same nature trail as it heads up-canyon to the west. It makes several switchbacks in the final 2 kms before arriving at the falls. This trail passes over private land all the way to just below Stewart Falls, so please don't deviate from it. It was built and is maintained by money personally donated by Sundance owner, Robert Redford. He allows people to use it as if it were a public access trail. The second route to Stewarts Falls is a trail from Aspen Grove, which runs across public lands nearly all the way. This trail is maintained by the Forest Service and they call it the **Stewart Cascades Trail**.

From the parking lot at the Theater-in-the-Pines Picnic Area, walk up the Aspen Grove Trail to the west only about 10 or 15 meters. From there, veer left or south, and walk along a less-used trail. There is no sign at that point indicating this different trail. A little further along, the trail veers to the

Stewart Falls, located not far to the west of Sundance Ski Resort and just below Cascade Cirque.

MAP 2, **STEWARTS FALLS TRAIL**--EAST PEAK, SECOND & SOUTHEAST SUMMITS & SOUTH PEAKS

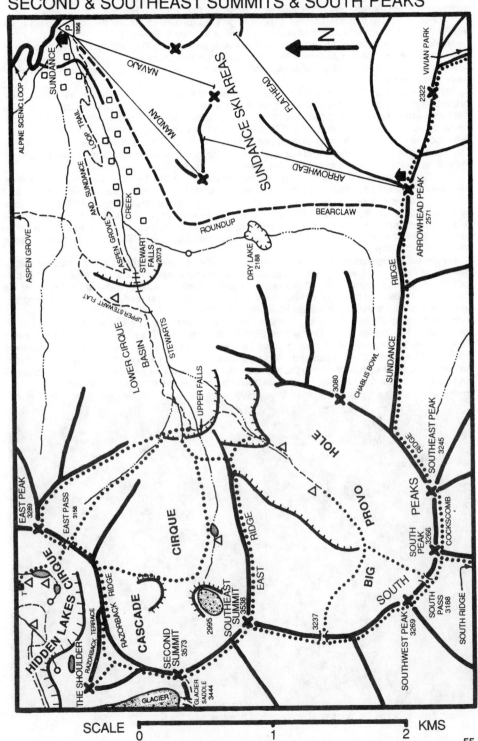

SCALE 0   1   2   KMS

right and runs west a short distance before making a sharp left turn. At that point, you will see the only sign for this trail, located right where the trail begins to climb the heavily timbered slope just above the picnic area. From there it runs to the southeast above the Aspen Grove Family Camp cabins.

Further along, the trail passes over a minor ridge then runs south around the base of East Peak and Elk Point. This is a well used and maintained trail all the way to Stewart Falls.

Stewart Falls is a series of cascades, about 4 or 5 altogether. The two right at the bottom are somewhere between 40 and 45 meters high, the highest on the mountain. If you visit this place in late spring or early summer(late May and June), it will be more impressive because of the higher volume of water in the stream.

Many people visit these falls each year, but few know anything about the hiking possibilities further up the mountain. Not far from the cascades is an old Forest Service trail which can be used to reach the cirque basins and peaks above. From the falls, walk northeast along the trail heading toward Aspen Grove. After about 500-600 meters, and just after passing through a grove of pine trees, look to your left or the west side, to find the beginning of the **Big Provo Hole Trail.** This trail hasn't been maintained in years and has almost been forgotten by the Forest Service, but it's easy to find and follow in most places to as far as the lower end of the Big Provo Hole.

The Big Provo Hole Trail begins by contouring(staying at the same elevation) to the left or southwest to a point just above the falls. This area is rather flat and open, and is often used by Boy Scouts and other groups for camping. The author calls this place **Upper Stewart Flat.** Continue on the trail to the south, but about 10 meters before it appears to cross the stream, you turn to the right. From there the trail runs uphill to the west and in between clumps of willows and oak brush. In this area the trail may be hard to follow if there haven't been any other hikers on it just prior to your arrival

Further up, the trail crosses two small streams then steepens just below a big cliff which the author calls **Upper Falls.** From spring until mid-summer, this will be a waterfall, but later when most of the snow fields have vanished above, it becomes dry(there's usually a trickle of water at the bottom of the falls however). The trail then runs directly below the falls to the left a short distance before turning up-canyon and into the lower end of the Big Provo Hole Cirque.

From the area of Upper Falls at the bottom of the Cascade Cirque, hikers will have a choice of several climbs to choose from. One will be **East Peak.** From the Upper Falls, walk up the slope to the northwest toward a big gully coming down from **East Pass,** at 3158 meters. The lower slope is covered with patches of oak brush and open meadows. Route-find up this steep gully until you're at the pass, then ridge-walk northeast to the summit. You could also veer to the right of the gully and get out onto a southeast ridge of East Peak. Go up whichever route seems easiest and safest.

Stewart Falls is below the Southeast and Second Summits and the Cascade Cirque.

Another fun hike and one that's for experienced and stronger climbers, would be to the top of the **Second Summit.** From the Upper Falls, walk up and to the right or northwest. You must look for the easiest way to get into the lower or bottom end of **Cascade Cirque.** Once inside this cirque, head straight up to the west.

About one km above Upper Falls, you'll see a mini-cirque basin on the upper left. This is the very last remnant of a former glacier which flowed down to the bottom of the Sundance Ski Resort perhaps 12,000 years ago. From the middle of Cascade Cirque, veer to the right or north and head for the top of **Razorback Ridge.** Just before you reach the top, there is one minor cliff you must scale, but anyone should be able to climb it. You can also get to the Razorback Ridge by climbing the gully running up to the East Pass, then climb southwest up the steep ridge to the top.

From the top of Razorback, walk west until you're confronted by a big steep buttress, then climb down to the north and onto the **Razorback Terrace**(read more on this route under Map 1). From there you can contour on deer trails to **The Shoulder,** thence to the south and up the north ridge of Second Summit. Then it's an easy walk south to the highest point, which is the second highest peak on Mt. Timpanogos.

From the Second Summit, you could then come down via the **East Ridge** of the **Southeast Summit.** Here's a description of that route from the Upper Falls. From the area of Upper Falls, stay on the trail going into the lower end of the Big Provo Hole. From the bottom of this cirque, head back to the north toward the lower end of East Ridge. This part is easy, as there seems to be a number of old sheep or deer trails in the area, but there will be one or two minor little cliffs to pass through before you reach the bottom of the East Ridge. You can also reach the bottom of the East Ridge from the lower part of Cascade Cirque, but it's more difficult than from the Big Provo Hole.

Once on the East Ridge simply head straight up. From lower in the canyon this appears to be a very difficult climb, but in reality it's very easy. Any one should be able to climb it. There are in some places little cliffs you must skirt around, but these are very minor obstacles. When you arrive at the summit you can climb the Second Summit and even go on to climb the main summit of Timpanogos, but that would be a long, long climb most people couldn't accomplish in one day. You could also return via Big Provo Hole, which is discussed next.

From the Upper Falls, walk up the trail into the **Big Provo Hole.** In about the middle of the basin, the trail gradually vanishes, and you'll be walking cross-country to where you want to go. There are lots of flowery meadows in this basin in mid-summer, one of its main attractions.

From this cirque basin you can climb the Southeast Summit by walking to its upper end and veering to the right or northwest. Head up a steep slope toward the low point in the ridge separating the Southeast Summit and Southwest Peak on the south side of Big Provo Hole. That little pass is

Flowers line the bottom of the Big Provo Hole Cirque.

labeled 3237 meters on the map. The part just below the ridgeline is steep, but shouldn't be dangerous. Once on the ridge, turn right and climb the south ridge of the Southeast Summit, a very easy walk.

From the Big Provo Hole, you can also climb one or more of the **South Peaks** of Mt. Timpanogos. One interesting route would be to climb to the pass(3237 m) between the Southeast Summit and **Southwest Peak,** then ridge-walk south. Or you could head straight for the saddle between Southwest Peak and South Peak. This steep, but easy-to-climb slope, will be covered with snow until August. You may want to have an ice ax or some kind of walking stick to aid in the ascent.

Once on the ridge, you can then climb right or left. If you head to the left, you can follow an old deer and goat trail to the top of **South Peak.** From there you can ridge-walk the cockscomb-like South Ridge over **Southeast Peak** down to **Arrowhead Peak,** then to Sundance via one of several ski trails or maintenance roads. The route down to Arrowhead is not difficult, but it's steep in places and *slow-and-go* all the way.

Distance and Time Needed The distance from either trailhead to Stewart Falls is about 2 1/2 or 3 kms, and can be walked by anyone in about one hour, each way. A trip from Aspen Grove to the top of East Peak, and back, will be 5 to 7 hours for most hikers(on this trip you could return--or begin the hike on the Aspen Grove Trail).

For those climbing up to the Razorback Ridge, then to the top of the Second and Southeast Summits, and returning via the East Ridge, you'll want all day with an early morning start(you could also go up or make the return trip via the Aspen Grove Trail, if you start at that trailhead). This long hike or climb is for advanced or more experienced climbers who are in good physical condition.

A trip up into the Big Provo Hole to one or more of the South Peaks will also be an all day affair, but won't be as long or as hard as the climb just previously mentioned. If you start at Sundance, climb into the Big Provo Hole, up to the South Peaks, then return via Arrowhead Peak and the Sundance ski slopes, it would be a very long all day hike.

Main Attractions There is a chance to see the highest waterfall on Mt. Timpanogos in Stewart Falls, and two glacier cirque basins which are almost unknown to the general public. Also, there are several new and relatively easy routes to the highest peaks on the mountain. These routes and peaks are also unknown to the public.

Elevations Aspen Grove Trailhead, 2109 meters; Sundance Parking Lot, 1856; bottom of Stewart Falls, 2073; East Peak, 3289; East Pass, 3158; Second Summit, 3573; Southeast Summit, 3538; Southwest Peak, 3269; South Peak, 3266; Southeast Peak, 3245; Arrowhead Peak, 2571 meters.

This foto was taken in the lower end of the Cascade Cirque. The Southeast Summit is above the small icefield.

The Southeast Summit and its East Ridge, as seen from the east end of Razorback Ridge.

From the top of the Second Summit, looking down into Cascade Cirque.

Water Since there are very few hikers and campers above Stewart Falls, this water should be good to drink as is, because most of the water there comes out just above the falls. Some may want to have a water bottle full at the start of either trail.

If you're there in early summer through the first part of August, or as long as there are some snowbanks on the upper slopes, there should always be a small trickle of water running somewhere in the upper cirque basins. However, always take a bottle of water, especially if you climb up to the peaks.

Boots or Shoes You can use about any comfortable shoe if your destination is only to Stewart Falls. But if you're out to climb any of the peaks, better use a more sturdy pair of hiking boots. A good pair of running-type shoes will get you up into the cirque basins OK.

Campsites There are a number of ready-made campsites at Upper Stewart Flat just above the falls. There are also a number of good sites in the two upper basins; but remember, in late summer and into early fall, these sites will be dry(especially the lower altitude Big Provo Hole). If the snowbanks are gone from the upper slopes, then you'd have to carry water from below up to your camp.

Winter Climbing You can drive to each trailhead on a year-round basis, so winter access is easy. During the winter ski season, the BYU lodge at Aspen Grove is open on Saturdays and they rent skis and snowshoes. They also groom some of the local trails. Because of this and all the skiers at Sundance, it's very likely the trail between Aspen Grove and Sundance will be compacted by previous use. If there's been traffic on the trail then it'll be easy walking with snowshoes or skis at least to Stewart Falls. Above that, it'll be wading in deep powder during the period from about the first of December on through mid or late March.

The best time to climb any of these peaks will be either early in the season, say sometime around the Thanksgiving weekend; or late in the season after about mid-March and into April. Of course, once you get onto one of the ridges, then you can count on the snow being wind-blown and crusted and relatively easy for walking about anytime during the winter.

Avalanche danger would have to be rated high for this entire section of the mountain. Some of the really big slides make it from the top all the way down to below Stewart Falls. It's a good idea to stay out of this area for the first several days after each snow storm. If you're planning a trip up any of these routes in the dead of winter, you might stay in touch with the Utah Avalanche Forecast Center, at 374-9770, 364-1581 or 621-2362. They give daily reports about the avalanche conditions in the back country all along the Wasatch Front. Usually the avalanche danger isn't high in the early part of winter or later on in April. However, right after any big storm there is great danger for 3 or 4 days, no matter what the time of year.

The East Ridge coming down from the Southeast Summit. Foto taken from near the beginning of
the Big Provo Hole Trail.

If you're hoping to climb the East Ridge to the top of Southeast Summit, the hardest part will be along the lower part of the Big Provo Hole Trail up to the Upper Falls. Forget the trail and head up-hill in the sunnier places on the right or north side of the lower cirque. Then walk under the Upper Falls into the lower end of the Big Provo Hole using basically the same route as in summer. Once on the East Ridge, it should be easy climbing.

Winter climbing on East Peak should be relatively easy from Stewart Falls and the area of the Upper Falls because you'll be on the sunny southeast face or gully all the way to the summit. If you stay in the gully part, you'll always have rock-hard snow to walk up, but you better not get into that situation for at least a week or 10 days after the last storm. Again, if you're not an expert on snow conditions or avalanches, contact the Avalanche Center for their opinion.

It's recommended you not even try the Razorback Ridge route to the Second Summit in winter, because of the steepness of the Razorback Terrace and the threat of avalanches there.

Getting into the Big Provo Hole should be fairly easy, but you'll always have some deep powder in the area of the Upper Falls and into the lower end of the Hole. After you get into the middle part of this Provo Cirque, then it should be easy walking. You'll need skis or snowshoes to reach this area, except in early winter or after about April first.

If you want to climb the South Peaks, it'll likely be easier to reach the ridge via the saddle or pass between the Southeast Summit and Southwest Peak. Once on the ridge, you can easily walk to all the other South Peaks. You can return down to the bottom of the cirque basin via the gully between South and Southwest Peaks. That route will have powdery snow in winter but should be easy going down-- but not going up.

Stewart Falls. Most of the water comes from a spring near the bottom part of the falls.

61

Sundance Ski Trails--Arrowhead Peak, South Peaks and the Big Provo Hole Cirque

Trailhead Location The trailhead to the hikes mentioned here is at Sundance Ski Resort. To get there, drive up Provo Canyon and turn north onto the Alpine Scenic Loop Road at Wildwood. After about 4 kms, you'll arrive at Sundance. Park in the main parking lot at the bottom of the ski lifts next to several buildings, one of which houses a small store and the Tree Room Restaurant.

Route Description The route described here is to the top of the lifts at Sundance which the skiing crowd calls **Arrowhead Peak**. The route also runs on to the South Peaks of Mt. Timpanogos. The official policy of the ski resort is, you are welcome to hike any of the ski runs or maintenance roads on the ski slopes in summer, but in winter cross-country skiing or snowshoeing in the same areas is forbidden.

In the summer season park in the large parking lot at the bottom of the ski lifts. Cross Stewarts Creek on one of 2 or 3 bridges and walk across the grassy area to the right or west side of the Mandan Lift. At that point you will see the maintenance road heading up the slope to the southwest. This particular road zig zags up the slope and eventually reaches the top of the Arrowhead Lift.

To reach the top of Arrowhead Peak, you can walk on this road all the way, but you can save time if you stay to the right and walk up part of the way on some of the ski runs on the far right-hand side of the area. The approximate route is shown on the map. Further up this is called the Roundup, then the Bearclaw Ski Run. Part of the time you will be walking along a roadway, but at other times you'll want to go straight up the ski slopes. On top of Arrowhead is a log cabin lodge where meals are served during the ski season. From this vantage point you can see the eastern slopes of Mt. Timpanogos as well as the northern half of Cascade Peak just to the south.

If you're interested in further hiking, you can continue up what the author is calling **Sundance Ridge** and to the top of the south rim of the Big Provo Cirque. From the lodge on Arrowhead, first walk down hill to the west, then look for hiker and deer-made trails running up the obvious ridge coming down from the west. At first follow one of these little trails, but as you get higher, the trails seem to fade away. When this happens just continue up right on top of the ridge. Near the top of Sundance Ridge, it steepens and you'll have to route-find around several minor ledges. This shouldn't be a problem for anyone.

From the top of the Sundance Ridge, you'll then be on a cockscomb-type ridge. The high points on this ridge the author calls the **South Peaks**. Begin walking to the west. It's a up and down hike, but it's fairly easy. Soon you will reach a major high point called here, the **Southeast Peak**. All the way along this cockscomb ridge you will have excellent views of the still higher summits of Timp to the right

Sundance in summer. The peaks left to right are; Southeast and Second Summits, and East Peak.

MAP 3, **SUNDANCE SKI TRAILS**--ARROWHEAD PEAK, SOUTH PEAKS, AND BIG PROVO HOLE

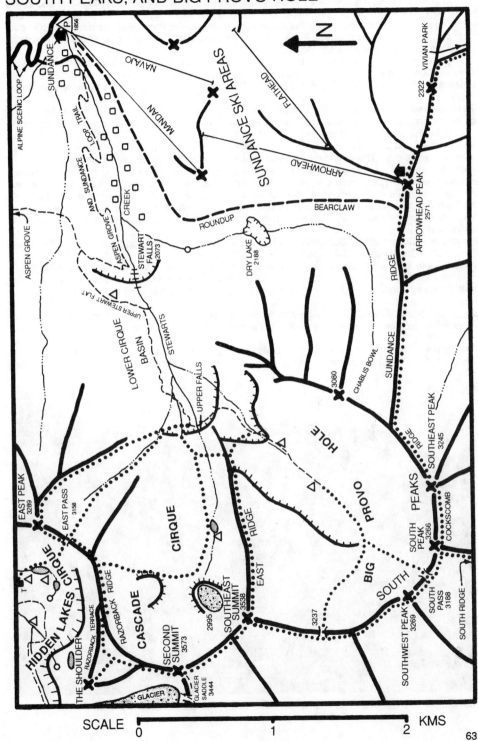

SCALE

0   1   2   KMS

or north, and of Provo Canyon and Cascade Peak to the left or south.

If you still have the energy to continue, the next major summit is called simply **South Peak**(if you were to begin climbing near Bridal Vail Falls, you would likely walk up the South Ridge and end at this peak). From the top of South Peak, head down the ridgeline to the northwest. At the low point of the ridge called **South Pass,** you can either go straight down into Big Provo Hole, or continue up to the north and to the top of **Southwest Peak.** This is the highest of the peaks around the south side of this cirque basin, reaching the altitude of 3269 meters.

If you're a really strong hiker, you could walk north and climb the **Southeast Summit** and go down its **East Ridge.** Most people however would be happy just to go down into the Big Provo Hole and return to Sundance via the Big Provo Hole Trail and Stewart Falls. Read more on these trails under Map 2.

Distance and Time Needed The distance from the parking lot at the bottom of the ski lifts to the top of Arrowhead Peak is about 4 kms. Fast hikers could walk up in about an hour and take perhaps 2-3 hours for the round-trip. Others may want about half a day for the trip. If you plan to go on to the South Peaks, and perhaps return via Big Provo Hole to Stewart Falls, then take a lunch and plan to spend the entire day. This long day hike would be for the more experienced and fit hikers.

Main Attractions A chance to see the ski resort in the summer season with green meadows instead of snowy slopes, some excellent views of Provo Canyon and Cascade Peak to the south, and the higher summits of Timpanogos to the northwest. If you combine this hike with a descent through the Big Provo Hole Cirque Basin, then you'll see a part of the mountain unknown to the average person who only climbs the main peak. The cockscomb ridge is an impressive site as seen from the rim of the cirque basin.

Elevations Bottom of the Sundance Ski Lifts, 1856 meters; Arrowhead Peak, 2571; Southeast Peak, 3245: South Peak, 3266; Southwest Peak, 3269 meters.

Water There is no water on the ski slopes or on the South Peaks. If you descend to the Big Provo Hole, you will find some small streams of water in early and mid-summer, but when the snowbanks melt, the water vanishes. This is usually in late July or early August in most years. Carry water with you.

Boots or Shoes If you're just going up to Arrowhead, then any comfortable shoe, such as running shoes will be just fine. However, if you plan to climb the South Peaks, then you'll need a more rugged pair of climbing boots.

Campsites Since there's no water on the ski slopes, camping is really out of the question there. However, if you're willing to carry a heavy pack up over the South Peaks, then head down into the

The Sundance ski slopes in summer. Arrowhead center, Sundance Ridge to the upper right.

cirque basin, you should find many excellent sites for camping. But do it no later than in mid-summer, otherwise you'll have a dry camp.

Winter Climbing The Sundance Ski Resort forbids anyone from hiking, snowshoeing or cross-country skiing up their slopes in winter. So winter climbing up this route is out of the question. If you want to climb the peaks above and to the west of Arrowhead, then you could wear skis on the lift to the top, then go cross-country from there to the South Peaks. They will not allow you on the ski lifts without skis.

You can also reach the top of Arrowhead Peak from the Provo Canyon side, which is discussed in the next section, under Map 4, Southeast Ridge. You could also reach the South Peaks from the South Ridge and from near Bridal Veil Falls in Provo Canyon. Read about that possibility under Map 5.

Log cabin at the top of the ski lifts on Arrowhead Peak.

<u>Southeast Ridge</u>--Arrowhead Peak, Slide Canyon and the South Peaks

Trailhead Location The route emphasized here is the climb up the Southeast Ridge of Timpanogos. To reach the starting point for this hike, drive up Provo Canyon to within about 500 meters of the Vivian Park bridge across the Provo River and the Chalet Cafe. In that area you will likely see a small trailer court and RV campground on the south side of the road called Frazier Park. As this book goes to press, the new canyon highway was being built, so it's not certain if this little park will change or not. Just park somewhere in the area about half a km west of the Chalet Cafe. The open ridge coming down from the north is the one you're interested in.

A second route of interest goes right up the bottom of Slide Canyon. This is not always the safest route to the top of the South Peaks, but many times it can be used as a way down instead of back-tracking along the ridge route. The trailhead for this route is right at the mouth of Slide Canyon and somewhere near the Olmsted Diversion Dam. It'll be 1 1/2 kms to the west or down-canyon from the Chalet Cafe. Park where there's space.

Route Description From the base of the Southeast Ridge walk to the left a bit and just into the lower end of the mini canyon as shown. Look for deer trails running to the right and through some maple trees. One will veer up and to the right. After a short distance look for other trails up through more trees on the lower part of the ridge. After you get through two minor stands of trees, it'll be clear sailing all the way to the top. There are several deer trails you can follow bypassing the occasional stands of oak brush. After the maple trees, there is no bushwhacking any where on the entire route.

Once on top of the eastern end of **Sundance Ridge,** veer to the west and after less than a km, you'll be at the lodge on top of **Arrowhead Peak.** The log cabin lodge at the top of the Arrowhead Lift has a restaurant in service when the resort is in operation. That's in winter time only.

From the lodge, walk downhill to the west a ways then begin climbing the upper part of Sundance Ridge. At first, you may follow some deer and hiker-made trails, but further along, simply walk up the ridgeline along the easiest route. Toward the top, it steepens and you'll have to route-find around a couple of minor ledges before reaching the cockscomb ridge above Big Provo Hole. There's nothing very difficult.

Once on the rocky ridge of the **South Peaks,** walk west and pass over the summits of **Southeast, South, and Southwest Peaks.** The way is an up-and-down walk, but generally easy. From this cockscomb ridge, you'll have fine views in all directions.

Looking west along the cockscomb South Peaks Ridge. Southwest Peak in right background.

MAP 4, **SOUTHEAST RIDGE**--ARROWHEAD PEAK, SLIDE CANYON, AND THE SOUTH PEAKS

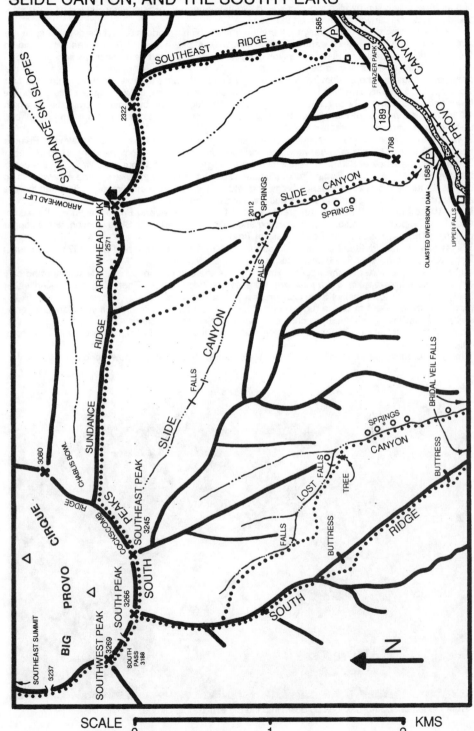

To return to the Provo Canyon Highway, you could use the South Ridge which is discussed under Map 5, or get down via **Slide Canyon.** The upper walls of Slide Canyon are very steep, but you can find an easy way down by climbing part way down the upper part of Sundance Ridge first, then walk south and into the canyon as shown on the map.

As you're going down Slide Canyon, there are about 4 high waterfalls or dryfalls(depending on the time of year) then 8 or 9 minor waterfalls lower down. Most of the higher falls you can get around on the east side. In the lower half of the canyon is a year-round flowing stream and many springs.

A short hike in winter would be up to some icy falls in lower Slide Canyon and in the area of the group of springs(but the avalanche danger is high there right after a snow storm or during the first warm spell of the year, usually in late February or March!). In summer, the walking is a little slow in the lower end of the canyon because it's full of dead trees brought down by winter snowslides—for which the canyon is famous. At the bottom of the drainage, the water seeps back into the ground without being tapped for culinary purposes.

Distance and Time Needed From the Southeast Ridge Car-park to the top of Arrowhead Peak is about 2 1/2 kms. This will take between one and two hours one way. From the car-park to the top of South Peak is about 7 or 8 kms. This will take the average hiker 4 or 5 hours one way. For the entire trip from the car-park to the South Peaks will take all day for the average hiker. Some may want to go only as far as the top of the Sundance Ridge and return. This is a slow and tiresome climb, but there is almost no bushwhacking and the way is easy and straight forward.

Main Attraction You'll have some great views of Cascade Peak and Provo Canyon to the south, and of Mt. Timpanogos. Also some interesting and unknown waterfalls in Slide Canyon, and a couple of new and untried routes to the South Peaks of Timp.

Elevations Either trailhead or car-park, about 1585 meters; Arrowhead Peak, 2571; Southeast Peak, 3245; South Peak, 3266; and Southwest Peak, 3269 meters.

Water There's no water on the ridges, except if you're there in late spring or early summer and can eat snow from snowbanks. Take your own water for the ridge routes. There is good drinking water from springs in the lower half of Slide Canyon on a permanent basis.

Boots or Shoes Best to take a rugged pair of hiking boots for this climb, but if you plan to go only as far as Arrowhead Peak, then you can get by wearing running-type shoes.

Campsites There are no desirable camping places on this climb. It is best suited for day climbing only.

Winter Climbing Because of the southerly exposure of this route, snow conditions for winter

From the top of South Peak looking down into the Big Provo Hole Cirque.

climbing should generally be good, with hard crusted snow much of the time. However, one discouraging thing about this route is that it's a long way to the higher peaks of the mountain. The distance from the trailhead to South Peak, is about double the distance as along the South Ridge, which begins near Bridal Veil Falls.

However, if you're goal is to reach Arrowhead Peak for some winter fotos of the southeast part of Timp or the east side of Cascade Peak, then this is the easiest way to make it to that point. If you stay right on the ridge all the way to Arrowhead, the threat of avalanche is almost zero. Above Arrowhead and on upper Sundance Ridge, avalanche danger is only slightly higher than on the lower slopes.

If you're in Slide Canyon, the avalanche danger is very high in the 4 or 5 days after a storm, or even longer if the temperatures continue to rise. After the big slides have come down, then it'll be easy walking on very hard snow in the bottom of the canyon. However, the best advice for inexperienced hikers would be to stay out of Slide Canyon in winter.

One word of caution. Wheather you're climbing up this Southeast Ridge in summer or in winter, keep in mind that you'll be on private land all the way until you're just west of the ski slopes. But since it's a steep mountain side with no development(except for the top of the ski lifts) or private property signs, it seems no one should care.

Winter on the South Peaks. South Peak left, Southwest Peak to the right.

South Ridge(Lost Creek) Route--South Peaks and Southeast, Second & Timp Summits

Trailhead Location The route discussed here is the best of any of the routes with the starting point in Provo Canyon. This is the South Ridge, or as an alternate, the Lost Creek route. It is the quickest and easiest way up to the South Peaks in summer, and it may be one of the best all-around routes to the summit of Timp in winter.

You must leave your car at the parking lot of the Bridal Veil Falls Resort or back down the road a ways, at or near the parking lot to the Bridal Veil Falls Park. As this book goes to press, the new Provo Canyon Highway has yet to be completed, so the best place to park is still unknown.

Route Description Park where you can somewhere in the Bridal Veil Falls area, then cross the new highway just west of the falls and locate the dirt road running underneath the big green Union or Olmsted Pipeline. This is a very large 3 meter-high pipeline which used to supply water for the Olmsted Power Plant at the mouth of the canyon. Follow this 4WD-type road as it angles up the steep slope to the west.

At about where the road reaches a high point, which is in a little canyon between two limestone ridges, leave the road on the right or north, and head up this little canyon. If you get right in the middle of the drainage, there will be a rocky flood debris talus slope which makes walking easy without bushwhacking. About 200 meters above the road, veer to the right again where a rock slide comes down from the lower part of the **South Ridge.** At the top of the South Ridge, veer left and route-find up through some waist-high oak brush. For about 200-300 meters you'll have to do some minor bushwhacking, but the author did it once in shorts with no scratched legs. So it's not a serious route problem.

Just above the brushy part a short distance, you'll have to turn to the left or west to avoid the first of two buttresses. After this minor detour, get back on the ridgetop and continue up. Further along, you'll come to the second buttress, which you must pass on the left again. The part up to the second buttress is rather steep, as is the second detour to the left, but it's not difficult or dangerous.

Above the second buttress, which is at about 2620 meters altitude, the going seems less steep and it's easier walking. The angle of the slope seems to ease a bit too. Below the second buttress the ridge is rocky with some oak brush to walk around, but above the ridgeline has grass and some Limber pines. In the last 500 meters, the ridge again becomes very rocky and a little rough and steep, but not difficult.

When you arrive on top of the **South Peak,** you will have a good look down into **Big Provo Hole,** as well as an unusual view of the main peaks to the north. Also, you'll have some interesting

Heading down near the top of the South Ridge in winter. Provo Canyon and Cascade Peak in the background.

MAP 5, **SOUTH RIDGE(LOST CREEK)**--SOUTH PEAKS, SOUTHEAST, SECOND AND TIMP SUMMITS

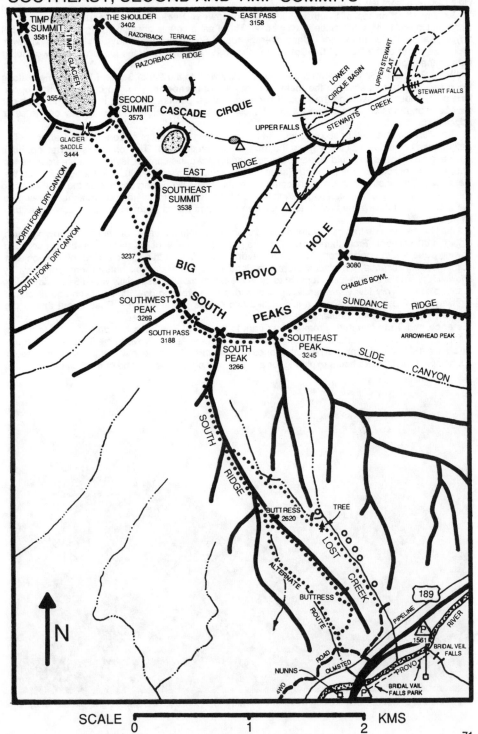

TIMP SUMMIT 3581

TIMP GLACIER

THE SHOULDER 3402

EAST PASS 3158

RAZORBACK TERRACE

RAZORBACK RIDGE

UPPER STEWART FLAT

LOWER CIRQUE BASIN

STEWART FALLS

3554

SECOND SUMMIT 3573

CASCADE CIRQUE

STEWARTS CREEK

GLACIER SADDLE 3444

EAST RIDGE

UPPER FALLS

NORTH FORK DRY CANYON

SOUTH FORK DRY CANYON

SOUTHEAST SUMMIT 3538

HOLE

3237

BIG

PROVO

3080

CHABLIS BOWL

SOUTHWEST PEAK 3269

SOUTH

PEAKS

SUNDANCE RIDGE

SOUTH PASS 3188

SOUTH PEAK 3266

SOUTHEAST PEAK 3245

ARROWHEAD PEAK

SLIDE CANYON

SOUTH

RIDGE

TREE

BUTTRESS 2620

LOST

CREEK

189

ALTERNATE BUTTRESS ROUTE

PIPELINE

P 1561

RIVER

BRIDAL VEIL FALLS

NUNNS

ROAD

OLMSTED

4WD

PROVO

BRIDAL VAIL FALLS PARK

P

BRIDAL VAIL FALLS PARK

N

SCALE 0   1   2 KMS

71

views of Cascade Peak to the south, and of course Utah Valley to the west. From South Peak you can walk east to the **Sundance Ridge**, then down to Arrowhead Peak, which is the highest part of Sundance ski slopes. In the summer season you can even get down into the lush green Big Provo Hole Cirque, a sight few people see.

As you stand on top of South and look at **Southwest Peak,** it first appears to be difficult to climb, but in reality its south slope is very easy. There are a couple of steep little gullies to climb, but anyone can do it, even in winter. Once over the top of Southwest, you'll have a short up and down walk until you're at the base of the **Southeast Summit.** From there to the top is very easy climbing right on the ridgeline.

From Southeast Summit, you'll have another easy walk to the top of **Second Summit** right along the ridge. If you're heading to the main peak of **Mt. Timpanogos,** you can cut across the upper face of the mountain avoiding the second and third highest peaks. However, in winter this short-cut may be prone to avalanche, so be aware of snow conditions. It might be best to stay on the safer ridgeline route.

An alternate route either up or down, can be used along the bottom of **Lost Creek Canyon.** The author once came down all the way via the route shown on the map. The top part is very steep, but if you have good knees it should be easy. If you're going down this canyon, less than a km from the top end, you will encounter a big waterfall(after the spring runoff it's a dryfall). Skirt around this on the west side. After another half km, you'll come to another high fall. Get around this on the west side and climb down a big pine tree standing next to the cliff face. The author climbed down about 8 meters to the ground. If you take the time to look you can likely find a less spectacular route down over this limestone cliff.

Just below the pine tree cliff, water begins flowing(in spring and early summer it'll be flowing much higher in the canyon). From there on down to the road at the mouth of the canyon will be a year-round flowing stream with good water. There are several minor falls in this lower end of the canyon, but nothing of significance. In places there are dead trees in the canyon bottom, brought down by snowslides. This is definitely not a place to be in the winter months, especially within 5 or 6 days after a snowstorm. Every few years really big snowslides come roaring down this canyon and block the highway and Provo River. Once a slide killed two people at the bottom. Read about that in the chapter, *Tragedies on Mt. Timpanogos.*

Distance and Time Needed From the car-park to the top of South Peak is only about 4 to 5 kms, but it has a rise of 1700 vertical meters(compare this with the Aspen Grove to the Timp Summit route, which is a 1500 meter climb!). The author once climbed this ridge route in winter in less than 5 hours, but he spent the first two hours exploring for an easy way onto the lower end of the South Ridge. Up

From the top of South Peak looking at Timp Summit(left), and Second Summit right(telefoto lens).

and back on that trip was about 7 hours. Most climbers would want this much time on a summer hike.

Many people would be happy just to top-out on one of the South Peaks, but strong climbers could make it to at least the Southeast or Second Summit in one long day. It would take a strong and enthusiastic climber with an early morning start to reach the Timp Summit and return in one day using this South Ridge route. Climbing it in summer is generally much faster and easier than in winter.

Main Attractions An almost unknown route up the summit ridge and some excellent views to the south and Cascade Peak, Bridal Veil Falls and Provo Canyon. One of the best routes to the top in winter time.

Elevations Car-park, 1561 meters; second buttress, 2620; South Peak, 3266; Southwest Peak, 3269; Southeast Summit, 3538; Second Summit, 3573; Timp Summit, 3581 meters.

Water There is no water what-so-ever on the South Ridge or the Summit Ridge, so take your own. From October through June each year, there should be some snowbanks around however. If you use Lost Creek Canyon as an alternate, you will find running water in the lower half of the canyon.

Boots or Shoes Best to have and use a rugged pair of hiking or climbing boots on this one.

Campsites Most people would consider climbing and hiking on this side of the mountain to be day hikes only, but you could camp on the ridge somewhere if you're out in winter. In summer you could lug a big pack up and camp in the bottom of Big Provo Hole, but there's no running water there unless it's early in the season or there are some snowbanks still around.

Winter Climbing This is one of the better routes onto the high peaks of the mountain during winter time. Here are some of the reasons. One, it has easy winter access, with the car-park along side a major highway. When the sun shines, the ridge is exposed to the sun for the entire day, which melts the snow, making it hard and crusty in the morning hours. This, along with the fact it's exposed to strong winds, makes for very easy walking most of the time. It's also a very simple and straight-line approach, making it easy to get down fast if the weather turns bad all of a sudden. In winter time an easy, fast and safe route down is important, especially in bad weather. And last, if you stay on the ridge, there is little avalanche danger(stay out of Lost Creek Canyon in winter time, unless you're a knowledgeable person on avalanches!).

The best time to climb this route in winter is about the same as far other routes; that is, in late March or April. That's when the snow will be hardest and easiest to walk on. Because it's a south facing ridge route, you can count on the snow being much harder at any one time than on any other route on the mountain, so it can be climbed throughout the winter. However, you will find some softer snow during and just after stormy periods in December, January and February.

If you wait until mid-April, then the lower 2/3 of the ridge will likely be free of snow, but each year

Looking east at the South Peaks from the top of Southwest Peak. Big Provo Hole to the left.

will be different. Here's another tip, try to do all or most of your climbing in the early morning hours when the snow is frozen. This is especially true in late winter or early spring. In the mornings before about 10 am, it's rock-hard. Later in the day the snow becomes soft and mushy. If it's wind-blown powder snow, it tends to ball-up on the bottom of your crampons when it's exposed to the sun.

Because this is one of the steeper routes on the mountain, you likely won't need snowshoes except during the dead of winter, and maybe it'll be too steep to use them then. If you do decide to try snowshoes, an intermediate size would be best. Also, snowshoes equipped with special crampons may work well on this route. Skis would likely be more of a hindrance than a help. The author has used crampons on this route several times in March and April, and they came in handy each time. Crampons add a touch of safety, although most of the time an experienced person with an ice ax and good rigid boots with lug soles can get by without them.

If you have the very best snow conditions, such as you find in late March or April, then a strong climber with an early morning start, could get all the way to the Timp Summit and back the same day. But most people would be happy just to get to the South Peaks, or maybe to the Southeast Summit. Most people who are serious about reaching the highest peak, would likely have to make a camp on the high ridge and do it in two days. If you try this, make sure you have a good weather forecast for several days in advance, because you'll likely have to put your tent on or near a ridgetop. If a storm blows in with your tent on any part of the summit ridge, you're in trouble. Having a period of good weather would be the single most important factor to having a successful winter climb on this route, especially if you plan to do it in two days. As previously stated, best to stay out of Lost Creek Canyon in winter.

From the top of South Peak, looking at higher peaks to the north. Southwest Peak to the left.

Looking down on Southwest Peak from the top of the Southeast Summit.

The southwest upper face of the Second and Southeast Summits. Timp Summit in the left background.

<u>Dry Canyon Trail</u>--Big Baldy, South Peaks and Southeast, Second & the Timp Summits

Trailhead Location The hikes featured here are along the trail and routes at the head of Dry Canyon, which is on the southwest face of Timpanogos. The trailhead is at the mouth of Dry Canyon, which is in the far eastern city limits of both Orem and Lindon.

To reach this trailhead, drive along State Street which is the old Highway 89 to the north end of Orem and to 20th North Street. This road is actually the boundary line between Orem and Lindon. It also goes by the name 200 South, which is a Lindon City street number. Once on this street, drive straight east. In 1989, there was lots of construction at the far eastern end of this road, so expect this street to change each year because of all the new homes being built right up next to the mountain.

At some point as you near the east end of 20th North--200 South Street, the pavement will end and you will be on a dirt road running up to the mouth of Dry Canyon. There will likely be a maze of roads, so route-find as best you can in the right direction. At the mouth of the canyon is a large debris flood basin dam built during the mid-1980's for flood control. You will pass to the left of this dam, then just a little ways further park where you can see the trail coming out of the canyon on the left or north side of the drainage.

Route Description The trail in Dry Canyon is used often and is maintained by the Forest Service. It's one of 3 major canyon trails on the southwest face of Timp. At the beginning of the trail is a sign stating it is #047, and that the Timpooneke Road is 4 1/2 miles(about 7 kms) ahead.

The trail runs up the left or north side of the canyon. After about 600 meters, you'll pass through a narrows called here the Great Blue Gate(so named because it's made of the Great Blue Limestone). After a short distance you'll pass a horse watering trough on the left. Just above that the canyon widens. For a ways the trail mingles with some old fire-break roads, but it's still easy to follow. Further up and on the south side of Big Baldy, you'll see terraces built in the early 1960's to stop erosion. The erosion was caused by overgrazing for about a century before the terracing was put in. Read more about this under *Livestock Grazing, Erosion and Terracing on the Mountain* in the back of this book.

After about 5 kms, you will arrive at a pass between Big Baldy and the main part of Mt. Timpanogos. This is called Baldy Saddle and is at 2540 meters altitude. From this saddle, you can walk to the southwest on a hiker and deer hunter-made trail up along a ridge to the top of **Big Baldy,** which is at 2669 meters. From this peak, you will have some interesting close-up views of the rest of Timpanogos. If you're planning to scale Timp along this route, it's recommended you take this short side-trip to Baldy, and look over your route before beginning the major climb. The best time for fotos

From the mouth of Dry Canyon. The Great Blue Limestone **gate in the** lower part of foto.

MAP 6, **DRY CANYON TRAIL**--BIG BALDY, SOUTH PEAKS AND SOUTHEAST, SECOND & TIMP SUMMITS

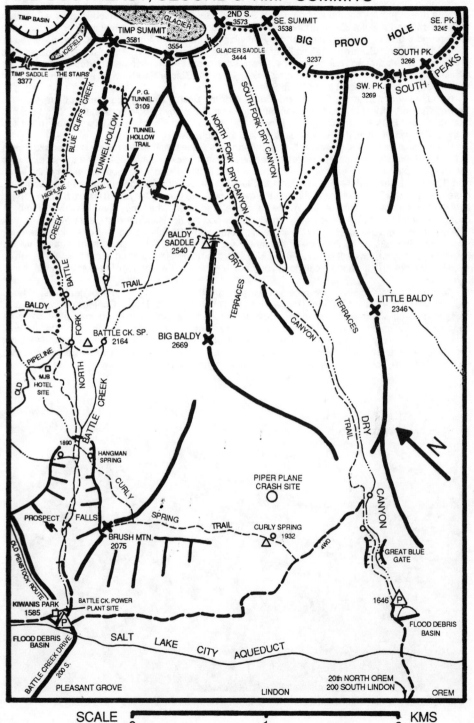

TIMP BASIN

GLACIER

2ND S. 3573

SE. SUMMIT 3538

SE. PK. 3245

TIMP SUMMIT 3581

3554

BIG

PROVO

HOLE

ICEFIELD

GLACIER SADDLE 3444

3237

SOUTH PK. 3266

TIMP SADDLE 3377

THE STAIRS

SW. PK. 3269

SOUTH

PEAKS

P. G. TUNNEL 3109

NORTH FORK DRY CANYON

SOUTH FORK DRY CANYON

BLUE CLIFFS CREEK

TUNNEL HOLLOW

TUNNEL HOLLOW TRAIL

HIGHLINE

TIMP

BATTLE CREEK

BALDY SADDLE 2540

DRY

LITTLE BALDY 2346

TRAIL

TERRACES

CANYON

TERRACES

BALDY

BATTLE CK. SP. 2164

BIG BALDY 2669

NORTH FORK

TERRACES

PIPELINE

OLD

BATTLE CREEK

MJB HOTEL SITE

DRY

1890

HANGMAN SPRING

CANYON

CURLY

PIPER PLANE CRASH SITE

TRAIL

N

PROSPECT

FALLS

SPRING

TRAIL

CURLY SPRING 1932

4WD

CANYON

OLD PENSTOCK ROUTE

BRUSH MTN. 2075

GREAT BLUE GATE

KIWANIS PARK 1585

BATTLE CK. POWER PLANT SITE

1646

P

FLOOD DEBRIS BASIN

P

FLOOD DEBRIS BASIN

BATTLE CREEK DRIVE

200 S.

SALT

LAKE

CITY

AQUEDUCT

PLEASANT GROVE

LINDON

20th NORTH OREM 200 SOUTH LINDON

OREM

SCALE
0   1   2

KMS

of the mountain from Big Baldy is in mid-morning when some shadows are on the mountain.

Perhaps the easiest way to reach the high peaks and the summit ridge, is to walk on one of several terraces running to the southeast from Baldy Saddle. Get on the first one which is about 40 meters from the trail and saddle. Once on this terrace, walk to the southeast on a mostly deer hunter-made trail around the bend and into the first canyon, which is the **North Fork of Dry Canyon.** If you're goal is the **Second Summit,** then walk straight up this canyon or gully. There are a couple of cliffs or dry falls to get around, but overall it's a very easy climb. It steepens at the top just before the Glacier Saddle which is at the head of the glacier. From the Glacier Saddle, walk east to the top of the Second Summit, or northwest to the Timp Summit.

If you're interested in the **Southeast Summit** or the **South Peaks,** you can get there from the Second Summit, or you can walk the same terrace from the Baldy Saddle on past the North Fork and into the **South Fork of Dry Canyon.** From there you can climb straight up this canyon to the top of the Southeast Summit, the South Peaks, or into the Big Provo Hole.

If your goal is the **Timp Summit,** then perhaps the easiest and fastest route is up an old trail in **Tunnel Hollow** to where an **old water tunnel** was begun back in July, 1902. The tunnel plan was set up by people living in Pleasant Grove. They wanted to tunnel under the mountain and tap the water from Emerald Lake, and have it run down to Pleasant Grove for irrigation and perhaps to generate more power at the Telluride Power Plant at the mouth of Battle Creek Canyon. It was just barely begun by Jake Nelson and his brother; Ike Wadley and Lee Warburton, when they were forced to stop by a court order from Provo City. Apparently Provo City owned the rights to Emerald Lake water.

To get on the **Tunnel Hollow Trail,** walk from Baldy Saddle along the one single terrace contouring northward along the face of the mountain. After about 200 meters, head straight up the mountain but angle to the left or north just a bit. There is no trail in this short section, so there will be some bushwhacking. It's not difficult however, because there are a number of deer trails in the waist-high brush.

About 200 meters above the terrace, you will find an old eroded trail going left or northwest. This is the first visible part of the Tunnel Hollow and the **Timp Highline Trail.** Contour northwest as it crosses a steep-sided erosional gully. Beyond the gully the trail is very obvious as it contours beneath a grey limestone cliff, then angles up to the right and into a minor canyon. After the trail crosses a second dry creek bed(it will have running water in early summer), you will surely lose it, but you can head straight up-slope to find it again further up. If you walk out on Big Baldy a ways, before going up the face, you can barely see this trail faintly on the mountain side. Follow it on the map.

From half way up the southwest face of Timp, looking down on the terraces of Big Baldy.

After a ways, the Tunnel Hollow Trail crosses a ridge from which you can see the Summit Hut at the top straight above you. From there the trail angles up toward the top. It's obvious this trail was man-made. A little further along, the trail seems to fade and you then have to route-find up near the bottom of the gully, which will have some running water as long as the snowbanks last on the upper face of the mountain.

Further up, and near the bottom of the upper-most basin, you will see a minor cliff band. Just below this and in between two early summer cascades, will be a horizontal natural opening to a cave. Apparently, the tunnel workers began in this natural cave, and barely got started putting up timbers, when the whole operation was called off. The cave or tunnel is only about 3 meters deep. There are still several rotted timbers inside, evidence that something happened there long ago.

If you're heading for the summit, climb over the narrow cliff band just above the tunnel opening and turn left. Walk in the direction of a minor pass in the ridge just north of Tunnel Hollow. Once on this ridge, climb up to the left of the ridgeline. If you stay on the ridge you'll be confronted with some cliffs. Route-find up the slope along the easiest way, then near the top veer right and end at the Summit Hut. Keep an eye out for the white Rocky Mountain goats along the summit ridge.

Distance and Time Needed Several years ago the author walked up the Dry Canyon Trail, then into and straight up the North Fork of Dry Canyon to the Second Summit. This took 2 hrs. and 52 min. This is much too fast for the average hiker however. Most people would want 5 or 6 hours for the ascent, and about 3 for the return trip on this particular route. The distance to the Second Summit would only be about 8 kms, but the vertical rise is just under 2000 meters. A long tough climb for anyone.

To reach the actual summit via Dry Canyon and Tunnel Hollow, should take about the same amount of time as to the Second Summit. A short and easy hike and one for the whole family would be to the top of Big Baldy. The distance is about 6 kms, and should take only a couple of hours to the top, or about half a day for the round-trip hike.

Best Time If you want a summertime hike but with some snow around, climb to the highest peaks from about the first week in June until mid-July. After mid-July, there is no snow on the peaks until perhaps late September or early October. The best time for summer hiking is from early June to about the middle of October. To climb Big Baldy, you can climb in May through October. Winter climbing is discussed below.

Main Attraction New and different routes to the top of Timp, a chance to see mountain goats, and probably no other hikers.

Elevations The trailhead, 1646 meters; Baldy Saddle, 2540; Big Baldy, 2669; Southeast Summit,

Deer hunting season. This big buck was shot in the North Fork of Dry Canyon(Joe Hilton foto).

3538; Second Summit, 3573; and the Timp Summit, 3581 meters.

Water When hiking on any of these routes, it's best to take all the water you'll need, because most of the time it'll be a very dry climb. There may or may not be water at the horse trough, and the spring just up-canyon has been tapped for culinary purposes.

If you're high on the mountain in June or during most of July, you will likely find some running water in the main canyons, but only if there are still some snowbanks above. When the snowbanks melt, the mountain is bone dry.

Boots or Shoes If you're out to just trail hike to Big Baldy, any comfortable shoe would be OK, but if you're heading up to the summit ridge, then it's best to take a pair of rugged hiking or climbing boots.

Campsites You could drop a tent about anywhere on the mountain, but there are no springs in the area covered in this description, so it's really not good for camping There are campsites on top of Baldy Saddle, but you'd have to walk down-hill to some springs on Battle Creek for water.

Winter Climbing The climb up Dry Canyon to around Baldy Saddle, then up any of the routes to the summit ridge, should be one of the easiest ways up the mountain in winter. The main reason being, the southwest face is exposed to the warm afternoon sun, thus there should be plenty of ridges or even avalanche chutes with hard crusty snow which makes walking easy. If you get on a north facing slope, it's deep powder all winter long.

In the bottom part of the canyon you will likely walk in other peoples tracks for a ways, but the further up you go and the deeper the snow becomes, and the fewer tracks you will see. Throughout most of the winter, you will likely have to use snowshoes or skis beginning about half way up to Baldy Saddle. You possibly can use them a little further above that too, then you'd want to get on the south facing side of one of the ridges. The one coming down from near the Glacier Saddle on the summit ridge to Baldy Saddle looks good for a winter assault. Ridges are generally a lot safer than gullies when it comes to avalanches.

Another possibility is to go up one of the canyons such as the North Fork of Dry Canyon. In the first 4 or 5 days after each storm, most slides come down, creating a rock-hard surface for walking on top of the snow itself. But to really feel safe in one of these canyons, the author recommends you wait and climb in them only if it's been maybe 10 days since the last storm, and in the morning hours only. That's when the snow will be frozen hard. On Timp's southwest face, avalanche danger will rise by about 11 am. One possible strategy would be to climb up a snowslide in the early morning hours, then return via a ridge route.

From the top of Big Baldy looking at the upper southwest face of Timp. Summit far left, Southeast Summit right. Barely visible is Timp Highline Trail in lower left, Tunnel Hollow Trail at far left.

Some last thoughts before leaving the avalanche situation. The author has made several ascents in this region during March and the first part of April, and the snow conditions were ideal. On each trip, the author went up and down in the canyon bottoms, and never felt in danger of snowslides. That was long after the previous storm. On an April 5 climb, he walked to Baldy Saddle, then up the bottom of North Fork of Dry Canyon to the Second and Southeast Summits, finally returning via the South Fork of Dry Canyon. The round-trip climb lasted 9 hours. March or early April is obviously the very best time of year to make any winter climb on any route on Timp.

If you're not so sure about the dangers of avalanches, maybe it's best to wait until late in the season to do you're winter climbing. Avalanche danger begins with deep snow in December and runs through March. For the latest word on avalanche danger, call 374-9770, 364-1581 or 621-2362. These are the three numbers of the Utah Avalanche Forecast Center in the Provo, Salt Lake and Ogden areas.

The summit ridge and cornices as seen from the top of the Southeast Summit.

Battle Creek Trail--Curly Spring Trail, Big Baldy, Pleasant Grove Water Tunnel and Timp Summit

Trailhead Location The trailhead for these hikes is located at the mouth of Battle Creek Canyon, which is at the upper east side of Pleasant Grove. To get there, make your way to the center of Pleasant Grove town and look for a major street running east named Battle Creek Drive. This is also known as 200 South Street. Follow it east until it ends near a large city water tank on the left side. About 100 meters beyond the tank is an unpaved parking lot next to the entrance to the Kiwanis Park. At this small city park is a large covered picnic site, a small grassy playground, some running water and a dilapidated toilet. This park sits right where the old Battle Creek Power Station caretakers home used to be. On the ridge to the north you can still see where the old penstock used to come down. There are even several fruit trees still clinging to life.

Most people will want to park at the Kiwanis Park, but with a strong vehicle, you can drive another 500 meters or so up-canyon. At the end of this road, all the water in Battle Creek(in summer time) enters a pipeline to be used for irrigation in the valley below.

The name **Battle Creek** came about because of an early encounter between some of the first white settlers and a band of Indians. The date was February 28, 1849. It seems that some cattle had been stolen by Indians near the small settlement of Willow Creek, which is now Draper in the south end of the Salt Lake Valley. Brigham Young sent John Scott and about 40 Mormons out to find the cattle. They went south into Utah Valley to the banks of the Provo River, where they found a band of Utes under the leadership of Little Chief. It seems Little Chief did his best to get along with the Mormons. He told them another small band of Utes had stolen the cattle and where they were camped. It was decided to send the son of Little Chief with the Mormons to find the thieves.

During the night, the Mormons made their way to the encampment of a small group of Utes at the mouth of the canyon east of what is now Pleasant Grove. They surrounded the camp and at dawn confronted the Utes. No one is certain who fired first, but in the end 4 Ute braves lay dead, including two named Roman Nose and Blue Shirt. Of the band of 17, four were men, the rest being women and children. The survivors were taken to Salt Lake City, where they were clothed and housed for a time, then eventually sent back to another group of Utes. Because of this first encounter between Indians and Mormons in Utah, the stream was named Battle Creek.

Route Description From the Kiwanis Park, which is the recommended place to leave your car, walk up the road half a km to the actual beginning of the trail. From there a good, well used trail runs up the canyon along side Battle Creek. After a short distance you cross the creek and come to an old prospect or adit on the left, where someone attempted to locate some minerals. Not far above the

From the ridge on the south side of Tunnel Hollow looking up at the summit.

MAP 7, **BATTLE CREEK TRAIL**--CURLY SPRING TRAIL, BIG BALDY, P. G. TUNNEL & TIMP SUMMIT

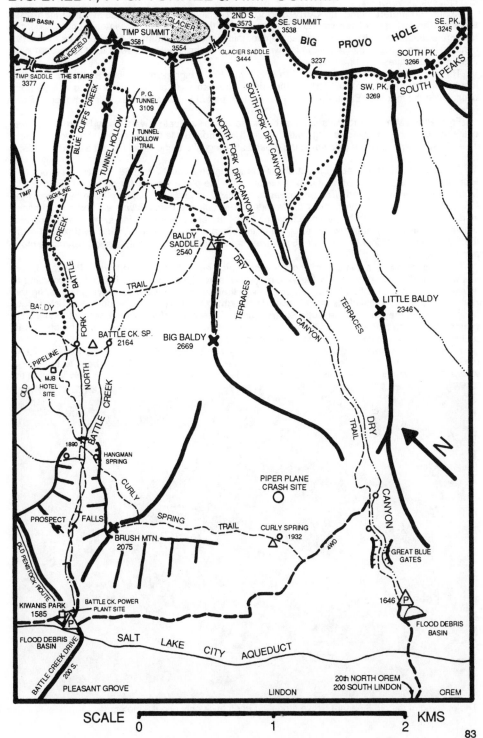

SCALE 0 1 2 KMS

prospect, is the highest waterfall on the face of Timp. It's generally referred to as the Lower Falls. About half a km past the falls is the beginning of the trail to Curly Spring. This trail veers to the right and crosses Battle Creek.

About 100 meters along the **Curly Spring Trail** is a slide area and a place called **Hangman Spring.** The spring has been tapped and connected to the Pleasant Grove water supply. According to some of the local residents of Pleasant Grove, this is the place where in the late years of the 19th century, a man hanged himself with his own belt. The author has never read anything about it, so there are many questions unanswered.

The Curly Spring Trail continues south until it reaches a high point between Big Baldy and what locals call **Brush Mountain.** If you turn right, you can walk a short distance to a high point overlooking the mouth of Battle Creek and the eastern part of Pleasant Grove. This is the top of Brush Mountain.

From Brush Mtn. walk to the southeast on the same walking path toward **Curly Spring.** This part of the trail is on the lower face of Big Baldy. About 3 kms from Battle Creek you will come to the spring. This is a small spring with a pipe set in the ground allowing hikers and wildlife to get a good safe drink from a trough.

An interesting event happened just above the spring on August 22, 1968. It was the wreck of a Piper Cub, which came down in the thick oak brush. The plane was hardly damaged and the pilot Mardon Dixon wasn't injured. The plane was later picked up and removed by a large helicopter from Hill Air Force Base. However, a day or two after the wreck and before it was airlifted out, someone went to the crash site and began to remove and haul the undamaged engine away. Joe Hilton and others, including the planes owner, returned to the site and it was thought their arrival scared away the thieves in the middle of the theft. Someone had carried the motor only a short distance before abandoning it.

Curly Spring gets it's name from another event which happened after the town of Pleasant Grove was well established and just after the Walker War was over(perhaps in the 1870's?). According to Howard R. Driggs in his book, *Timpanogos Town,* there were two white cowboys riding along the foothills of Timp southeast of Pleasant Grove. They sighted two Indians coming down the Timpanogos Trail(along what may be now the Curly Spring Trail?). They hid until the braves were into the valley, then the two riders began chasing them. One of the braves managed to escape, but the other was captured by the two whites. The captive was taken into town.

After a time the brave told the Mormons his family was camped at a spring at the foot of what we now call Big Baldy. Regardless of the intentions, the Mormons took the Indian back to the spring where the encampment was, only to find it abandoned. The whites and the Indian then followed the

The opening of the old Pleasant Grove tunnel. It goes back only about 3 meters.

tracks until they overtook the small band. In the group were the families of the two braves and the fellow who had been chased but escaped. Why the Indians had been chased in the first place is unclear, but the settlers took the two families back to Pleasant Grove where they camped in their tepees for the winter. Evidently one reason for the sudden kindness on the part of the Mormons was the fact that the captured Indian, very soon after his struggle to escape the two cowboys, became blind. After the event, he was always known to the settlers as *Blind Pete.* The other brave camped at the spring was called *Curly.* Thus the name of the waterhole has been called **Curly Spring** ever since.

Returning now to the junction of Battle Creek and the Curly Spring Trail. If you continue up Battle Creek, you will soon be out of the canyon and into a more level area with trees and meadows. About a km above the beginning of the Curly Spring Trail you will come to what appears to be an old road running across the trail. This is actually an old **pipeline route.** The pipeline ran from Battle Creek Spring to a holding pond above the mouth of Battle Creek. Then the water went down a penstock to the power plant where Kiwanis Park is today. Read more on this pipeline under Map 8.

From the pipeline crossing, which nowadays is covered with lots of tall grass, the trail continues up and east another 100 meters to where the forest opens up into a large nearly flat meadow. At that point the trail runs north, then east another half km, to where it meets the **Baldy Trail.** You can stay on the trail all the way, but if you're heading for Big Baldy or the Tunnel Hollow Trail, you can also walk straight up the slope through the maple forest from the first large meadow. See the map. This cuts the distance to the Baldy Trail in half.

Once on the Baldy Trail, walk to the southeast toward **Baldy Saddle,** the pass between Big Baldy and the summit region of Mt. Timpanogos. From Baldy Saddle you can walk to the southwest along a hiker and deer hunter-made trail to the top of **Big Baldy.** The trail along the ridge is pretty good in most places, but it fades in others. It's an easy walk for just less than a km. From the top of Big Baldy, you will have some good views of Timp and its southwest face.

If you're planning to climb to the top of Timp from this area, then you'll have several routes to choose from. From Baldy Saddle, walk east up the slope about 40 meters and get on the first of several terraces in that area. On top of this first terrace is a hiker and deer hunter-made trail running southeast along the face of the mountain. It soon turns the corner and heads into the bottom of the **North Fork of Dry Canyon.** Inside the North Fork there are several waterfalls, which dry up when the snowbanks melt. You can get around these easily. If you walk up the bottom of North Fork it will lead to the **Glacier Saddle** at the head of the Timp Glacier, and to both the **Second** or the **Timp Summits.** You can also climb to the **Southeast Summit,** or even the **South Peaks** from this

Timp Summit in the background. The opening to the old tunnel is in the middle at the bottom of the picture.

canyon route.

Another alternate to the North Fork is the South Fork of Dry Canyon. You can get there on the same terrace trail you take to get into the North Fork, but just continue around one more ridge. The **South Fork** route would put you closer to the Southeast Summit, South Peaks and the **Big Provo Hole.**

If you want to climb to the **Timp Summit** and perhaps visit an old historic site along the way, then use the route and trail in **Tunnel Hollow.** To start this climb, walk north from Baldy Saddle along the one single terrace running in that direction. After about 200 meters, head straight up the slope but veer a little to the left. After about another 200 meters, you should locate what the old stockmen used to call the **Timp Highline Trail,** which is also the first part of the **Tunnel Hollow Trail**(it must begin at Baldy Saddle, but the author never did find it down in that area). At any rate, you can surely find the trail as it crosses a deep recently eroded gully. On the other side it becomes very visible.

Once on this trail, follow it as it contours beneath some big grey limestone cliffs. It then angles up to the right and into the next little drainage above some cliffs. Just after you cross this second drainage(which will have running water in the early part of summer) you will likely lose the trail. The Timp Highline Trail continues to contour around the next ridge and into **Tunnel Hollow,** but on that ridge is where the Tunnel Hollow Trail takes off and runs up-slope. From about where you cross the creek bed you can head straight up and intercept the trail higher up.

Once on the Tunnel Hollow Trail, it's easy to follow but it is fading. It soon crosses the ridge on the south side of Tunnel Hollow where you will then see the **Summit Hut** at the head of this canyon. The trail angles up toward the middle of the drainage then gradually disappears. Further up, and just as you're at the bottom of the upper basin, you will see what appears to be a natural cave with a wide mouth in between two early-summer waterfalls(later in the season there is no water). This is where several men from Pleasant Grove wanted to tunnel under the mountain and tap the water from Emerald Lake back in about July 1902. The men were reportedly Jake Nelson and his brother; Ike Wadley and Lee Warburton.

Their plan was to get more water for irrigation and/or hydroelectric power in their area of the valley below. But apparently when Provo City found out about the scheme, they brought a lawsuit against the Telluride Power Company and the project was halted just as it began. Apparently all court records have been lost on this case, so there are no accurate records available. Inside the cave you can still see several old rotting timbers which were to be used in the tunnel, but hardly anything else which resembles a tunnel. The cave is only about 3 meters deep, and about 8 meters wide at the entrance.

To reach the summit of Timp, get on top of the little cliff just above the tunnel or cave opening, and turn left or north. Walk up to the little pass or saddle on the ridge north of Tunnel Hollow. Once on the

The north face of Big Baldy, as seen from the upper Battle Creek Trail.

ridge, head up but to the left and toward the middle of the next drainage north to avoid the cliffs above. Once past another rock band or cliff, head straight up or veer to the right and get on the upper part of the ridge, then go on to the summit.

From the Battle Creek Trailhead and Trail, there is still another route to the summit of Timp. When you first get on the Baldy Trail, you will round one corner and cross the middle part of the **North Fork of Battle Creek.** Some of the old timers used to call this **Blue Cliffs Creek.** Where the trail crosses this creek you will find water on a year-round basis. If you head up this gully or canyon, it will lead you to the summit. It's a rough and rocky route in places, but there is no bushwhacking. In winter, big avalanches come roaring down this canyon, and the resulting snowfield stays until the middle of summer each year. It might be easier to climb this route in the early part of summer, at which time you can walk straight up the snowslide. Some kind of a walking stick or an ice ax might help during an early or mid-summer climb, but crampons won't help much. This route might be the easiest and fastest all-around route to the top of Timp on the southwest face.

Distance and Time Needed From the trailhead to the beginning of Curly Spring Trail is about 2 kms. It's steep, but most people can walk this part in half an hour or 45 min. From the trail junction to Curly Spring is about 3 kms, and this is an easy 45 min. or one hour walk. Round-trip to Curly Spring would be maybe 3-4 hours for the average hiker.

To walk to the top of Big Baldy is to walk about 5 or 6 kms, which is a couple of hours for most, or about half a day for the round-trip hike. For those heading to the top of Timp, plan on a long all day climb round-trip. Years ago the author walked up the Blue Cliffs Creek Drainage to the top and back in 5 or 6 hours or thereabouts. Recently, he climbed to Big Baldy, then went up to the Pleasant Grove Water Tunnel opening and to the summit, which included some exploring around, and made the summit in just over 4 hours. The round-trip hike that day lasted 9 hrs. 20 min. Take a lunch and get an early start if you plan to climb to the summit.

Best Time Warm weather type hiking with very little or no snow on the Curly Spring or Baldy Routes begins in about May and extends through the month of October. These lower altitude hikes however, are most enjoyable in May or the first part of June and again in September and October. In other words make these hikes in cooler weather, or in the early mornings in summer, especially the one to Curly Spring.

Summer climbing to the summit area would begin sometime in June, but each year is different. In June and early July, expect to find lots of avalanche snow in the bottoms of the upper canyons. By sometime around mid-July, there aren't many snowbanks left, and the mountain is high and dry. The summer season would end on the higher peaks by about mid-October or around the time of the deer hunt(the Saturday nearest the 20th of October).

The lower falls in Battle Creek Canyon. It's only about one km from the trailhead to this waterfall.

From the top of Roberts Horn, one has a fine view down on Emerald Lake and the shelter. (telefoto lens).

Looking south along the ridge from the Summit Hut. The Second Summit is at the far left.

The upper southwest face of Mt. Timpanogos. The Summit Hut is in the upper right hand part of the picture.

A look at the final part of the summit trail and the top of Timp from a point just above the Stairs.

Main Attractions Here are a couple of short hikes which can be done either early or late in the season. Sometimes they can make fun winter hikes as well. There is also an old historic trail up to where some Pleasant Grove people wanted to build a tunnel on the face of Timp. Also, there are several different routes to Timp's highest peaks.

Elevations The Kiwanis Park Trailhead, 1585 meters; Battle Creek and Curly Spring Trail junction, 1890; Curly Spring, 1932; Baldy Saddle, 2540; Big Baldy, 2669; Pleasant Grove Water Tunnel opening, 3109; and Timp Summit, 3581 meters.

Water It's probably safer not to drink the water in the lower end of Battle Creek. But there is good water coming down a side drainage from the north just below where the Curly Spring Trail begins. Also, at Curly Spring, Battle Creek Spring, lower Blue Cliffs Creek, and along the Baldy Trail as it crosses Blue Cliffs Creek and upper Battle Creek. In late spring and early summer there is some running water in each of the major canyons on the face of the mountain, but they all dry up in mid-summer or when the snowbanks melt off the upper part of the mountain.

Boots or Shoes Any kind of comfortable shoe will do in summer if you're just hiking the trails to Curly Spring or up to Big Baldy. But if you plan to attempt the summit, then more rigid and rugged hiking or climbing boots are best.

Campsites In the spring or fall one could camp at Curly Spring, but it's not normally used for camping. You could also camp near the springs in the middle part of Battle Creek or Blue Cliffs Creek just below the steeper face of the mountain. That's near good water sources. If you're heading for the summit in early summer, when there's some running water in the upper canyons, then you could camp about anywhere on the face, if you can locate a flat spot large enough for your tent. Another option would be to take a one gallon(3.78 liters) jug, fill it with water at one of the springs, then make camp at Baldy Saddle.

Winter Climbing Climbing to Timp's highest summit along one of these routes would be one of the better and easier ways for a winter ascent. But perhaps they're not quite as easy as walking up the Dry Canyon Trail.

As with any of the different routes up Timp in winter, the very best time to climb is near the end of March and the first part of April. The reasons are; the temperatures are warmer, there are more daylight hours, and most importantly, the snow is usually hard enough for you to walk on without sinking in too far. If you're there early in the season without a lot of snow, then it should be easy walking too, but if it's a half meter deep(20 inches) or more, then you'll have to use snowshoes or skis on the lower slopes.

Any time from about December first until early or late March, you'll have to use snowshoes or skis

Timp Summit and summit ridge as seen from the Glacier Saddle.

from somewhere near the lower Battle Creek waterfall. From there you'll likely have deep soft snow all the way to Baldy Saddle. From the Saddle it's likely best to head straight up the slope to the first ridge north of North Fork of Dry Canyon. Once on this upper ridge, you should have hard crusty snow all the way up. The higher up you go, the harder the snow will be on the south facing ridgetop. If it's been a week or two since the last snowstorm, then you possibly could go up the bottom of the North Fork of Dry Canyon. But during the dead of winter, there will always be some threat of avalanches in the canyon bottoms.

Another possibility(if it's been a week or two since the last storm)is to head up the hard-packed snowslide in the morning, then return on a ridge route in the afternoon when the snow is more prone to avalanche. On the other hand, if you're there right after a storm with lots of new snow, even the ridgetops can be prone to avalanche. Snowslides are definitely a problem in the dead of winter on any of these routes.

An alternate route up the face would be to go up Battle Creek Canyon to where the Battle Creek Trail intercepts the Baldy Trail and from there head up the ridge to the left or north of Blue Cliffs Creek. Stay on the sunny side of the ridge and it should be easy walking. Near the top you'll have some cliffs to get around. Do that on the right or south side. That's where the Aspen Grove Trail zig zags up through the cliffs at the Stairs.

If you were to go up the ridge between Tunnel Hollow and Blue Cliffs Creek, you'd have at least two sets of cliffs to skirt. The one very near the summit might be too difficult to pass on the right or south side, at least for the average climber. Under the best and safest conditions, you could also walk right up the bottom of upper Blue Cliffs Creek Canyon.

At the top of Mt. Timpanogos during a March ascent of the mountain.

Battle Creek & Grove Creek Loop Trail--Pleasant Grove Pipeline, Little Mountain and the Letter "G" Hikes

Trailhead Location There are two trailheads involved here; one is at the mouth of Battle Creek, the other at the mouth of Grove Creek. Both of these canyons drain the southwest slopes of Timpanogos and both streams come down to the Pleasant Grove City limits.

To get to the mouth of Battle Creek Canyon, find your way to the center of Pleasant Grove and look for the street named Battle Creek Drive, which is the same as 200 South. Drive east until this street ends at the Kiwanis Park right at the mouth of the canyon. Most people will want to park at the entrance to the Kiwanis Park. This is the same trailhead as discussed under Map 7.

To find the trailhead on Grove Creek, make your way to the middle of Pleasant Grove, then go north on about any street until you reach 500 North Street, which is also named Grove Creek Drive. Head east on this street until it turns to the right. At that point, you veer to the left and drive up a dirt road along side the flood debris basin and straight into the canyon. People with cars will want to park near the flood dam, but those with higher clearance vehicles may want to drive into the canyon maybe another 300 meters.

Route Description There are several hikes here, one of which is a loop hike from Grove Creek to Battle Creek. You can walk this loop in either direction, but it will be discussed here beginning on Grove Creek.

From where you park your car, walk up **Grove Creek Canyon.** Just into the canyon will be a short 4WD segment of road going down to the creek on the right. It ends at the stream where the water enters a pipeline. But stay on the trail instead, which veers to the left. At first the trail runs along the canyon bottom, but a little further up it makes a sharp left turn and begins to climb the canyon wall. After one more switchback, it again heads up canyon high on the north wall.

From the second switchback you will walk about two kms along a good trail until finally you'll be at the head of the steep-sided canyon. Just above some waterfalls or cascades, the trail crosses the upper part of Grove Creek and makes a couple of zig zags up through the pines on the east side. Once the trail gets out of the canyon bottom and through the pines, it levels off a bit as it passes through several meadows and past a couple of springs, then it finally runs beside **Grove Creek Spring** on the right. This spring is in the middle of a large clearing and the water seeps out of the gravels. This is the best place around to get a good drink.

From this spring you will have two routes to choose from. If you continue northeast toward the mountain, you will soon come to the **Timpooneke Road,** which starts on the north side of the

The old Battle Creek Hydroelectric Power Station completed in 1907(Eva Proctor foto).

MAP 8, BATTLE CREEK & GROVE CREEK LOOP TRAIL--P. G. PIPELINE, LITTLE MTN. & "G" HIKES

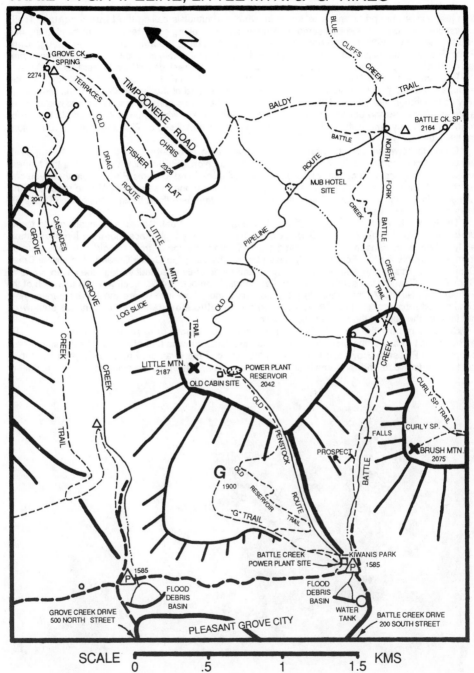

SCALE

0   .5   1   1.5   KMS

mountain at the Timpooneke Campground. At the road, turn right and walk this good road nearly to its end on the southeast side on **Chris Fisher Flat**. At that point is a sign pointing out the beginning of the Baldy Trail which heads for Baldy Saddle.

Back to Grove Creek Spring. Instead of walking up to the Timpooneke Road, you can make a right turn just above the spring and walk south on what the author is calling the **Little Mountain Trail**. At first this trail contours through some quaking aspens and along some terracing put there in the late 1950's and early 1960's to stop erosion. Beyond the terracing, the trail runs into and through Chris Fisher Flat, and meets a road on the south side of this large mountain meadow. Once on this road turn left and walk to the end of the Timpooneke Road on the southeast side of Chris Fisher Flat.

From the end of the Timpooneke Road, take the **Baldy Trail** in the direction of Big Baldy, but after about a km turn right at the sign and walk down the upper end of the **Battle Creek Trail**. It winds its way down through a large meadow for about half a km, then turns abruptly to the right and heads down a steep section. At the bottom of this 100 meter steep place is what appears to be an old terrace or road. It's actually where the old **Battle Creek Power Plant Feeder Pipeline** used to run. More on this later.

Continue down-canyon through some meadows, then at about where the **Curly Spring Trail** heads off to the south, you'll be inside Battle Creek Canyon. Further down you'll pass the highest waterfall on the face of Timp and will end the hike at the road and **Kiwanis Park**. From there you can easily get back to your car on Grove Creek by walking along one of several 4WD-type roads running along the foot of the mountain. One of these roads runs from one flood basin to the other. This is an easy and fast 2 km walk.

The high point on the big ridge between Battle and Grove Creek Canyons, is locally called **Little Mountain**. It's also been called **G Mountain**. It's not a very high place, but its a fun hike either early or late in the season. You can get there from either canyon or from the old penstock route up from the Kiwanis Park. For simplicity, let's start out by going up Grove Creek to the Grove Creek Spring. From this spring, walk south on a good and moderately used trail through the terraces and to Chris Fisher Flat. On the south side of this flat the trail intersects a 4WD track which is a branch of the Timpooneke Road. At this track, turn right or west and follow it to where the Forest Service has constructed a barricade. From there continue on the **Little Mountain Trail** as it heads southwest not far from the edge of the Grove Creek Canyon Gorge.

Somewhere near the top of Little Mountain, is an **old loggers drag route** off the mountain. The author wasn't aware of the place when he made this hike, but was told of it later. As the story goes, people from Pleasant Grove used to go upon the face of Timp to an area north of Sagebrush Flat, to cut logs for firewood and for home and corral construction. This practice goes back to the middle of

The cable car running to the top of Little Mountain, sometime between 1907 and 1917(Eva Proctor foto).

the 19th century just after the first pioneers arrived in the valley. Much later in time the same method of getting logs off the mountain was used by Fred Smith and Joe Walker of Pleasant Grove in the late 1920's and early 1930's.

Townspeople would cut the logs in the warm season, then use horses to pull the logs down to Grove Creek Spring with the help of an old wagon wheel axle setup. From there the old drag line route contoured southwest along the mountain side just below and to the west of Chris Fisher Flat. When they got to about the summit of Little Mountain, there were two different routes used to get the logs down to the valley. Joe Walker used to wait until there was deep snow on the ground, then he would pull one log down the face of the mountain very near where the letter "G" is on the mountain today. This would make a groove. Then after the snow was allowed to melt a little, then refreeze, other logs could be sent down the chute all the way off the mountain, which was near where his farm was located.

Fred Smith lived nearer the mouth of Grove Creek Canyon, so he would dump his logs off to the northwest and into the middle part of Grove Creek Canyon. Because it was an all-rock route and very steep, Smith could do this trick even in summer time without snow. His logs landed at the bottom of the canyon about 500 meters above the end of the first switchback along the canyon trail. From there, horses were used to pull the logs down to his home. As you walk up Grove Creek Canyon and along the Little Mountain Trail, be aware of these places and look for the traces of this old logging route. This information comes from Joe Hilton and Wes Walker of Pleasant Grove, who were told about it by other old-timers before them.

Now back to the Little Mountain Hike. Once you're on top of the highest point of the mountain, walk south about 200 meters to what remains of the old **Battle Creek Power Plant Reservoir.** Before 1957, water was stored there before being released into the penstock which powered the electric plant at the mouth of Battle Creek Canyon. Today the old reservoir is dry, but it's still there and clearly visible. The next part of the hike is along the old feeder pipeline route which began at Battle Creek Spring.

To walk this **old pipeline trail,** begin at the northern end of the reservoir. You will clearly see what appears to be an old road of some kind running north from the reservoir. After only a short distance, you will see the remains of some old iron wheels. Someone thought they may have been used in the early construction days to drag loads of pipe along this trail. In this same area you will see portions of the old wooden pipeline which have been buried under ground.

Continue walking the trail as it contours eastward around the ridges and minor drainages. Not far from the reservoir you will begin to see remains of the old pipeline still above ground in some places. When the pipeline was in use, it was entirely above ground and visible for inspection, but after the power plant was closed, the Walker Construction Company of Pleasant Grove got the contract to

The old wooden feeder pipeline running from Battle Creek Spring as it appeared in 1988.

destroy it. They dug a trench in most places and buried it. Where it ran over rocky ledges it was left lying above ground.

In the middle parts of this pipeline route, water was transported over the deepest drainage by way of a siphon, but the walking trail presently runs up-canyon a short distance, then doubles back to the pipeline on the other side. The last part of this trail runs through a fine forest of hardwoods comprised mostly of maple and aspen trees. Near the upper end, the well-used Battle Creek Trail crosses the pipeline route. If you continue, this pipeline trail runs on to the southeast and into the North Fork of Battle Creek which local sheep and cattlemen used to call Blue Cliffs Creek. From there it contours around one last ridge and ends at **Battle Creek Spring**(actually the beginning of the wooden feeder pipeline).

About twelve years after they closed down the power plant and pipeline in about 1957, Pleasant Grove City installed a **new pipeline** from Battle Creek Spring down the canyon and into town. It's used today for culinary purposes in Pleasant Grove. This new pipeline runs down in the same general area as the Battle Creek Trail. You can see the line in places and hear the running water as it gushes down the steep grade.

This new 30 cm(12") pipeline was installed by Niels Fugal Sons Construction of Pleasant Grove. It was begun in 1969 and finished in 1970. They hauled the pipe up on the mountain along the Timpooneke Road on a flatbed truck, then one crew worked its way down canyon, while another started up from the bottom. It's been said the only 4WD vehicle ever driven down Battle Creek Canyon was one which was used in the pipeline construction. To get it passed the Lower Battle Creek Falls, they had to drill holes into the canyon wall to build up the downhill side with railway ties

Here's a short history of the **Battle Creek Hydroelectric Power Plant** which was at the mouth of Battle Creek Canyon. Survey work was first begun in about 1905 and construction started in 1906 by the Telluride Power Company. This was the same company owned by Lucien L. and brother Paul N. Nunn, who built the Nunns Power Plant in Provo Canyon(that hydroelectric plant sent power to the mining town of Ophir in the Oquirrh Mountains).

According to the late Sam Hilton who lived and worked at the Battle Creek plant from 1932 until it shut down in 1957, it required the use of 20 horses and two steam engines to move the transformers and generator up to the Battle Creek plant site. About 60 meters of track would be laid into place, then they would pull the equipment up to the top of the track, disassemble all of the track below, and start over again. Sam also stated that for awhile water was piped from the head of Grove Creek to the top of Little Mountain to supplement the normal water supply from Battle Creek sources.

The building of the pipeline, reservoir, penstock and plant itself was finished by 1907. The construction was under the supervision of Robert Fairbanks, brother of movie star Douglas Fairbanks. Fairbanks left the power business in 1912 when Utah Power and Light bought out Telluride, and went to Hollywood to become a Fox studio executive.

Ed Warburton standing in front of his cabin on Little Mountain
sometime between 1907 and 1917(Eva Proctor foto).

96

To aid construction efforts, they first built a simple tramway from the mouth of the canyon where the electric plant was located, up to where the old reservoir is located today, and used it to transport pipe and other equipment and materials to the top of Little Mountain. The tram was about 1200 meters long, with an elevation rise of over 400 meters. It consisted of a narrow set of tracks, upon which rode a small car, similar to ore cars in mines. Fastened to the front of the car was a cable, which was attacted to a pulley at the upper end of the line on top of the mountain. At the base of the mountain was a large drum which was attached to a motor of some kind. The motor would reel in the cable, sending the cable-car up the mountain. It was used while the Warburtons were on the mountain but torn down some time before Sam Hilton arrived at the plant in 1932.

The steel pipe used for the penstock was riveted sections which was larger in diameter at the top than at the bottom. At the time, American manufacturers of steel were far behind in orders and couldn't supply the Telluride Company needs. Consequently, specially constructed steel pipe had to be shipped from Germany and carried by railroad from Galveston, Texas.

The feeder pipeline running to the mountain-top reservoir from Battle Creek Spring, was made with wooden tongue & groove slats. These were held together by steel rings placed a short distance apart. It was laid above ground but where there were sharp turns, the wooden parts were replaced by steel elbows. Several of these are clearly visible along the old pipeline route today. It brought water from Battle Creek and Blue Cliffs Creek Springs to the power plant reservoir, then it was sent downhill to the hydroelectric plant in the steel penstock pipe.

Just a few meters north of the old reservoir is where **Ed Warburton's Cabin** used to stand. This was the caretakers home and it had two rooms; a bedroom and a kitchen, and electric lights. The only people to ever live there was Ed Warburton and his family, from about 1907 until 1917. One of his children is Eva Proctor, born in 1902, and presently living in Pleasant Grove. Most of this information comes from her keen memory.

The Warburtons(wife Tina, and daughters Eva and Pearl) lived there during the summer seasons which was from the end of April to the first part of September each year. That's when the children were out of school. During the winter the family stayed in the valley. In those early years some people used the tramway to get up and down the mountain, but the Warburtons usually got to the top of Little Mountain on horse back along the now-fading reservoir trail(discussed below).

One unusual event which took place on Little Mountain in about 1915 is told in Ed Warburton's bear story. It started out with a Sunday visit to town for the whole family. After they returned, Ed discovered bear tracks around the cabin and some of the chickens and pigs dead. Ed got his rifle and with Tina rode uphill toward the Grove Creek Trail. At one point Ed got off the horse and left Tina to

Ed Warburton's Bear in about 1915. Wife Tina is on the left(Eva Proctor foto).

watch. He went around a hillside, but soon after, Tina saw the bear come out of the brush. It stood up on it's hind legs momentarily, then headed up hill. Tina hollered, Ed came running, then shot it. They got an old skid-like contraption and hauled the bear back to the cabin. When Alma Christiansen heard the news, he went to the mountain and took a number of pictures. Still later they took the carcass down to the valley where it was skinned. Eventually it became a rug in the Warburton's living room.

During the winter seasons, Ed would go up the mountain to keep an eye on things. His job was to check the water level of the reservoir and make sure the pipeline was in good repair. Ed could easily see the markers indicating the water level from the cabin with a pair of binoculars. In the early years the water level and the amount of water going down the penstock was manually operated. Warburton would keep in touch with the power plant below via telefone. When they finally perfected an automatic float device to regulate the water going into the penstock, the need for a full time caretaker ended. That was in about 1917.

After only about 5 years of operating the plant, Telluride Power Company was sold by Nunn to the newly formed Utah Power and Light. That was in September of 1912, but the sale of the water rights was signed on January 13, 1913. UP&L operated it from then until it closed down in 1957. At the same time, Nunn also sold the Nunns and Olmsted Hydroelectric Power Stations in the lower Provo Canyon. This was the beginning of UP&L.

Sometime after the Warburtons moved out of the reservoir cabin, it was torn down. Part of the lumber was moved east to a place nearer the beginning of the pipeline. Another cabin was built and the local workers used to call this the **MJB Hotel.** It was a one room cabin measuring about 4 x 4 meters. It had a cook stove, a table and a pair of bunk beds inside. In winter time the workers usually got to the pipeline and cabin via the Reservoir Trail up the face of Little Mountain. In summer they usually went up the Battle Creek Trail.

The MJB Hotel cabin was used on a part-time basis year-round, but it was used full-time for a week or two in the late spring or early summer season. During this period of time, UP&L would send a work crew to the mountain, temporarily shut off the water in the pipeline, then do some major repairs if needed. The water was shut off for one to two weeks at a time. The rest of the year, and during one week intervals, workers would walk the pipeline inspecting it for leaks. Most repairs were made with water in the pipe. Snowshoes were used for winter travel along the pipeline.

If you're interested in seeing the old reservoir on top of Little Mountain, you can also use the old **penstock route** or **Reservoir Trail** to get there. You could go right up the ridge, but it's very steep at the bottom, and too much foot traffic there will help erode the mountain side even more than it already is. The best way up is to walk east from the Kiwanis Park covered picnic site, past a couple of

Repairing the Pleasant Grove feeder pipeline. Joe Hilton left, and Bud Marshal and Byron Carter(Joe Hilton foto).

apricot trees, then turn left or north, and walk along a trail heading toward an old yellow metal tank of some kind on the hillside less than a 100 meters away. This is the trail which runs to the letter "G" on the hillside, and the old original Reservoir Trail to Ed Warburton's Cabin. Walk this trail for 400 meters or so, then when you arrive on top of a minor bench or terrace, look to the right for another trail cutting back south toward the ridgetop. Once on the ridge look to the north again for a sign of this fading trail. If you can locate the trail, you can follow it much of the way up, but it's hard to find in many places.

If you can't locate the Reservoir Trail, just head for the ridge and walk up. Along the way you will see places where the old penstock used to be fastened to the mountain. Higher up, the slope becomes more gentle, and you will see old poles which apparently supported the old telefone lines. At the very end is the old reservoir.

At the same time the old wooden feeder pipeline was being buried in about 1960, the steel penstock was also being removed. Walker Construction did this job at the same time they did the terracing on the mountain sides. This riveted pipe was removed with great pains from both the top and the bottom. Later it was sold to a sign company in Salt Lake City, which used it to mount some of the taller signs seen around that valley.

There is one last hike worth mentioning in the area. It's to the **letter "G"** on the mountain side between Battle Creek and Grove Creek Canyons. The trail begins at the Kiwanis Park. Walk east from the park, past two apricot trees, then turn left and walk up the trail past a yellow metal tank. Once you get on this trail, it's easy to follow. From the park to the "G" is only about 1 1/2 kms, and it's an easy walk for the whole family.

According to Ora Thorne of Pleasant Grove, the letter "G" was first made in the spring of 1921. It was a school project for the boys of the senior class at Pleasant Grove High. The teachers who supervised the project were Junious Hayes and Alma Kirk. They would go as a group to the mountain either in the afternoons or on weekends, and gather rocks from all over the hillside. These rocks were placed in the form of a letter "G". When the rocks were in place, they were covered with a white coating of lime. They hauled the lime up the mountain in a wheelbarrow-type contraption. They got water from a nearby spring to mix with the lime, then poured it over the rocks to make it visible from the valley below.

The old "G" remained the same for many years, and often the school and community went to the mountain to maintain and white-wash it. In March, April and May of 1986, plans were made to make a more permanent and maintenance-free structure. The high school, Kiwanis Club and community got together and renovated it. The National Guard helped by declaring the project a practice drill, and used one of their own helicopters to transport material from the Kiwanis Park to the letter "G" site. Boyd Fugal of Niels Fugal Sons Company helped ramrod the operation and donated trucks for transporting materials.

They made the letter by driving metal stakes into the hillside, then a heavy gage steel wire mesh was laid out above the ground. Finally, thin aluminum strips or bands were interlaced into the steel wire. There are electric wires in place on the letter, and all they have to do is haul a small electric generator up the mountain to light it up for special occasions, such as Strawberry Days, Homecoming at the high school, etc.

Distance and Time Needed The distance from the trailhead on Grove Creek up to Grove Creek Spring is about 5 kms. From this spring near the Timpooneke Road to the beginning of the Battle Creek Trail is about 3 kms more. From there to the Battle Creek Trailhead is another 4 or 5 kms. From the Kiwanis Park back to the trailhead on Grove Creek is about 2 kms or less. This adds up to about 14 or 15 kms, and can be done in about 4 to 6 hours by most hikers.

If you were to walk up Grove Creek to Little Mountain, and on the old feeder pipeline to the Battle Creek Trail, then down-canyon and back to your car on Grove Creek, it would be roughly 15 or 16 kms long. This would take about 5 to 7 hours to walk. The author did this one once in 4 hrs. 42 min. But that's too fast for most people. However, if you were to go up along the old penstock route, walk along the old feeder pipeline, then return to the Kiwanis Park via Battle Creek, it would mean walking 8 or 9 kms and will take 4 to 5 hours for most people. Most could walk from the Kiwanis Park to the letter "G", and back in about one hour or slightly more.

Best Time There are no real high points on any of these trails, the highest place being only 2328 meters at Chris Fisher Flat. This means you could do any of these warm weather hikes beginning some time in April. You could also hike until the end of October, or even into November in some years, without getting into too much snow. April, May, June, September and October might be the best times to hike.

Main Attractions Several short easy hikes for the whole family for about a 6 or maybe 7 month period. Some interesting old historic sites as well as some good views of the towns at the bottom of the mountain. In winter, you can do any of these trails with snowshoes or skis without fear of avalanches.

Elevations Each trailhead, 1585 meters; Grove Creek Spring, 2274; Chris Fisher Flat, 2328; Little Mountain, 2187; and Battle Creek Spring, 2164 meters.

Water There is good drinking water at any of the springs shown on the map. The water in the upper end of Grove Creek should be good where the trail crosses the stream. The further up Battle Creek you go, the better the water will be. Just below where the Curly Spring Trail leaves Battle Creek is a small drainage on the north side, which should also have good water.

Boots or Shoes You can wear about any kind of comfortable shoe on any of these hikes, but the penstock route is a bit rougher. Thick-soled running shoes would work well on any of these trails.

Campsites There are several fine sites in the area of all the springs in upper Grove Creek. You could also find some campsites in the area of Battle Creek Spring. There are many good sites around, but they're all dry except for those just mentioned.

Winter Climbing If you're not interested in reaching the summit of Timp, but would just like to do some cross-country skiing or snowshoeing, this would be an excellent area to visit. The canyon easiest to ascend in winter time would likely be Grove Creek. The trail there is not quite as steep as the one in Battle Creek Canyon, and it's up on the south-facing side of the canyon wall. This means the snow would either melt quickly and not be too deep, or it would be hard and crusty and easy to walk on much of the time.   Traveling there should be reasonably easy up to near the head of the canyon. Avalanche danger in the canyon would be minimal, except maybe right after some heavy snow storms

Once you get to the flats below the upper face of Timp, you'll find many semi-level places for cross-country skiing. If you were to try doing the loop between these two major canyons, it's recommended you go up Grove, and down Battle Creek. You'll need skis or snowshoes all the time between about Thanksgiving weekend and the mid-March. In March the snow will normally be hard in the mornings, but will begin to soften up by about 11 am. By April the snow will be gone from the these lower slopes.

A short and interesting winter hike would be up Battle Creek to the falls which will be frozen solid throughout the 3 coldest months of the year--December, January and February. The hikes to the letter "G" and up the penstock ridge, should normally be easy with very little snow even in the dead of winter.

What remains of the old reservoir on top of Little Mountain. Big Baldy in the background.

The MJB Hotel as it looked back in the late 1940's(Joe Hilton foto).

An up-close look at the new letter G, built of aluminum stripping raised up off the ground.

Grove Creek Trail--Mahogany Mountain, Timp Highline Trail and Bomber & North Peaks

Trailhead Location All the peaks and hikes on this map are best reached via the trailhead at the mouth of Grove Creek Canyon. To get to this starting point, make your way to the center of Pleasant Grove and locate the east-west running street named Grove Creek Drive. In the center of town this same road is more commonly known as 500 North Street. Once on this street, drive east to where the paved road turns right or south, next to a flood debris basin dam. At that point, you turn to the left and proceed into the mouth of Grove Creek Canyon on a dirt road. You can drive 300 meters or so into the canyon, but most people with cars would prefer to park just above the dam and walk from there.

Discussed here are trails and routes to three important peaks. They are Mahogany Mountain, Bomber Peak and the North Peak. The author has given the name *Bomber* to one of the higher peaks along Timp's summit ridge, because that's where a B-25 Bomber crashed on March 9, 1955. Also discussed here is a fading early-day livestock trail old-timers called the Timp Highline Trail.

Route Description From the trailhead walk up the 4WD-type road about 300 meters to where there's a fork. The right hand track runs up-canyon only a short distance to where it ends at a diversion dam and pipeline intake. You take the path on the left which is the Grove Creek Trail. At first this trail runs up-stream near the creek bed, then it makes a sharp left turn and angles up-slope. Further on, it makes one more switchback, then heads up-canyon high above Grove Creek.

As you near the upper end of the canyon, you will cross the creek, then zig zag up through some pines and finally reach terrain that's not so steep. A short distance above the steep part of the canyon, you will come to the best spring in the area called **Grove Creek Spring**. Continue on the trail going straight up-hill until you reach the **Timpooneke Road**. From that place, the upper part of the mountain will be in full view, and just in front of you will be Bomber and North Peaks. To your left and behind will be Mahogany Mountain.

To climb **Bomber or North Peaks,** use essentially the same route for either, at least at the bottom part of the mountain. From where the Grove Creek Trail intersects the Timpooneke Road, turn left or north and walk along the road about 100-150 meters. Then look to the right or east for a minor drainage. Walk up this dry creek bed some where between 100 and 200 meters. At some convenient point, perhaps at a deer trail, turn left or northeast, and walk through some small aspen trees and other brush for another 200 meters or so. By that time you should be in an opening at the bottom of the canyon leading straight up to the col or low point between North and Bomber Peaks. Once you locate this opening, it'll be clear sailing all the way to the **summit ridge.**

Part of the Timp Highline Trail as seen in the upper East Fork of Grove Creek half way up the southwest face.

MAP 9, **GROVE CREEK TRAIL**--MAHOGANY MTN., TIMP HIGHLINE TRAIL AND BOMBER & NORTH PEAKS

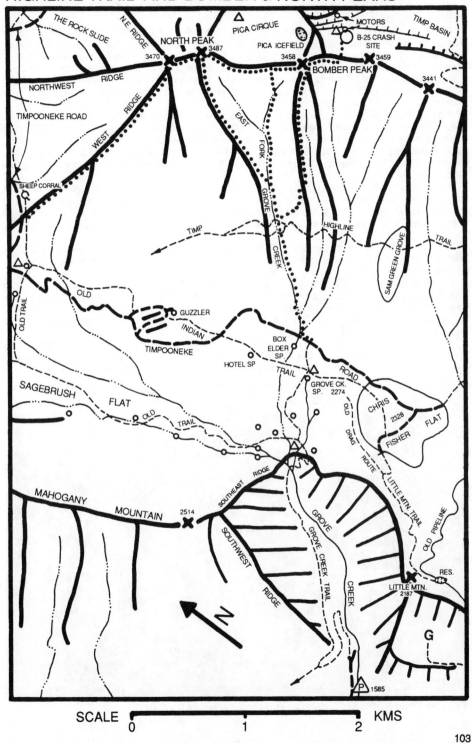

SCALE

0   1   2   KMS

At first, head straight up the bottom of the drainage to avoid bushwhacking on either side. The dry creek bed makes an easy route all the way to the top. About one km from the road, you'll be in an area that isn't as steep as above or below. You may see part of the old Timp Highline Trail in this area. It's especially easy to see as it runs to the south.

Once on the Highline Trail, you could walk south to the first ridge, then ridge-walk straight up the mountain to the top of the northern part of Bomber Peak, at 3458 meters. Or you could continue up the bottom of the canyon to the summit ridge, then turn to the right or south and walk up to Bomber. Once on the peak, walk to a point about half way between the two summits. You will then see a chute or gully heading straight down to the northeast side of the mountain. Climb down this steep gully or couloir to below the cliffs, look to the right a bit, and you will see the scattered remains of a **B-25 Bomber.**

Most of the wreckage is on the lip of the first terrace or bench below the summit ridge. Included there is one of the two engines and the main part of the now-crushed fuselage. About 200 meters straight down the slope and over two more minor benches, will be seen several other parts of the plane, including the other motor. This plane went down the night of March 9, 1955 in a snowstorm. Five men were killed. Read the full story on Map 13. The normal route to this crash site is up the Timpooneke Trail.

To climb North Peak(some people call it Twin Peaks), at 3487 meters, make your way up the bottom of the same canyon you may have taken to Bomber Peak, but when you reach the summit ridge, turn left and walk northwest to the top. From the area where the Timp Highline Trail crosses the East Fork of Grove Creek, you could also get on the first ridge to the north and ridge-walk to the summit.

North Peak has two summits and can be climbed from about 5 or 6 different ridge routes. By itself, it's an imposing mass of rock, especially as seen from the north. It has a very impressive northeast face, which is discussed under Map 12.

From the top of North Peak, you can go down the same way you went up, or you can try a new route few people climb. From the northern summit, head down the mountain in a westerly direction. Near the top, it is mostly a west or northwest face, but a little further down two more-or-less distinctive ridges begin. One is a Northwest Ridge, the other is the **West Ridge.** If you've come up from Grove Creek, better use the West Ridge to get down.

The West Ridge is a rugged route, but anyone can make it up or down. In a couple of places you'll have to skirt around some cliffs, but it's not a difficult route. It's just steep and rugged enough to make it interesting. Near the bottom, the slope eases a bit and you'll end the trip on deer trails just

From the Timp Highline Trail looking up at the south slopes of North Peak.

MAHOGANY MOUNTAIN HIKE

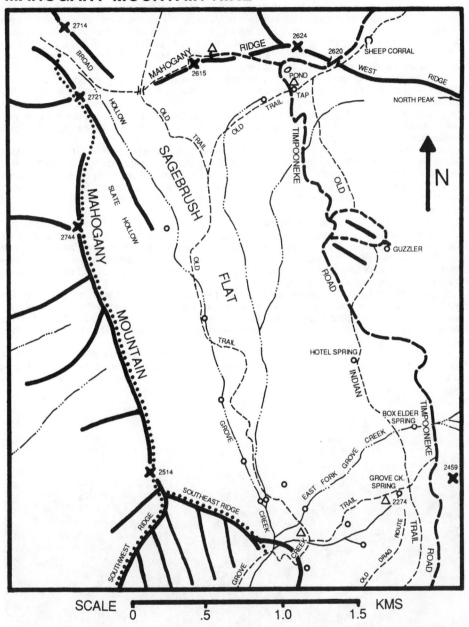

SCALE 0 .5 1.0 1.5 KMS

above the Timpooneke Road. Once on the road, walk south to the Grove Creek Trail, and back down the canyon.

Here's an idea for healthy and enthusiastic climbers. It's perhaps the easiest way to the top of **Mahogany Mountain.** When you reach the bottom of the west ridge of North Peak, walk along the road for 500 meters until it makes a hard left turn, then instead of returning south to Grove Creek, locate an old deer hunter's road running west from the bend. Walk this old road for about 700-800 meters until you come to a camping place and a barricade erected by the Forest Service. At that point, the road ends but a trail begins.

Continue west on the trail. Not far from the end of the road, the trail ascends a rounded knoll and from there you'll have a clear view of the east face of Mahogany. From the knoll, continue west on the same trail. Further along, it seems to fade in places, but if you do lose it, head northwest between two of the peaks on Mahogany Ridge, called Broad Hollow. Still further, you will find a trail but then you'll have to turn left or south and climb the northern ridge of Mahogany. From the summit, you'll have some unique views of the upper face of Timp.

From the top, the easiest and fastest way down is to walk south along the top of Mahogany Mountain. For the most part there are deer trails you can follow, or there is simply no vegetation on the ridgetop, so walking is easy. As you approach the south end of the mountain, you will have a choice of two ways down to the trailhead. One will be the **southeast ridge,** which if taken, will take you down to about where the Grove Creek Trail crosses the stream at the head of the canyon. This route is steep, but not really difficult or dangerous.

The second route down(or up) Mahogany Mountain, is via a **southwest ridge.** The author hasn't tired this one, but it doesn't look any harder or more difficult than the southeast ridge. You will have to route-find around a couple of cliffs however. This ridge comes to an end on the lower end of the Grove Creek Trail. The author has described the climb up Mahogany from the north end, but if you only want to climb this mountain and nothing else, then you could climb it from either of these two ridges just mentioned.

The **Timp Highline Trail** is one that few people know about. It is an old sheep and cattle trail located about half way up the main face of Timpanogos. It runs along the face between the 2750 and 2900 meter contour lines. It probably evolved over the years and some parts are clearly man-made and still very visible today. It could make an interesting hike, but since it only runs along the face on a contour line, it doesn't help hikers who want to reach the summit. Surely it's used more during the deer hunt each year than at any other time.

To get on this old trail, it's probably best to start at Baldy Saddle, which is the pass between Big Baldy and Timp's main summit ridge(see Map 7 for a look at the south end of the trail). From the saddle, walk north along the one terrace for 200 meters, then head up another 200 meters but veer a little to the left. You should find the trail in that area, then walk on it across an erosional gully, then under some big gray cliffs.

Finally the trail angles up and into another minor drainage, where it contacts the Tunnel Hollow Trail. From that point on, contour or walk at about the same elevation as it runs to the northwest along the face. It runs through several big groves of pine trees, including one called Sam Green Grove. It's

Looking south at Utah Valley from the summit of North Peak.

clearly visible as it crosses the East Fork of Grove Creek. From that area north, it seems to fade, but old timers say it runs north and ends at or near the sheep corral at the bottom of the West Ridge of North Peak. This hike could be done from either Battle Creek or Grove Creek Trailheads. Horsemen would likely be more interested in locating and riding this old trail than hikers.

Distance and Time Needed The distance from the trailhead at the mouth of Grove Creek Canyon to the top of either North or Bomber Peak, is about 8 to 10 kms, depending on the route taken. Most climbers would want anywhere from 4 to 6 hours for the ascent, and another 3 hours coming down.

On one trip, the author climbed North Peak from the trailhead on Grove Creek in 2 hrs. 55 min. He then climbed down the West Ridge and to the top of Mahogany Mtn., and walked south along the mountain top to the southeast ridge, then back to the trailhead in 7 hrs. and 25 min., round-trip. The average person shouldn't try these two peaks on the same day. If you just wanted to climb to the top of Mahogany Mtn., most could do the round-trip in about half a day. If you're out to do the Timp Highline Trail, better plan on a long all-day trip. This one can be done from Battle Creek Canyon as well.

Best Time A summer climb to the top of North and/or Bomber Peaks, can be made from about June 1 until mid or late October, but this varies each year. If you do either of these two climbs early in summer with snow in the East Fork of Grove Creek, then an ice ax and crampons will help.

If you want to see the wreckage of the B-25, then you'd better wait until about mid-August, otherwise parts of it will be under snow. If you want to climb Mahogany via one of the southern ridges, then that can be done from the first part of April until the first of November. But again each year is different.

Main Attraction A couple of high summits few people climb, an old semi-historic plane crash site and stock trail, and great views in all directions. On Mahogany, you will have fine views of the upper face of Mt. Timpanogos.

Elevations The trailhead, 1585 meters; Grove Creek Spring, 2274; Bomber Peak, 3459; North Peak, 3487; Mahogany Mountain, 2744 meters.

Water Good water can be found in the upper part of Grove Creek, and at springs near the trail. The best is at Grove Creek Spring. In early summer, there should always be some running water below snowbanks on the mountain, otherwise it's a dry climb. There's a small spring with a pipe and tap just south of the little pond near the road on the Mahogany Mtn. Map. Mahogany Mountain Ridge is dry except for possible snowbanks in spring or fall. Better carry some water with you on any of these trips.

Boots or Shoes A rugged pair of hiking or climbing boots would be best for any of these climbs.

From North Peak, looking at the north face of Bomber Peak, with the Timp Summit in the background.

Campsites Somewhere near a good water source, such as Grove Creek Spring. Near the bottom end of the West Ridge of North Peak is a spring and tap, which might be a good place to camp if you're on the mountain in your car.

Winter Climbing In the dead of winter, say from the first of December until mid-March, you will need either snowshoes or skis beginning about half way up the Grove Creek Canyon Trail. Once you get out and above this rugged gorge, the steepness of the route lessens along the flats up to the bottom of the upper face. Up to that point it should be easy, even when the snow is powdery as it is in the middle of winter.

From the base of the upper face of Timp and its summit ridge, you will normally want to pick out one of the prominent ridges to walk on to the top. Stay on the south facing part of the ridge. That's where the snow will be the hardest, the easiest to walk on, and the part that's safest from avalanches. Both of the ridges on either side of the East Fork of Grove Creek should be good for a winter ascent.

If you're on the mountain and it's been a week to 10 days since the last storm, then you may be safe in going straight up in the bottom of the East Fork of Grove Creek Canyon--at least in the morning hours. When you descend in the afternoon, it might be safest to do so on one of the ridges. New slides can occur if the temperatures are on the rise, even if all the big slides have already fallen right after a storm. If you'd like expert opinion on the avalanche situation, call one of these numbers; 374-9770, 364-1581, or 621-2362. This is the Utah Avalanche Forecast Center.

The very best time to climb North or Bomber Peak in winter, is in March or early April. At that time the snow on the southwest face of Timp is really getting melted down, making morning climbing very easy on a hard crust(You can also make an easy climb near the end of the foggy periods in the middle of winter. That's when the mountains are warmer and sunnier than the valley below). Also, in late winter or early spring there seem to be fewer snowslides, except of course, right after a storm. The temperatures are higher and the days are longer, otherwise you'll have to wear about the same kind of clothes.

The author once made an ascent of the north summit of Bomber Peak from the trailhead in Grove Creek Canyon on a March 16. It had been warm for 2 weeks prior to the climb. He found no snow on the trail until he crossed the upper part of Grove Creek. From there on up, he was on rock-hard snow all the way. He raced up the bottom of the East Fork of Grove Creek trying to beat incoming clouds. The time was 2 hrs., 52 min., while the round-trip was 5 hrs. 32 min. The snow conditions were ideal and snowshoes weren't needed. The snow stayed hard until about 11 am, then began to soften on the lower flats.

Mahogany Mountain should be a relatively easy climb in winter. The best route up would likely be

From the north part of North Peak, looking southeast. Timp Summit in the far background.

to start at the flood basin at the mouth of the canyon and walk straight up the steep southwest ridge. Since this is facing directly south, what little snow there will be, should be very hard and crusty in the morning hours. You will have to skirt several cliffs along this route, but there should be no avalanche danger.

From the top of the North Peak looking southeast. Pica Cirque in the lower left hand corner.

North Peak as seen from the top of Mahogany Mountain.

The Timpanogos Cave Hike

Trailhead Location The hike here is to the Timpanogos Cave, better known locally as the Timp Cave, which is located in the lower part of American Fork Canyon. The map shows one square km, all of which is the Timpanogos Cave National Monument. To get there, drive east into the canyon from the Alpine exit on I-15; or from American Fork or Pleasant Grove. The road in the canyon is called the Alpine Scenic Loop(Utah State Highway 92), and the visitor center is located near mile post 10. Drive to the visitor center and park.

Route Description To begin this hike, you must first enter the monument visitor center. There you must purchase your ticket, which is also a reservation for a time slot and designated cave tour. While there you can also purchase books, maps and color slides, and during the busy summer season, food and drinks in a nearby snack bar. You can also view a slide show or video presentation about the cave and monument before going up to the cave.

To begin the hike, walk out the east side door of the visitor center directly onto the cave trail. The trail is paved all the way and moderately steep, but it's easy walking. Along the way you will see numbers placed beside the trail. These are part of a self-guided tour which explains vegetation and rock formations along the way. To better appreciate this walk, buy the little booklet entitled, *Along the Way to the Caves,* at the visitor center before you leave. Just before you arrive at the cave entrance you will pass a restroom. Use this if you need to, as the cave tour will last up to an hour. There is also another old emergency-only type restroom just beyond the exit.

At or very near the entrance is The Grotto, a shady resting place if you're there in the middle of a hot summer day. There is also a water fountain inside The Grotto. You must wait there until your cave tour, at which time your guide will open the locked cave door and your tour will begin.

The first cave you enter will actually be Hansen Cave, the part of the cave system first discovered. There's not much to see in this part, because back in 1892-3, the cave was mined of most of it's decorative features(called *onyx* at that time).

From Hansen Cave, there is a 26 meter-long man-made tunnel, connecting it to the Middle Cave. This part of the cave system was the last to be discovered, so it was not vandalized. The Middle Cave has a small lake, and one room called Coral Gardens.

From the Middle Cave, there is another man-made tunnel extending 57 meters to the lower part of Timpanogos Cave. This cave is the most beautiful of the three, mainly because it was never mined and was spared from vandals. In it are a couple of small ponds or lakes, the famous Great Heart of

A scene inside the Timpanogos Cave.

MAP 10, **THE TIMPANOGOS CAVE HIKE**

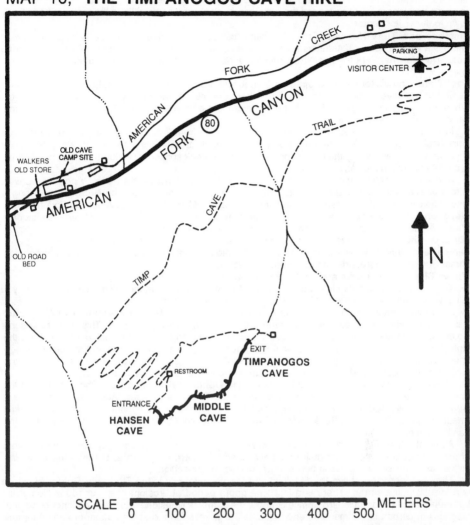

SCALE 0 100 200 300 400 500 METERS

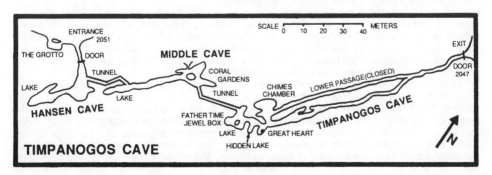

TIMPANOGOS CAVE

Timpanogos, and perhaps the best and largest room of all, Chimes Chamber. Normally the guides will allow you to get up close to the walls for good fotographs in this last room. From Chimes Chamber, you walk up along a fault line toward the exit, then back around some cliffs to the main trail and back down to the visitor center.

Distance and Time Needed From the visitor center to the cave's entrance is about 2.4 kms. There is a vertical rise of 324 meters from the road to the entrance. The round-trip hike will be about 6 kms. The National Park Service(NPS), recommends about 3 hours for the round-trip hike and cave tour.

Best Time The visitor center is open on a year-round basis from 8 am to 4:30 pm daily, 7 days a week, but the caves tours are run only from about the middle part of May until about mid-October. When the cave tours begin and end is partly dependent on the weather so the opening and closing dates are different each year.

In the busy summer season the visitor center is open from 7 am until 6 pm daily, and the cave tours begin about 8 am and run until 4:30 pm. At the visitor center is a snack bar, which is usually open on a daily basis when the cave is open. During the peak season, cave tours can run as often as every 10 minutes, depending on demand.

At the visitor center you can see a slide show in a small auditorium and a video TV program as well, before or after your hike and cave tour. For the summer season of 1989, the NPS is considering a reservation system. If you have any questions call the TCNM at 756-5238(an American Fork number).

Elevations The visitor center sits at 1727 meters, while the cave entrance is 2051 meters altitude.

Water At the visitor center and at The Grotto near the entrance of the cave.

Boots or Shoes Any comfortable walking shoe, but running shoes are excellent.

Campsites There is no overnight camping in the national monument, but there are a number of U.S. Forest Service campgrounds and picnic sites further up-canyon.

Winter Climbing The cave and the trail to the cave are closed in winter.

Geology From the time you leave the visitor center until you arrive at the the mouth of the cave, you will have walked through roughly 275 million years of geologic history.

At the very bottom of the trail the rock exposed is called the **Mutual Formation or Quartzite.** It is a Precambrian rock, dating back to sometime before 600 million years ago. This figure represents the end of Precambrian times and the beginning of the Cambrian period. The next formation above the Mutual is the **Tintic Quartzite.** It's a Cambrian rock dating from about 565 to 600 million years ago. These two formations actually began as sandstone, then throughout the eons of time, and after being subjected to pressure and heat, they evolved and re-crystalized into quartzite.

Above the Tintic are the less visible rocks of the **Ophir Shale Formation.** This is also from the Cambrian time period, but since it's on top or above the Tintic, it's younger. Above the Ophir, most of the rocks you will see are limestone, all of which were formed at the bottom of an ocean. The first limestone layer is the **Maxfield Formation.** It is the youngest of the three formations of the Cambrian period.

Above the Maxfield, there is an unconformity. This means there is a time gap between two layers of rock. It usually means that rock may have been laid down at one time, but then the area was uplifted and erosion took place in between two periods of deposition.

The next formation above the Maxfield and the unconformity is the **Fitchville Dolomite,** which is a Mississippian strata. There is a lost time gap(a period of erosion) of about 150 million years between these two formations(Dolomite is about the same as limestone, but it has a higher content of magnesium carbonate. Limestone and dolomite are always formed at the bottom of an ocean, and from the deposition of sea shells and other marine life).

The next layer above the Fitchville Formation is the **Gardison Limestone.** It's hard for the untrained eye to see the difference between these layers, but the Gardison has more white chert veins than the next formation above. The Gardison is immediately below the formation in which the cave is located. That next band of rock is called the **Deseret Limestone.** The Deseret is a Mississippian formation which is about 340 million years old. It's identifiable by large amounts of black chert. All three Timpanogos Caves are located in this geologic formation.

Immediately above the caves and the Deseret Formation is the **Humbug,** then **Great Blue Limestones.** They are both Mississippian in age.

Development of Timpanogos Cave This cave is very similar to other limestone caves throughout the world. The way it developed is also the same, except this cave was created along a fault line. In a limestone cave there are basically two stages of development. The first stage is when the cavities and passage ways are **dissolved** away. This is caused by rainwater and snowmelt percolating down through the cracks or along fault lines. Limestone cannot be dissolved by mineral-free soft rainwater; however, as the rain reaches the ground, it reacts with carbon dioxide from

GEOLOGY CROSS SECTION--AMERICAN FORK CANYON

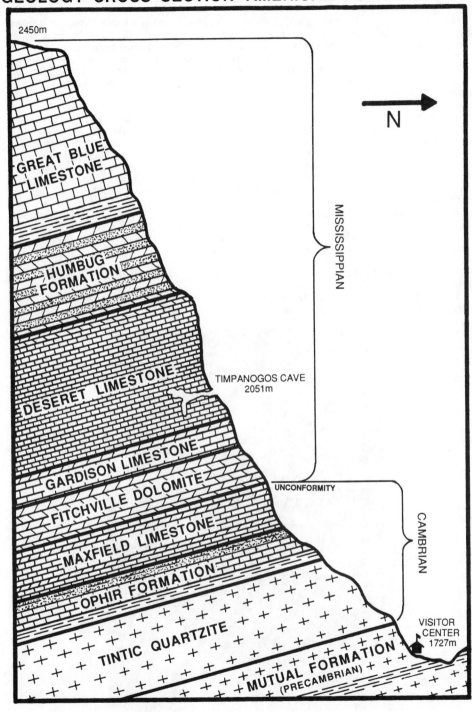

113

decaying leaves and roots of trees, and becomes carbonic acid. This weak acid then seeps into the ground by way of cracks.

Once inside the rock, the water gradually moves down until it reaches the water table. As it moves down it dissolves limestone, creating cavities, chambers and tunnels. During wet periods, these chambers might be full of water, but later during dry periods, the mineralized water would flow out. Thus, during the dissolving stage, there was a constant renewal of water. Some geologists think most of the Timpanogos Cave system was made when the cave was at or near the water table. If this was the case, it must have been made long ago, because the water table today is at the bottom of American Fork Canyon, 324 meters or more below. However, others feel it is younger than that, so the age of the cave is still unknown.

The second stage is that of **deposition.** After the water table is lowered, or when the cave area is raised and becomes dry, this stage begins. An opening to the cave and atmosphere is likely made at some point in time. The process in this stage is almost the reverse of stage one, but this time there is less water and more air for evaporation. When the water with the dissolved minerals is exposed to air, the carbonic acid breaks down and the carbon dioxide is lost to the air(like opening a can of soda pop). In the process the water loses it's ability to hold suspended matter, which in this case is calcite. The calcite is then deposited on the ceilings, walls or floors of the cave as evaporation takes place.

The basic limestone cave structures are called stalactites, stalagmites, columns, flowstone, drapery, and rimstone. Timpanogos Cave has all of these, plus helictites, something unique to this limestone cave. If you're interested in further explanations about this cave's features, you can buy a publication at the visitor center entitled, *Timpanogos Cave.*

History of the Discovery and Development of Timpanogos Cave National Monument

Much of the information in this section comes from a 1968 thesis from BYU by Gary V. Keetch, entitled *The Changing Impact of Man in American Fork Canyon.* Also, from an unpublished manuscript

At the mouth of Timpanogos Cave sometime in the 1920's.

available at the visitor center titled, *The History of Timpanogos Cave National Monument, American Fork Canyon, Utah.* This is an excellent information source up to about the early 1960's.

In the fall of 1887, Martin Hansen discovered a beautiful cave high up on the south wall of American Fork Canyon. One day when it was time to return to his home in American Fork, Hansen left his ax by the partially trimmed tree on which he had been working. That night a light snow fell. Returning to work the next morning, Hansen noticed the tracks of a mountain lion in the snow near the fallen tree. He followed the tracks onto some higher ledges, which led him into an opening in the cliff face. This cave became known as Hansen's Cave.

During the following winter, Martin Hansen interested several other men in his discovery and they joined together to open the cave to the public. With the aid of his brother-in-law, Richard Steele, and Charles and Joseph Burgess, they hacked out a rough trail from the canyon bottom to the cave entrance. The path went almost straight up for 365 meters with little or no attention given to making switchbacks. Hansen apparently had no legal claim to the cave, but in order to protect it he placed a wooden door over the natural entrance.

For about 3 or 4 years after the discovery, Hansen conducted groups through the cave on request; a small fee being collected for his guide service. Despite the locked door, some people periodically broke into the cave to destroy or remove dripstone formations. Sometime during 1891, Hansen stopped taking groups through the cave and did not return for a year or two.

Reportedly, during the winter of 1892-93, a few men from a neighboring town mined the cave for it's onyx deposits. These men had located the cave as a mining claim and were reportedly working on contract with the Duke-Onyx Company of Chicago, Illinois. They stripped the cave of some of its decorations and partially destroyed its scenic value.

It is known that at least two freight cars of onyx were removed, but no records have been found to reveal the destination. It is rumored that at least two freight cars of material were shipped to New York City and used for decorative purposes in the construction of the American Museum of Natural History. Another building in which some of the flowstone may have been used is the Mormon Temple in Salt Lake City.

It was not until 1915 that the present Timpanogos Cave was discovered by James W. Gough Jr. He and Frank Johnson of Lehi, discovered the cave while Gough's parents were visiting the old Hansen Cave. He was primarily interested in the mining possibilities of the cave and in August of 1915, his family filed on the location and named the claim the Lone Star Lode. However, shortly after filing the Goughs moved to Idaho, and little or none of the necessary assessment work was done to validate the claim. In order to conceal the entrance before they left, young Gough piled rocks over the opening, and apparently no one entered the cave again until 1921.

The Middle Cave was discovered by George Heber Hansen and Wayne Hansen while deer hunting on about October 20, 1921. This was about 8 weeks after the Timp Cave was re-discovered on August 14.

In Gary Keetch's thesis on the canyon, he quotes a letter from James W. Gough, Jr. Apparently over the years there was some controversy as to just who discovered Timpanogos Cave. This letter has cleared up any controversy. By reading the letter carefully, it appears other people, perhaps Indians, had known of the cave even earlier. Here is that letter dated December 13, 1960.

During the summer of 1914 or 1915, I, James W. Gough, Jr. went with my parents and a group of people from Lehi, Utah, to visit the old Hansen Cave. This group consisted of the following named men and their wives: James W. Gough, Sr., Harmon Johnson, Lavon Fox, Wilma Johnson, Thomas A. Taylor. There were also two boys 14 or 15 years of age; Frank Johnson and myself.

While the adults of the party were visiting the cave, Frank Johnson and I, who had been to the cave at other times, took a hike. In going up over some steep ledges we found ourselves in a position in which we could not get back down the way we went up. After several hours of trying to find a way down, we finally discovered a notch in the canyon wall which would allow us to descend. To do this, I held on to the roots of a tree and dangled over the side while Frank, clinging to my body, slowly climbed down and then dropped to the ledge five feet [1 1/2 meters] below. I then dropped to the ledge and was only prevented from plunging over the edge of a vertical drop of about 300 feet [100 meters] by Frank who grasped me.

Proceeding around the ledge, we discovered a place that looked mineralized. I started digging into a fissure which showed some mineralization that looked similar to mineralized rock I had seen at the Scranton mine. While digging, it soon become apparent that I was breaking into an opening or hole in the mountain side. Pulling the rock and soil away from the opening, it was soon large enough for me to look into. Looking down into the hole, I could see another opening about ten feet [3 meters] below which admitted daylight. This aroused the curiosity of Frank and myself, and further investigation revealed that a large slab of rock had been placed in the entrance way to a cave. This slab was almost completely buried and covered with top soil, and only the upper portion was sticking out. Grass growing in the soil showed that it had been sealed up for a good many years. By taking another rock and pounding the "key" that held the slab in place, I broke the "key" and the slab plunged down into the cave. My curiosity was aroused to the point where I had to go down into the cave and see what was in it. Lighting a piece of candle which I had been carrying in my pocket, I persuaded Frank to go with me down into the opening.

While climbing down, something suddenly knocked my hat off. Thoughts of bears and mountain lions raced through my head and I decided to get out of the cave as fast as possible. Attempting to scramble back up the slope, my foot hit a slick, mossy spot; I slipped, lost my grip, and slid to the bottom of the slope about ten feet [3 meters] below. In falling, I had lost my light and my hat. Everything about me, as I sat, was darkness and dusty. At first I was very frightened, as I thought a bear would get me. Up above I could hear Frank laughing and laughing; then he called down and said that it had been a bat that had knocked my hat off and not a bear. It was not long before the dust cleared away and once my eyes had become accustomed to the change from broad daylight, I could see fairly well with the light that came through the opening above. Frank came down to where I was, and together we explored the cave until we came to a deep hole in the floor. We were blocked from exploring deeper into the cave by the pit in the floor as we could see no way around it. We then left the newly found cave and returned to Hansen's Cave to tell our folks of the discovery.

When we arrived there we found them just coming out of the cave. After we had told our folks of the find, we all rushed around to the entrance to explore it. The group entered the cave, but was also halted by the pit. Some of the men then went outside to get a log which was used to bridge the hole in the cave floor. After crossing the log bridge, the party explored the cave as deeply as what is now known as the "Heart of Timpanogos." Near the Heart, the cavern branched into a number of passageways going in many directions. Fearing we would become lost if we went too far into the maze, it was decided to stop exploring at this point and return in about two weeks with better and more equipment than we had on hand. More rope, string for marking the trail, carbide lanterns were needed, or so we thought.

Two weeks later a party consisting of my father James C. Gough, Sr., myself, and perhaps two or three other people, the names now forgotten, returned and fully explored the cave. In the bottom of the cave we found a beautiful lake, ice cold and crystal clear. The many openings or side passageways, which we had at first feared would lead into a bewildering maze, were actually only short passageways, and there was no real danger of getting lost. When we returned to the entranceway we noticed some bones at the bottom of the slope; these had been broken by the slab of rock which had covered the entranceway when it fell.

About one month later, after we had explored the entire cave system, Thomas A. Taylor took a mutual group of about 15-20 boys and girls through the cave. After the mutual group's trip the cave was commonly known, and many other groups went through the cave.

Approximately one year later, because of the fracture that looked mineralized, my father and I staked the cave ground for a mineral claim. I sent a sample of the rock to John Hutchings, who lived in Scranton at the time, to have it analyzed. Hutchings found the sample contained 3% zinc. About six months later John Hutchings moved to Lehi, Utah, and being so interested in the cave, he was taken in as a third partner, each holding a one-third interest in the claim.

Over the period of years that we held the claim to the cave ground, I went to the cave twenty-one times. On the last trip to the cave before I left to work in Shelley, Idaho, I took a powder box to the cave. This box contained powder caps, fuses, and carbide. It had been given to me by John Hutchings in Scranton, and was left in the cave for future use.

signed James W. Gough, Jr.

In 1921 the cave was re-discovered by Vearl J. Manwill(a son of a Forest Service employee), who had lived as a boy at the South Fork Ranger Station. In the summer of 1921, after he and a group of friends from Payson had climbed Mount Timpanogos on the annual mountain climb, they decided to do some exploring and see if they could find the mysterious cave in American Fork Canyon. They found the cave just as Mr. Gough had left it. The following letter is the personal account of the re-discovery of the Timpanogos Cave by Manwill. This letter is featured in the thesis by Gary Keetch.

I was born in Payson, Utah, November 15, 1900, to John V. and Elizabeth Keele Manwill. Father was a farmer of moderate means, but about 1908, he went to work for the Forest Service as a Ranger. For about a year he was stationed at Vernon, in Tooele County, then he got transferred to American Fork Canyon in 1909.....

We lived at the South Fork Ranger Station in the summer and in American Fork in the winter where we went to school. The summers were very interesting, but we saw very few people. Mostly miners, ore haulers, prospectors, sheep herders, and on holidays, covered wagons of campers would sometimes come up from the valley to picnic. Occasionally an artist or explorer would stay over at our house for a night. On these occasions, as a boy, I was fascinated by some of their stories of legends about Indian gold mines, exploring, and prospecting.

I later learned that there was a cave about a mile down the canyon called Hansen's cave, and my mother told me of going through it with some University of Utah students of 1898, and described its beauty. I later got a chance to go through it, and it was very beautiful.

We spent nine summers in the canyon, and on several occasions, I took school chums through the cave using candles for light. In 1918, father was transferred from American Fork to the Strawberry Valley ranger station, so he moved back to Payson so the boys could work the farm in the summer time.

We missed the canyon very much so we organized a small hiking club and every other week-end we would go camping, mountain climbing or exploring. In the summer of 1921, we went on the annual Timpanogos Mountain Climb, then in camp that evening we planned our next trip.

I remembered reading an article in the American Fork Citizen that was entitled, "Rumors of Mysterious Cave in American Fork Canyon." We assumed that someone knew where it was, so we decided to go up to the canyon on August 14, 1921, and go through it. We went to see Martin Hansen(discoverer of Hansen's Cave) and he said he had heard rumors, but knew nothing about its where-abouts, but if we were going to look for it, to look for it in the general area and level as Hansen Cave, as it was formed on a fault and if the fault extended through the rocks that would be the logical place to look.

We then proceeded up the canyon and went through Hansen's Cave. We had carbide miner's lamps, candles and also a couple of cameras and a flash gun for taking pictures. At this time we were very disappointed, as the onyx and beauty of the cave had been practically all stripped off. We didn't take any pictures, but proceeded to the entrance where we decided to separate and do exploring. I went alone and went to the west, then climbed up over the ledges to the top and then turned back east and down the east side of the big ledges. I stopped to rest at a point about the same level as Hansen's Cave. but about 3/4 mile[one km] east and as my eyes scanned the mountainside, I noticed next to the ledge an artificial appearance like masonry with vegetation partially growing over it about thirty feet [10 meters] west of where I sat. I walked over to it and kicked at it and one of the rocks came loose, rolling down an incline inside of the mountain. I opened it up and the hole was about two feet [half a meter] in diameter. I immediately called the rest of the group and we proceeded to explore it. At the foot of the first incline, about 30 feet[10 meters] down, was a room of rather spacious dimensions and on the floor was part of an old dynamite box(all soggy and mouldy). This indicated that someone had been there before and then sealed up the entrance and had either lost the location or was keeping it secret.

We then proceeded to explore it. It was a thrilling experience as there were no trails or tracks to follow. In places we had to lay on our stomachs and squeeze through. Other places we had to make ourselves into human bridges or ladders to help the ladies along. About halfway through, half of the party become frightened and turned back. However, three of the men and two ladies proceeded all the way and we took pictures of what is now called "Father Time Jewel Box."

We then went back out and joined the rest of the party and closed up the entrance, much the way we found it and went back down to the canyon bottom where we were camped and that night by the light of campfire, discussed our find and talked about ways and means to preserve its beauty for posterity instead of allowing it to be vandalized as Hansen's Cave had been. We decided to start by organizing an outdoor club dedicated to the objective of preserving the cave, which we did.

We called it the Payson Alpine Club and I was elected President and my sister Elva Manwill, secretary. We decided to return in about two weeks and measure, map, and photograph the cave then turn our information over to the proper authorities for their assistance.

We returned the following week(actually two weeks) with a party of twenty-two, but so much time was spent showing it to the other group that we did no measuring, but did take a few pictures. When we left the cave, we were met near the mouth by Deputy Supervisor Mann and Ranger West of the Forest Service who demanded to know what we were doing there. When we explained they did not believe us. They seemed to think that we were the persons who were keeping the whereabouts of the cave a secret and were attempting to commercialize on it. So they, at that time, nailed up a sign on a nearby tree declaring the location a public service site, and then told us to vacate at once and they would investigate our story.

A day later an article appeared in a Salt Lake Newspaper titled, "Forest Rangers Discover Mysterious Cave." We were not mentioned in the article. From this point on it was taken over by the Forest Service, the Wasatch Mountain Club, and a Dr. Hopkins(dentist) of Salt Lake City made valuable contributions by pictures and other assistance in preserving the cave.

I did not go near it again for several years, and it was not until about November, 1926, when I read an article in the Improvement Era Magazine[LDS Church publication] that stated that the U. S. Geological Survey gave me official recognition for the discovery, that my name was linked with the discovery. I later learned that considerable investigation, law suits, claims, and counter claims had brought to light the truth about it. But I am glad that I have contributed in part toward its preservation.

signed Vearl J. Manwill

Below is a third letter written by Wayne E. Hansen concerning the discovery of Middle Cave. It is featured in an unpublished document at the visitor center called, The History of Timpanogos Cave National Monument.

On or about October 20, 1921, my Uncle, George Heber Hansen and myself, then a young man of 18 years, journeyed to American Fork Canyon to hunt deer. We made the journey by horse and buggy.

We traveled up the canyon to the location now known as Timpanogos Cave Camp, left the horse and buggy there and made our way on foot up the canyon to Tank Canyon, just below the old Hanging Rock. We traveled up Tank Canyon climbing to the top ridge. Then we proceeded to hunt in the ledges and pines back down the canyon to a point across from the old Hansen Cave and new Timpanogos Cave. It was about mid-day and we sat down here to eat our lunch.

While eating and resting, we were looking across the canyon with a pair of field glasses which Uncle Heber had brought along. First we located the entrance of Grandfather's old cave then the new Timpanogos Cave.

Because of a story told by Grandfather Hansen, about another opening in the immediate vicinity of his cave, we were trying to find this opening with the glasses and thus found another opening about midway between Timpanogos and Hansen Caves, on about the same level. To us, across the canyon it appeared to be two or three feet[about a meter] in diameter. We talked about it and decided as we had not sighted any deer we would go across an try to locate this new opening.

From where we were we came down to the canyon bottom where we had left the buggy, over what we then called "Rattlesnake Slide" a very rugged and rocky trail as I remember it. Leaving everything we were carrying except our rifles, we climbed the trail to the Hansen Cave. Then taking a course around and up the canyon, on about the same level, we worked our way through brush, timber, and ledges until we found this new opening.

We found it to be an opening of about four to five feet[about a meter and a half] in height and three feet[a meter] wide. It was bigger than it had appeared to be from across the canyon. It seemed to be the opening of a huge crack in the canyon wall. We ventured into the opening as far as we dared, using what matches we had. The opening, we found, slanted downward. The floor of the opening ended abruptly going straight down.

It was decided to tell Grandfather about it and get a party together and come back. When we arrived back at American Fork that evening(with no deer), we told Grandfather and others of the family about it. Everyone was excited about what we had found, so a party was formed and a date set to go back and explore this new cave.

Members of this first party as I remember them were: Grandfather, Martin Hansen, my two uncles, George Heber Hansen and Thomas Hansen, one of my two elder brothers, Edmund R. Hansen or Leo T. Hansen, myself, and Richard H. Hansen, father of Wayne T. Hansen.

We took along with us, about 60 feet[20 meters] of hay derrick rope, other small ropes, flashlights, candles, hand picks and other things we thought we would need. We arrived at the new cave the morning of October 24, or 25, 1921, secured the derrick rope at the top of the opening, letting the end fall down over the edge of the ledge inside.

As I remember, Uncle Heber was the first man to attempt to go down into the cave. We did not know how far down it would be or if we had enough rope. So we had dropped rocks down and they did not seem to fall too far before we heard them strike bottom. Soon Uncle Heber shouted that he was on the bottom and we all followed him down into the cave.

We spent about two or three hours exploring this new cave that day, but later another party went up and made the second trip through.

This second party was a bigger bunch. Included were my two brother-in-laws, Leo Throne and Junius Adams, my father, Richard H. Hansen, my younger brother, Martin E. Hansen, both of my elder brothers, Uncle Heber and myself. Grandfather did not make this trip because of his age and because the other trip had been quite hard on him.

It was during this second exploration that an incident occurred which will not be forgotten by the members. In order to get out of the cave, one must climb hand over hand up about 60 feet[20 meters] of rope, pulling yourself over the ledge at the top. In a few places on the way up, you could brace yourself against the walls of the huge crack, but most of the climb was hang on to the rope and pull.

We spent another hour or two climbing around and exploring and were on our way out of the cave when Leo Thorne, who was climbing out and had reached the top at the ledge, fainted and fell to the bottom. landing in an upright position feet first. Because of working the midnight shift at the Lehi Sugar Factory, then riding a bicycle from American Fork and climbing the trail to the cave, Leo must have been exhausted. This causing him to faint and fall. I was sent down the canyon to the Number two Utah Power and Light Plant to phone for Dr. Kelley and help. While I was gone the others in the party tied Leo to the derrick rope in an upright position and in this manner hoisted him up and out of the cave. Fortunately Leo was not injured seriously but he still carries the scars of this fall.

There could be other details and people, who may be involved in this account. I do not mean to leave anyone out of this account. This is as I remember it this October of 1956.
Signed Wayne E. Hansen

The Forest Service was not in a position to assume the cost of running and maintaining the cave because of lack of funds. So Forest Supervisor Parkinson told the Commercial Club of American Fork, at a club meeting on September 8, 1921, that the Service was planning to build a trail and would enlarge passageways inside the cave in order to make all rooms accessible. But, he suggested that the electric lighting and other improvements would have to be done by local people. According to Keetch's thesis, Parkinson later wrote a letter to the club, part of which went like this:

The Forest Service cannot afford to keep a guard there continuously. If you sold 1200 tickets it would keep one man busy guiding people through the cave. If the club cares to hire a man of it's own to protect the cave, we can issue a special use permit for it so that you can charge whatever admission is deemed proper.

This letter cleared the way for an organization, separate from any federal agency, to administer and operate the cave as a tourist attraction. This was apparently a common practice during that time, and as a result the Timpanogos Outdoor Committee was organized to administer the cave. Actually the Timpanogos Committee affiliated themselves with the Utah Outdoor Association in Salt Lake City, so they would not have to formally file for a use permit. So complete control of the cave remained in the hands of the local people; subordinate, of course, to the Forest Service. The Timpanogos Committee served until January 1, 1947, after 24 years of service.

The Forest Service, with the help of the Timpanogos Committee, administered the cave from 1921 to 1933. Because of conflicts with public service sites and mining claims in the area, Regional Forester, R. H. Tuthledge of Ogden wrote to the Forester in Washington D. C. asking that Timpanogos Cave National Monument be established. On October 14, 1922, President Warren G. Harding created Timpanogos Cave National Monument by proclamation. The Forest Service continued to administer the cave area until July 10, 1933. In that year Ranger Vivian N. West was released and Superintendent Preston P. Patraw was appointed to manage the monument for the National Park Service.

Over the years many improvements have been made in and around the cave site. The first trail system was actually begun back in about 1888, by Martin Hansen and 3 other men. This was to the entrance to Hansen's Cave. This was a very rough trail and went nearly straight up the mountain. After the Forest Service got involved with preservation of the site, they started to build a trail to the mouth of Timpanogos Cave in the fall of 1921, right after Thanksgiving. Most of the major work was completed by January 1922, and the final touches were performed later that spring.

It was soon after the trail was completed and cave tours began, that the Forest Service hired L. L. Hammer to protect the cave from vandalism and act as guide. He lived in a tent at Cave Camp during the summer of 1922. In about mid-summer, a man named Basil Walker of Pleasant Grove, also moved to Cave Camp and pitched a tent for his family. Walker was the concessionaire, who also worked for the Timp Cave Committee during the summers and sold tickets for cave tours. Money from ticket sales went to the committee for cave improvements and the people guiding tours.

In the fall of 1922, Mich Halliday replaced the aging Hammer as Ranger-in-Charge at Cave Camp. During the fall of 1922 and into 1923, Halliday was placed in charge of building a four-room rangers home and a small store, gas station and ticket office at the bottom of the trail. Basil Walker was also involved with the construction. Walker earned money from the store which was a small frame building with a stone foundation perched on the side of the hill next to the road. During the summers he used a mule to haul soda pop and other goodies up the mountain to the entrance of Timpanogos Cave.

Mich Halliday worked as custodian until the spring of 1933, then there were a series of rangers who replaced him and guarded the cave. Thomas Walker began work as custodian in 1934, then after several other men worked in the same job, Thomas returned as full superintendent in 1946. He had the job until 1969.

Basil Walker lived in the cabin-store during the summers until 1941, then retired from the job as concessionaire. There have been many other concessioners since that time. Sometime in about the late 1950's or early 1960's the original store and ticket office was finally torn down. In this area today, you can still see some evidence of the site of the old store as well as Cave Camp across the road.

Over the years several trails were built and rebuilt. In 1933, the Civilian Conservation Corp(CCC) began to build a trail from the middle of the Timpanogos Cave Trail, around the cliffs to the entrance to Hansen's Cave. In 1936, the CCC's finally finished that part of the trail, but it wasn't used much because the Hansen Cave had been robbed of it's glitter back in the 1890's. It wasn't much to look at when compared to the Timpanogos Cave.

During the period of 1936 and 1937, there were tunnels built between the three separate caves finally connecting the Hansen, Middle and Timpanogos Caves. In 1939 tours of the three-cave system were first begun. This added a new dimension to the national monument. In 1941, a new and better trail was begun on the lower part of the mountain, but because of the war, it wasn't completed until 1952.

This new trail began at the same location as the present-day visitor center. For several years, there were two small buildings at the base of this new trail. One was a National Park Service office where tickets were sold; the other was a refreshment stand. In 1956 and 1957 the trail was paved for the first time. Since those years, there have been only minor modifications of the trail. In the mid-1960's a new building was begun, and in 1966 the present visitor center was dedicated.

Throughout the years there have been a number of different lighting systems placed in the cave. The first explorers used candles and carbide lamps, the type used in mining. But when the site was made a national monument, a better system was needed. In 1922, the first electric lights went into Timpanogos Cave. It was a 2300 volt system which included a 160 kg transformer. Inside the cave there were holes drilled into the walls where wooden pegs were placed. The wiring and lights were strung out and hung from the pegs.

By 1924, the first lighting scheme was replaced by a second. This was a 6600 volt system. It was finished during the winter of 1924-25. This system involved concealment of wiring and cables, and used back or indirect lighting in the cave. There was a huge cable involved, which took 24 men 1 hr. and 40 min. to carry to the cave.

In 1939, the lighting was extended from Timpanogos Cave into Middle and Hansen Caves for the first time. This took place upon completion of the two tunnels connecting the three. This system was good for 40 years, then was finally replaced again with new lighting in 1979.

At the bottom of the foto is the original cabin and ticket
office built by Basil Walker in 1922-1923.
(Lucile Walker foto)

Carrying the electric cable up the Timpanogos Cave Trail in 1938(NPS foto).

Mutual Dell Trailhead--Bear Canyon Trail

Trailhead Location The hike here is up Bear Canyon, which is in the South Fork of American Fork Canyon. The trailhead is located at Mutual Dell Summer Camp. As you drive up the canyon, you will first pass the Timpanogos Cave National Monument, then some picnic sites and campgrounds. At the junction of the North and South Forks, turn right or east and drive another 2 kms or so along the Alpine Scenic Loop Road, until you see a paved road and buildings on the right or south side of the creek.

Mutual Dell consists of about 10 hectares(25 acres) of land leased from the Forest Service by several LDS stakes in American Fork, Pleasant Grove, Highland and Alpine. But you can still enter the camp area to reach the Bear Canyon Trailhead. There is public access to the trailhead and although sometimes they shut or even lock the gate, they cannot keep you out if you're walking up to the trailhead. On occasions the gate may be closed, but if it is you can open it and drive in, or just park along the road and walk in. If you drive in to the trailhead parking place, it might be best to check with the caretakers first, so they won't lock the gate on you. On Sundays they always lock the gate so you'll have to park on the road and walk in on that day.

Just inside the gate the paved road splits. The one on the left goes past the caretakers log cabin, then to the lodge and other facilities. The one on the right runs uphill and ends at a parking lot about 300 meters from the gate. At the parking lot look for the trailhead sign at the west end.

Route Description At the beginning, the trail heads south, then veers to the right or west a ways, before heading straight up Bear Canyon. This is one of the best and most used trails on the mountain. The reason of course, is that it begins at a busy summer camp. It runs along the east side of the canyon and through heavy timber all the way.

In the upper end of the canyon you will hear running water to the west. If you're thirsty, you'll have to climb down a ways to a spring. Further along, you may or may not notice another old side trail veering to the south as the main trail begins to turn west and zig zags up to the road. This branch trail running up across the Timpooneke Road and to the west end of the upper Timpooneke Campground, is the old trail which once connected Mutual Dell to the Timpooneke Trail, the one that runs up to the summit of Timp from the north.

The main trail today ends for the most part at the Timpooneke Road at 2408 meters. At that point is an undeveloped campsite in the pines next to the road. If you cross the road, you may find the trail again as it continues to the west around the north face of Timp. Apparently this was originally an old Indian Trail, then was re-built and maintained by the Forest Service before the Timpooneke Road was built in about 1959. It seems to end, or perhaps just fade, at another campsite at 2507 meters.

Distance and Time Needed There's a sign at the Mutual Dell Trailhead stating the distance to the

The trail in Bear Canyon. This is a heavily wooded trail all the way to the Timpooneke Road.

MAP 11, **MUTUAL DELL TRAILHEAD**--AND THE BEAR CANYON TRAIL

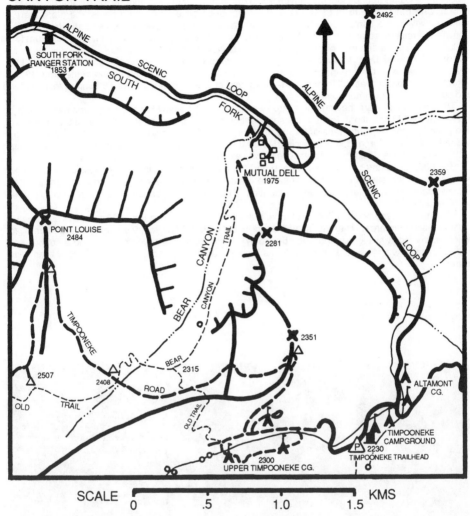

SCALE 0 .5 1.0 1.5 KMS

Timpooneke Road is 2 miles, or 3 kms. A similar sign at the Timpooneke Road states it's the same distance back down to Mutual Dell. The average person can make it from the trailhead to Timpooneke Road in about one hour, so it should be about two hours for the round-trip hike.

Best Time This trail should be clear of snow sometime in early May, so you can make warm weather or snow-free hikes until about the first part of November. Mutual Dell is open and used on a year-round basis. The caretaker also lives at the Dell year-round. Ski touring should be good in winter.

Main Attractions Easy access, a well maintained foot trail and a short hike for the entire family. However, you won't get a view of the mountain or anything else until you get to the Timpooneke Road because of the heavy timber.

Elevations The Mutual Dell Trailhead, 1975 meters; Timpooneke Road, 2408 meters.

Water At the trailhead and picnic sites, and again in the upper part of Bear Canyon. You'll have to walk over and down to the spring when you hear running water to the west of the trail. Otherwise there is no drinking or running water right on the trail.

Boots or Shoes Any comfortable boot or shoe will be fine.

Campsites There are many campgrounds in lower American Fork Canyon, and at the Alta and Timpooneke Campgrounds just up-canyon from Mutual Dell near the Timpooneke Trailhead.

Winter Climbing The road to Mutual Dell is kept open on a year-round basis, therefore there is some activity at the camp year-round. With all the people in the area, it's likely the trail up Bear Canyon will receive some use even during winter time. It should be a fun ski tour, with no threat from avalanches. You'll need skis or snowshoes from late November until into April.

History of Mutual Dell Mutual Dell began as a camp organized and maintained by various LDS wards and stakes in the American Fork and Pleasant Grove areas. It first began in the early 1920's. Forest Service policy was different in those days, and at that time they allowed 6 families to lease land and build cabins or summer homes.

Throughout the years the immediate area was maintained both by the summer home owners and by the Mutual Dell Association. Each of the summer homes was on a acre of land(about 2/5 of a hectare), and each had to pay rental fees of $15 annually in the 1920's and $195 in 1979. However, as time passed and policy changed, it was decided to gradually do away with the privilege of summer homes. In the 1970's, it was decided to allow the leases to expire on the remaining two homes.

By 1986, all summer homes were gone and the association was in sole possession of a new 99 year lease on the site. In order to renew the lease, the Forest Service had those in charge of the summer camp renovate and build up the facilities. This reportedly cost the 9 LDS stakes involved half a million dollars.

At Mutual Dell today you will find a lodge, the third to be built since the 1920's. In it is a recreation room and sleeping area. There is also an open-air but covered pavilion, 9 camping or picnic units, for which reservations are needed(for members only). They also have a youth camp and a softball field and volleyball court. Near the entrance to the facility is a new log cabin where a caretaker lives year-round.

Ripe raspberries ready to eat in the middle of Woolly Hole Cirque.

The northeast face of North Peak.

Autumn scene of North Peak, from along the Alpine Scenic Loop Road near the Timp Divide.

Upper Timpooneke Campground Routes--North, Forgotten and Bomber Peaks

Trailhead Location   The peaks discussed here include those at the northern end of Mt. Timpanogos. To begin the climbs on this map, head up American Fork Canyon along the Alpine Scenic Loop Road in the direction of the Timpooneke Campground; or come in from the Provo Canyon side, drive past Sundance and Aspen Grove, and head for Timpooneke. When you arrive in the upper end of American Fork Canyon, watch for the sign pointing out the direction to the Timpooneke Campground and Trailhead. This is a short paved side road heading off to the west. Just as you turn off the loop road, you will be in the lower part of the Timpooneke Campground.

Drive along this road and soon you'll come to the Timpooneke Trailhead parking area. This is the beginning of the Timpooneke Trail, discussed under Map 13. Continue to the west as the paved road winds up towards the upper part of the Timpooneke Campground. After a short distance the paved road ends, and a good gravel road continues as far as the campground's two entrances. At the sharp bend of the road, and at the sign pointing to campsites 15-32, turn left. Drive about 200 meters until the road makes another sharp left turn and crosses a bridge. Park on the right just before the bridge and at the beginning of an old road.

Route Description   You will be parking at a barrier or locked gate at the beginning of an old road running uphill to the west and toward North Peak. Walk up this road past some springs and willows. As you walk, the road will gradually fade into a trail after about 200 meters. This old road was used to install intake pipes at a spring to capture drinking water for the campgrounds below. After you pass the beginning of a pipeline(hidden), you will cross the creek bed to the left side. When the trail gradually fades, begin walking in the dry rocky creek bed. In the late spring and early summer(May and June), there will surely be some water in this small creek bed.

You will have to walk up this cobblestone corridor, because all of this lower glacier cirque basin is covered with willows and brush of various kinds. Gradually the creek bed veers to the left or south and steepens. Soon you will be near a rock band making up the lower lip of **Woolly Hole.** Toward the top there will be a very steep gully with several small springs which flow year-round. Stay in the gully until it becomes so steep you can't go any further. At that point look to the right or west, for a narrow but walkable bench or terrace. Walk along this until you're out of the ravine, then climb up beside it on the west side. Very soon you will be in the lower end of Woolly Hole cirque basin.

From Woolly Hole, you will have several climbs, routes and peaks to choose from. One will be the North Ridge of North Peak. Another will be to climb onto the the summit ridge then to the North Peak. You can also climb what the author is calling Forgotten and Bomber Peaks.

The upper Timpooneke Campground and trailhead to the north peaks. Parking is on the right.

MAP 12, **UPPER TIMPOONEKE CG. ROUTES**-- NORTH, FORGOTTEN AND BOMBER PEAKS

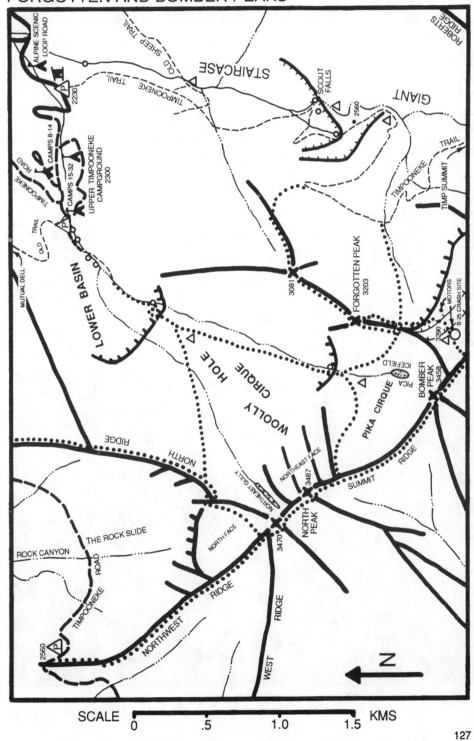

SCALE

0   .5   1.0   1.5 KMS

To climb the **North Ridge of North Peak,** veer to the right or west from the lower end of Woolly Hole. You will be confronted with a broad easy-to-climb talus slope. Aim for the ridge to the right or north of the northeast face and big gully or couloir coming down the right side of the North Peak. When you arrive on the ridge and at a point that's semi-flat(less steep), look for a ramp heading to the north along the east face of the main ridge coming down from the summit area. Walk to the north along this ramp.

When you arrive at the end of the ramp, make a 180 degree left turn and head up along the ridge itself or out onto the upper north face of the northern part of North Peak. This is a little steep, but not difficult or dangerous. However, in late spring with some steep snow fields, it could be risky for inexperienced hikers. An ice ax and crampons would help at that time and place. At the top of this face, walk a short distance to the southeast to the two summits of the North Peak.

Before leaving the North Ridge, it must be mentioned there is an alternative way up this almost-never-used route. First, look at Map 11, and the Bear Canyon Trail. Shown on that map is a campsite at 2507 meters. That place is about 4 or 5 kms along the Timpooneke Road from the upper Timpooneke Campground. Turn to the south onto a little side road to reach that point. At the 2507 meter campsite, walk west and onto the lower end of the North Ridge.

At the lower levels of this ridge, it's usually best to walk through the pine trees on the west side, because there is less brush. For the first half km, there will be a some brush around, but hardly any bushwhacking. Higher up, the walking is along an open alpine ridge up to where the ramp is found which has just been discussed.

There are other possible routes up North Peak from the Timpooneke Road. One route almost never tried or even heard of, is the **Northwest Ridge.** As you drive this good dirt and gravel Timpooneke Road around the north side of the North Peak, you will pass right under the north face and at the bottom of the Rock Slide. Just beyond this, the road heads around to the bottom end of the Northwest Ridge. Park somewhere along the road and climb up on this ridge. The author hasn't been on the very northern end of it, but has come down this ridge twice. He got off above where the ridge and road meet. On this lower north end of the ridge there could be some bushwhacking, but it can't be very much. Higher up, it's an easy walk through pine trees, then up the much steeper upper rocky part, and finally to the North Peak.

Now back to the routes up from the Timpooneke Campground. From the lower end of the Woolly Hole, walk straight south to the head of this middle glacier basin(Timpooneke Campground is in the lower basin, Woolly Hole is in the middle basin, and Pica Cirque is the highest basin of the series). If you like, you could veer right or west and climb some route up the Northeast Face of the North Peak,

Climbing a steep gully just below the lip of the Woolly Hole Cirque.

but this is for experienced climbers with proper equipment only.

The author once tried climbing the **Northeast Gully,** which has either snow or ice the year-round, but there was a continuous barrage of small pebbles and rocks whistling down. Someone properly equipped with a helmet, ice ax and crampons, could make it, but it's not recommended because of the rockfall danger.

At the head of Woolly Hole, is a steep place and some minor cliffs separating it from the bottom end of **Pica Cirque.** The easiest way up this part is to veer right or west once again and go up some goat or deer trails into Pica Cirque. If your goal is the North Peak, then once into Pica Cirque, veer right and climb up the steep but easy-to-climb east face of the peak.

Another interesting climb is to the top of what the author is calling **Forgotten Peak.** From the top of this moderately high summit, you will have some fine views of the North Peak, Bomber Peak and the B-25 crash site, and the summit of Timp far to the south. To get there, walk to the south or upper end of Pica Cirque, but veer to the east and head for the pass or saddle between Forgotten and Bomber Peaks. It's very easy getting up to that point on a deer and goat trail. From the pass, walk along the ridge on one side or the other to the north. The east side seems easiest. Several parts of this short ridge are very steep and jagged, but with care anyone should be able to handle it.

From the top of Forgotten, you have a choice of three ways down. First is the same way you came up. Second is to walk north along the ridgetop until one ridge veers to the right or northeast. Walk down this one a ways and at a convenient place go down to the east to where you will see the **Timpooneke Trail.** From there walk on down to the Timpooneke Trailhead. The third way down would be to return to the pass between Forgotten and Bomber, then walk down the slope to the east until you meet the Timpooneke Trail.

The normal route to **Bomber Peak** and the site of the **B-25 bomber** which crashed in March of 1955, is via the Timpooneke Trail. That route is discussed under Map 13. However, you can get to the crash site from Pica Cirque as well. From the pass between Forgotten and Bomber Peaks, scramble up to the south. There are some steep places, but pick out the easiest way up. It's not difficult, but you will have to route-find. Once you reach some ground that's not so steep, walk in a south-southeast direction and toward the highest bench below the summit ridge of the two peaks of Bomber. You will soon reach the crash site. One motor is there with most of the other wreckage; the other is 200 meters down-slope.

Distance and Time Needed Since most climbs here are more vertical than horizontal, it's almost meaningless to speak in terms of distances or kms. It's only 3, 4 or 5 kms at the most, to any of these summits.

The quickest way up North Peak is via the North Ridge. Most people should make it up in about 3 hours, but some may need longer. The round-trip might be 5 or 6 hours, depending on the way you come down. The trip will be more interesting if you come down a different route. It will take about the same amount of time to climb North Peak via Pica Cirque and the east face. The recommended route would be to climb up the North Ridge, and come down the east face to Pica and Woolly Hole Cirques.

The time and distance to Forgotten Peak is roughly the same as going up North Peak. Getting to the bomber crash site is also about the same distance. Some people may want to take a lunch and spend the whole day visiting several peaks or places on this map.

Best Time Normally by about mid-June you can get into these areas, but in the upper basins and on the higher slopes, there will be lots of snow at that time. It's probably best to wait until about the 4th of July or mid-July, then most of the higher snows will have melted, and the flowers will just be starting to bloom. If your goal is the B-25 crash site, better wait until about mid-August, because snowbanks will cover most of the fuselage until then. The motors will be exposed and clear of snow in early or mid-July, if not a little earlier.

Main Attractions Unusual views from the tops of all these summits, very few(if any) other hikers or climbers, and a chance to climb peaks unknown to most people. This isn't the normal route, but you can also see the bomber wreck. If you scan the cliffs and crags closely, you will likely see some mountain goats as you perch yourself on the top of Forgotten Peak.

Elevations Upper Timpooneke Campground and trailhead, 2300 meters; the base of the North Ridge, 2507(see Map 11); base of Northwest Ridge, 2560; North Peak, 3487 and 3470; Bomber Peak, 3458; Forgotten Peak, 3203; and the B-25 crash site, about 3290 meters.

Water There will be water in taps at the Timpooneke Campground and in the creek running through the campsites(with all the campers around, it's best not to drink from the creek!). There's a small spring or two about a km above the trailhead at the head of the lower cirque basin. There should also be a small spring at the steep place between Woolly Hole and Pica Cirque. At the head of Pica Cirque, there should be some small year-round snowbanks or very small icefields, so it's likely you will find some water there about any time.

Boots or Shoes Take rugged hiking or climbing boots on all of these routes.

Campsites Next to the trailhead is a campground, which is a fee-use site, or you can backpack into the upper basins and camp anywhere. If there are still snowbanks around, then water should be plentiful. The lower part of Woolly Hole has some meadows, grass, trees and wild raspberries(ripe in late August and early September), while at the bottom of Pica Cirque there are some grassy meadows.

Winter Climbing This would be one part of the mountain not so good for winter climbing. The main reason is, you'll be on north facing slopes and the snow will be deep and powdery throughout the winter. To do any winter-type climbing here, you'll have to do it early, perhaps around Thanksgiving weekend; or very late, such as in early or mid-April. In between these two dates, it would be very difficult to do any fast climbing because of the soft and deep snow.

An exception to this general rule, might be if you could get upon the North or Northwest Ridges. Once on either of these ridges you should find the upper parts, those areas above timberline, to have very hard wind-blown snow. You would have to use snowshoes or skis to get up to the higher parts on either ridge.

Avalanche danger in or around these cirque basins would be about the same as on any other part of the mountain. This means high danger if you're there soon after any storm. If you stay on a ridgetop, there will be less of a threat from avalanches.

Climbing one difficult route on the North Peak

Just days before this book went to press, the author received a letter from technical climber Joel Bown of Park City, in which he described a difficult route he made up the north face of the North Peak. Part of his letter went like this.

The first climb we did was up the center of the north face of the North Peak. Four of us, Dave George, Tom Stephens, John Zaratian, and myself bivvyed at the base of the face in late April or early May of 1969, I think. We were able to climb through the nearly vertical rock band that spans the bottom of the face by using several steep ice gullies. As I recall, the rock was so bad that the only protection available was from ice screws. After about 3 or 4 pitches of steep ice, we were able to climb the remainder of the face with crampons and ice axes on firm moderately steep snow. We began the climb using headlamps an hour or two before dawn and summited the North Peak about 7:30 am. It required about 3 more hours to work our way along the ridge to the main Timp summit. We descended using the standard hiking route[Timpooneke Trail].

This climb is probably the best technical route on Timp due to the fact it can be done completely on snow and ice. I would guess the gullies are full of ice for a month or two almost every spring. An early

A wide-angle lens view from the lower Woolly Hole. The northeast face of North Peak is on the right, and the north face of Bomber Peak is in the upper left of the foto.

start is certainly the safest bet and also makes it likely that the descent can be made without plunging into too much deep snow.

From the top of Forgotten Peak, one has a fine view of the north face of Bomber Peak.

The east face of North Peak, as seen from the top of Forgotten Peak.

Timpooneke Trail--Forgotten & Bomber Peaks(B-25 Crash Site) and the Second & Timp Summits

Trailhead Location The route discussed here is the second most popular trail to the summit of Mt. Timpanogos. This is the Timpooneke Trail which begins at the Timpooneke Campground at the head of the South Fork of American Fork Canyon. By taking this trail you can climb Forgotten and Bomber Peaks, see the crash site of the B-25 bomber, visit Emerald Lake and the Timp Glacier, and reach Timp's two highest summits.

To get to this trailhead, drive up American Fork Canyon past Mutual Dell along the South Fork and to the sign which points out the Timpooneke Campground to the right. Take this paved side road into and through the lower part of the campground and to a large parking lot which is the Timpooneke Trailhead.

Route Description At the very beginning of the trail are several signs and a small Forest Service shelter where you can see and read maps and other information. Then the trail heads straight up through a glacier valley known as the **Giant Staircase.** After less than a km you'll come to an open meadow, but the trail veers to the right and continues through the forest. If you were to go down into this meadow and turn left, you would find and walk on an old sheep or cattle trail of some kind veering to the northeast. There will be water running through this meadow in the spring and early summer.

About one and a half kms from the trailhead you will begin to climb and will pass several places where spring water crosses the trail. In this area you will see a sign pointing out the way to an overlook of **Scout Falls.** It appears to be a large spring on the side of the mountain which cascades down into the creek bed.

Just above the Scout Falls Overlook, there are several switchbacks and more places where spring water crosses the trail. Above these zig zags you will arrive in the **Middle Basin** which is at about 2560 meters altitude. In this area there is lots of avalanche debris scattered around, and snowdrifts from the previous winter which stay until mid-summer each year.

In about the center of the Middle Basin the trail veers to the right or west and makes a big loop in order to gain altitude before arriving into the upper glacier cirque called Timpanogos Basin. The western side of this loop passes along the bottom of a big slope coming down from the pass between Forgotten and Bomber Peaks. If you're interested in climbing a peak that's really unknown or forgotten, try **Forgotten Peak.**

Head straight up this slope to the west, which in winter time will be an avalanche chute. At the top you will come to a pass, where you can look down into Pica Cirque. From the pass walk north along the

From Timpanogos Basin and where the trails divide. To the south is the north face of Timp's main summit.

MAP 13, **TIMPOONEKE TRAIL**--FORGOTTEN & BOMBER PEAKS(B-25 CRASH SITE), SECOND AND TIMP SUMMITS

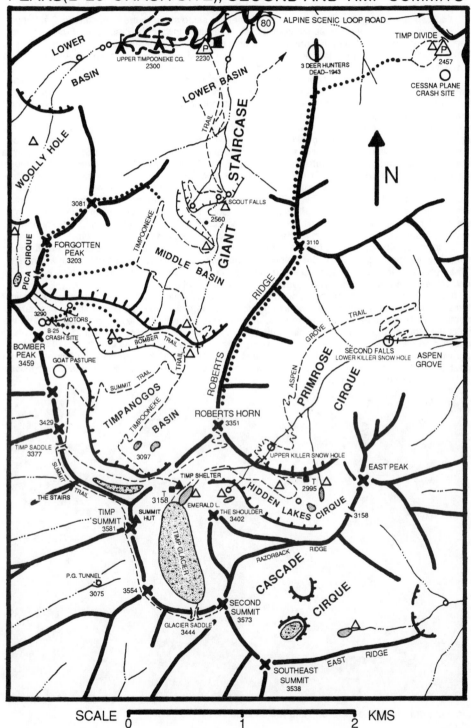

SCALE

0   1   2   KMS

ridge to the top of Forgotten. This is a rugged ridge route, so in places it's best to walk down off the ridge itself on the east side. From the summit of Forgotten you will have some unusual views of the North Peak as well as Bomber and the main Timp Summit. You can also see the wreck of the B-25.

You can leave Forgotten Peak by walking down the same slope to the Timpooneke Trail, or you can walk south and up a steep series of little cliffs or terraces toward the crash site. From there you can walk southeast and rejoin the trail to the summit of Timp. Or from the top of Forgotten Peak, you could ridge-walk to the northeast and at a convenient place head straight down the steep slope to reach the Timpooneke Trail in the Middle Basin.

Continuing now on the Timpooneke Trail. From the Middle Basin, the trail makes several minor switchbacks as it heads up the steep escarpment of the upper part of the Middle Basin. Finally you will arrive on the rim of the **Timpanogos Basin.** At that point you will see the summit, the Second Summit and the Timp Glacier for the first time.

When you first arrive at the lip of the Timp Basin, you will see two short trails veering off to the right. The first one has a little sign which reads *Toilet.* In past years there was a cement and rock toilet just off the main trail, but that has been taken down. In the future, the Forest Service may build a new and better *outhouse* at that same location. Since Timp is now part of America's Wilderness System, man-made features are frowned upon, so the toilet issue is a problem for the Forest Service.

If you want to visit the **B-25 crash site,** locate the second little trail veering off to the right or west just beyond the *toilet trail.* This trail has developed as a result of local people going to the crash site. Walk west on the **Bomber Trail** as it contours along the lip of the Timp Basin. After about half a km, you'll come to a mini-basin which will have a couple of small ponds and a small stream until the middle of summer. In the fall when all the seasonal snow has melted this part dries up.

From these little ponds you have a choice of two routes to the crash site. One is to continue to contour along the lip of the Timp Basin about another half km. At about that point look for a wing flap. When you see this, head straight up-slope to the southwest. One bench above the wing flap will be one of the plane's two engines and several other pieces of metal wreckage.

From this lower engine site, again head straight up the hill about 200 meters. After about two minor terraces, you will arrive on a major bench, the first such terrace below the summit ridge of what the author calls **Bomber Peak,** at 3459 meters. At that point you will see the second motor right on the lip of the terrace, and 25 meters up-slope the twisted and crushed remains of the B-25 bomber which crashed on March 9, 1955. The two engines can likely be seen as early as late June, but the rest of the wreckage will be covered with snow until about mid-August. Each year will be different. If your goal is the summit of Bomber Peak, then look for a steep, but easy-to-climb chute coming down between the two parts of this peak.

In many gray limestone rocks on Timp you can find fossils like these.

From the mini-basin and the two little ponds, you could also get to the crash site by making a bee-line to the west, and heading for the low point in the ridge between the north and south summits of Bomber Peak. You'll have to route-find up through about 3 terraces, but there isn't anything difficult along the way. If you want to visit and see both motors, then the first route described is the best to use. Read the full story about this plane crash below.

From the crash site, you could return to the Timpooneke Trail along the same route you used to arrive at the site, but if you want to continue on to the summit, it's best to walk to the southeast along the same bench or terrace as the crash site. Heading southeast first, you will gradually turn and walk south along the eastern face of the summit ridge. In a place or two you will have to route-find around some minor ledges, but after only about one km you should see at about the same elevation as the crash site, the upper part of the summit trail.

If you take this route, you will have a good chance to see some **Rocky Mountain Goats.** As you walk along, watch along the east face of the summit ridge. The billies seem to always be up high and on the more rugged ridgetops. They are always white, so they are most easily seen in the late summer or fall seasons when the snow has melted. The nannies and kids on the other hand, may be down lower and in some meadows, possibly on the same level as the crash site.

On two occasions the author has seen and fotographed up close, groups of 13 and 17 nannies and kids in the area shown on the map as *goat pasture*. This is very near the summit trail. A telefoto lens will give you some excellent close-ups. The author got to within 12-14 meters of the goats, then they began to be nervous. Other hikers have stated they have met billies right on the summit trail, and it was the hiker who had to go around to get past these ornery critters. Read the full story of the transplanting of goats in the back of this book.

Now back to the Timpooneke Trail near where the toilet used to be. If you continue on this trail for about 200-300 meters you will come to a junction. Straight ahead is the trail which heads directly for **Emerald Lake** and the **Timp Shelter.** To the right, will be the trail heading directly to the summit. Turn right at the junction and walk along this very good trail as it winds its way through the middle of the lush green meadows of the Timp Basin. Mid to late July is when it's at its greenest and by the first of August the flowers are at their best. After a km or so, the trail zig zags up through a rock band to a bench, where you may see the goats.

Soon you will be at the **Timp Saddle,** at 3377 meters elevation. Arriving at this place will give you you're first view of Utah Valley. This pass is the meeting place of the Timpooneke and Aspen Grove Trails. Continue on to the south, then after a ways you will zig zag up through a steep mini-canyon called **The Stairs** and onto the upper summit ridge. Finally you will arrive at the top and the little **Summit Hut,** which at one time was called the **Glass House.** It was originally built back in

The north face of the Timp Summit as seen from the Timp Saddle.

1928 by the Forest Service. They put glass in it and made it into a kind of observatory. The glass has long since been blown out and it doesn't make much of a shelter any more. Read more about this hut under the *History of the Annual Timp Hike* in the introduction of this book.

From the summit you can walk south along the ridgeline directly above the **Timp Glacier.** When you reach the **Glacier Saddle** you can then climb up a simple hiker-made trail to the top of the **Second Summit,** or slide and walk down the glacier to **Emerald Lake.** From there you can walk west a ways, and if you have the energy, can try for the summit of **Roberts Horn.** From the Horn you can walk back to the Timpanogos Basin and the Timpooneke Trail.

Distance and Time Needed The sign at the Timpooneke Trailhead reads: Emerald Lake--6.5 miles(10.5 kms), Timp Summit--9.1 miles(14.7 kms), and Timpanogos Campground(Aspen Grove)--12 miles(19.3 kms).

Most people can hike to Emerald Lake in about 3 to 4 hours and the summit(without going to the lake) in 4 to 6 hours. By taking this normal route to the B-25 crash site it should take only about 3 hours one way for the average person. For those who are interested in seeing the crash site, the summit, then down the glacier to the lake, and back to the Timpooneke Trailhead, it would take most people around 8 to 10 hours. This hike would be too much for the average person, and only strong and fit hikers should attempt this semi-marathon. Most hikers however could see the B-25 and the Timp Summit and return in one day OK.

Best Time The normal hiking season for this route on Timp is from about mid-July until well into September. However, it should be reasonably easy and safe to do it from early July until late October, depending on the year. For those who have some pretty good boots, it could be hiked even in June, but you'd be on snow for at least half the distance in the upper basins. For an early season hike such as this, an ice ax or some kind of walking stick would be handy.

If you want to include a side trip to the crash site and see all the wreckage, better wait until after about mid or late August, otherwise the main part of the wreck will be covered by snow. In late summer the two airplane engines will be surrounded by a carpet of flowers.

Main Attractions There are many waterfalls along what is called the Giant Staircase, at least in early and mid-summer. There is the B-25 crash site, the most spectacular of the three plane wrecks that have occurred on the mountain. There is a good chance you will see some Rocky Mountain Goats, and have some good views of the valley, the glacier and Emerald Lake from the summit. This is perhaps the best all-around hike on the mountain.

Elevations The Timpooneke Trailhead, 2230 meters; Middle Basin, about 2600; Forgotten Peak, 3203; B-25 crash site, 3290; Bomber Peak, 3459; Timp Saddle, 3377; Timp Summit, 3581; Glacier

Rocky Mountain Goats resting on snowbanks during a warm summer day.

Saddle, 3444; Second Summit, 3573; and Emerald Lake, 3158 meters.

Water For the most part, water is not a problem on this route, but in dry years some of the regular waterholes can dry up. An example was the very warm and dry summer of 1988, which was preceded by one of the driest winters on record. In August and September of 1988, the creek running down the Giant Staircase was bone dry and the only water available was in the springs in the area of Scout Falls. The Timp Basin at the same time was dry, making the only water high on the mountain, either on the Timp Glacier or in Emerald Lake.

For most of the summer, and as long as there are visible snowdrifts on the upper part of the mountain there will be some water running down the creek from the Timp Basin most of the way to the lower Timpooneke Campground. This water is normally good to drink as is, but try to drink where the water comes from a spring. Regardless of the season, it's best to start the hike with a full water bottle.

Boots or Shoes You can make all these hikes with a pair of common running shoe or anything comfortable, but if you're heading for the top of Bomber or Forgotten Peaks use a more rugged hiking or climbing boot.

Campsites There are a number of previously-used camp sites along this trail. One site is in the first meadow you come to, where the old sheep trail is found. Also in the Middle Basin near Scout Falls. This would be a good one, because you will always have water nearby even if you're there at the end of a dry summer. There are also many old camping places in the pine trees in the area at or near the lip of the Timp Basin and in the general area of the old toilet. Or you could camp near the B-25 crash site, somewhere in the Timp Basin, or around Emerald Lake. Please leave a clean campsite.

Winter Climbing This is not the ideal route to take if you're planning a winter climb of Mt. Timpanogos. The main reason is, you'll be walking south and up the north-facing slopes of the mountain. The snow on the north slopes is always shaded, therefore very soft and powdery throughout the winter season. Another disadvantage to using this as a winter route is you will have to ski or snowshoe from the area of Mutual Dell up the road to the trailhead. That part of the route along the Alpine Loop will be groomed for snowmobiles, so it'll be easy walking, but it still adds an extra 5 kms at the beginning of the actual climb.

Of course this climb can be done, but you'd have to use skis or snowshoes all the way. The general slope isn't too steep, except where the cliffs are located between the Middle and Timp Basins. This would be the most difficult part of the entire trip, getting up from the Middle to Timp Basin. If you knew where the trail was and followed along in the same general area, it shouldn't be too difficult; but the snow along that cliff band would be soft deep powder throughout the winter season.

Another possible way up through the cliff band in winter would be to go up where you see the

The Rocky Mountain billy goats tend to stay on the ridgetops during the summer months. Timp and Second Summits in the background.

137

cascades and waterfalls during summer. Of course right after a stormy period, there will be danger from avalanches. But because of the occasional avalanches, it should be a very hard compacted snow surface throughout most of the winter season.

If you do attempt a winter time hike up the Timpooneke Trail, it might be best to go early in the season, say around Thanksgiving weekend, or wait until early or mid-April. Even in April, you will surely sink into deep snow on the north face of the rock band just below Timp Basin. Avalanche danger on this route would be similar to other routes on the mountain. Along the Giant Staircase, avalanche snows come down to the valley floor from all sides.

History of the B-25 Crash Here's the story behind the crash of the B-25. The information comes from old newspaper clippings and from eye witness accounts to the rescue. Most of the people involved in the rescue attempt and bringing the bodies off the mountain were from Salt Lake or the Air Force. Other eye witnesses were from the towns of American Fork, Pleasant Grove and Alpine.

In the late afternoon of March 9, 1955, the weather in northern Utah was stormy as a cold front passed through the region. That day Brighton Ski Resort got 35 cms(14 inches) of snow, and other mountain areas received nearly half a meter(18"). Valley locations received both rain and snow.

The plane officially known as an Air Force TB-25(the T stands for trainer), with the aeronautical number 30050, had began its flight in Great Falls, Montana earlier in the day. The plane carried a crew of three and two passengers. Aboard the plane were Maj. D.C. Holley, pilot; 1st Lt. H.E. St. John, co-pilot; Airman 1-C D.H. Dempsey, crew chief; and M.J. McNalty and D.R. Cubbage, both civilians. All were stationed or working in Great Falls.

The B-25 had made a refueling stop at Hill Air Force Base near Ogden, Utah, Wednesday afternoon, March 9, 1955, and was on its way to March Air Force Base in Riverside, California. The plane passed over Salt Lake City and apparently made radio contact at 7:37 pm. At that time of year it would have been just after dark. Shortly after this time it dropped out of radar sight. It failed to make radio contact over the Utah County station, presumably the Provo Airport.

Somehow the World War II bomber got off course because of the bad weather. Perhaps their instruments were malfunctioning. At any rate, they were blown way off course to the east and crashed on the first bench below the summit of what the author is calling Bomber Peak. The crash site is on the northeast side of the peak at an altitude of approximately 3290 meters.

The next morning, Thursday, March 10, the clouds and storm abated somewhat and when the clouds finally lifted, 18 search planes were sent out looking for the B-25, as well as a twin-engined Beechcraft. This second plane had last made radio contact with Ft. Bridger, Wyoming at 5:14 pm, as

Timp Shelter at Emerald Lake. Looking south at the glacier with the summit of Timp to the right.
A June 1st foto from the early 1980's.

it headed for Salt Lake City, the same day the B-25 went down. The Beechcraft was carrying 5 people as it left Rock Springs, Wyoming, destined for California(it was found later in the spring on the north slope of the Uinta Mountains).

In the late afternoon of Thursday, March 10, the wreckage of the B-25 was spotted by the pilot of an Air Force C-47. The Provo Daily Herald quoted the pilot as stating, *it was pretty well broken up, and there was no sign of life.* That evening the Air Force, Wasatch National Forest, and the National Ski Patrol personnel planned a rescue attempt for the next day.

In the early morning hours of Friday, March 11, a rescue party led by Alta avalanche expert and Wasatch National Forest ranger Monte Atwater, began the trek up the mountain. Others in the group were Wallace(Smokey) Saling of Pleasant Grove, a Uinta National Forest ranger; Jim Shane, Harold Goodro, Jim McConkie, and Bob Wright, all of Salt lake City and the National Ski Patrol. Also, Robert J. Miller of Nephi and the Uinta National Forest, and T-Sergeant William Hyatt and A-1c Roger Record, 44th Air Rescue Squadron, Lowry AFB in Colorado.

The rescue party used a snowcat, apparently belonging to the American Telephone and Telegraph Company, because two of their employees John H. Risch and Gerald B. Rusho, were operating the machine. They went up American Fork Canyon to the area of the Timpooneke Ranger Station, which is next to the Timpooneke Campground and Trailhead. From there they headed up the mountain along the Giant Staircase in the general area of the present-day Timpooneke Trail.

To help the ground party, an Air Force Albatross was to be used in spotting the wreckage and guiding them to the site. But the weather was still very bad and the ground party got no help from the air. However, Sheriff Theron T. Hall and his department did post a radio operated car somewhere near Timp Cave. The ground party carried a walkie-talkie radio and had hoped to make contact with the search plane and/or the Sheriff's department. It's unknown if they succeeded.

As it turned out, the ground party apparently did not locate the crash site on Friday, but went back up the mountain again Saturday morning, March 12. They toiled all day, but most of the party turned back because of the threat of avalanches. That part of the group was apparently hoping to get one or more recoil-less rifles to trigger avalanches. However, three of the party continued to search the higher cliffs and crags of the mountain. That morning an Air Force rescue plane again flew over the mountain and spotted the wreckage, and this helped Jim Shane to see the site. Later he and two other members of the group identified as Harold Goodro and Lee Stoerts, all members of the National Ski Patrol, made it to the scene. They found three bodies, but because of the late hour, they had to get off the mountain before darkness set in. They made no attempt to bring out any of the victims that night.

Sunday, March 13, was apparently another day of bad weather, because nothing happened in the

Wreckage of the B-25 bomber which crashed on March 9, 1955. As it looked in 1988.

way of rescue attempts. This is what the Provo Daily Herald reported in the Monday March 14 newspaper. *Jim Shane and another group of skiers had planned to spend Monday night in the Timpooneke Ranger Station, then get an early 5 am start on Tuesday morning. They were hoping the skies would be clear enough so an Air Force plane could drop supplies, such as aluminum sleds and snow shovels, onto the mountain.*

The Tuesday, March 15 newspaper reported that an Air Force plane had indeed dropped the rescue supplies on the mountain, and that the ground party had found the parachute package and were on there way to the crash site. The Wednesday, March 16, edition of the Herald reported 4 bodies had been brought down the mountain, but they were unable to locate the fifth. The weather continued to be stormy, so at that time, it was not clear as to when they would mount another search attempt.

Apparently the weather remained bad for some time, because the March 29 edition of the Herald reported that the Air Force had requested the area be closed to the public until the last body was found. The paper stated, *Uinta Forest Supervisor James L. Jacobs today relayed the order from Acting Regional Forester A.G. Nord of Ogden, which closes the area to all except those with particular and necessary business in that region, in which case a special permit must be obtained from the Air Force and the Forest Service.*

All of the above information comes from Provo Daily Herald newspaper accounts of the accident and rescue attempt. However, there were other stories surrounding the rescue attempt and subsequent searches for the bodies. One unusual story comes from a person who wishes to remain anonymous. The day was Friday, March 11. Three young men from the valley went up Grove Creek Canyon, then headed toward the north end of the mountain where they went up what they called Porcupine Ridge. American Fork Canyon had been blocked off to all traffic as soon as the Air Force knew the plane was on Mt. Timpanogos, so this unauthorized group had to use an alternate route to get to the crash site. They found the wreckage the day before the official ground party arrived on the scene.

They found what remained of the plane mostly covered with snow, because of the continued snowstorm. They could still see the marks in the snow where the wing tip had first made contact, then the impact area itself. They found parts of bodies scattered about. The most gruesome sight at the scene was the planes pilot who was still fastened into his seat. He was apparently in an upright position, but was decapitated.

One of the motors of the B-25. One motor is 200 meters down-slope from the main wreckage.

Two or three weeks after the wreck, Joe Hilton and Bob Penrod made it to the crash scene via Grove Creek Canyon and the southwest face of Timp. They made it up to the ridge running between the two summits of Bomber Peak, but the snow cornice was so large, they had trouble finding a route down the other side. Finally they located a place without a cornice and went down. The fotos he took show the wreckage was just about as it is today, but it's been flattened over the years because of all the heavy winter snows. They found parts of bodies scattered about and the altimeter. This was apparently taken off the mountain later by the Air Force.

In the Daily Herald for Monday, May 30, 1955, the final story on the crash was written. It was titled, *LAST BODY RECOVERED FROM TIMP. Finish was written late Saturday[May 28, 1955] to one of Central Utah's worst air disasters when a party of mountain climbers returned the fifth and last body down off Mount Timpanogos from the wreckage of an Air Force B-25 which crashed there earlier this spring.* The last body was that of Airman Second Class Doyle H. Dempsey.

It must have been in about late June when Don Devey and Galyn Blackburn of Alpine went to the scene using horses. They found pajamas and other clothing scattered about and parts of bodies including one whole leg with red hair.

Sometime in the early summer of 1955, the Air Force hired Leonard Walker of Lindon to go to the mountain and gather some of the remaining parts and bring them down by packhorse. Walker also took gasoline to the crash site and burned the wreckage. It was later covered with green paint so other search planes wouldn't confuse it for other downed aircraft.

A June 11, 1955 foto of the B-25 crash site before it was burned. Notice the wheel still in place
(Bob Penrod foto).

The eastern side of Timp as seen from near the dam on Deer Creek Reservoir. The Heber Creeper is to the lower right.

Mt. Timpanogos as seen from the Deer Creek Island Resort in the lower Heber Valley.

An October scene and the northeast face of North Peak.

Snow Cornices along the ridge between the Second and Southeast Summits.

Roberts Ridge Route--Roberts Horn

Trailhead Location The climb featured here is to the top of Roberts Horn via a big northern ridge called the Roberts Ridge. The starting point for this climb is the Timp Divide. The Timp Divide is the high point along the Alpine Scenic Loop Road between American Fork Canyon and the North Fork of Provo Canyon.

At one time you could pull off the road right at the Divide and drive an old deer hunters track for half a km to the southwest, but in the summer of 1988, the Forest Service blocked off that road and re-vegetated the place to stop erosion. Now you have to park in a large parking area right at the Divide, and walk along the old track.

Route Description From the parking place next to the Timp Divide, you can walk either one of the two tracks shown on the map, but the best is probably the one to the north. This track winds through the forest for about half a km, then ends. From where it ends, just set your sights on the northern end of the Roberts Ridge and start walking through the trees. For the most part it's easy walking through an open aspen forest. At times you can use deer trails, but they don't usually go in your direction.

Half way between the end of the track and the ridge, is a shallow drainage. In the bottom of this are a number of dead trees on the ground, but it's still easy walking. The hardest part of the entire trip may be going up the steep eastern slope toward the top of the ridge. On that slope are various kinds of willows and small aspen trees. Once you reach the ridgetop, the walking is easy as you wander back and forth from one side of the ridge to the other looking for the easiest route. The higher you go, the easier the going is because there will be less brush and willows.

Incidentally, it's at this extreme northern end of Roberts Ridge, where three deer hunters were caught unprepared in an early winter snowstorm back in October of 1943, and froze to death. Read all the details of that event in the chapter on *Tragedies on Mt. Timpanogos*.

After you've been on the ridge about one km, it's very open and all you'll find on top are some pine trees and grass. From the high point on the ridge marked 3110 meters, you will have some excellent views of Roberts Horn and the even higher peaks and summits beyond. From that point, you will descend a ways, then begin to climb the section of the ridge that's at or near timber line. In places you'll have to walk on one side of the ridge or the other to avoid rocky buttresses, but all in all it's still easy walking.

From the top of Roberts Horn you will have perhaps the best view anywhere of the higher peaks of Mt. Timpanogos. From left to right will be East Peak, Razorback Ridge, Second Summit, The Shoulder, Timp Glacier, Emerald Lake, Timp Summit, Timp Basin, and Bomber, North and Forgotten

From the 3110 meter peak along the Roberts Ridge, looking southwest at the Second Summit, Roberts Horn, and Timp Summit in the right background.

144

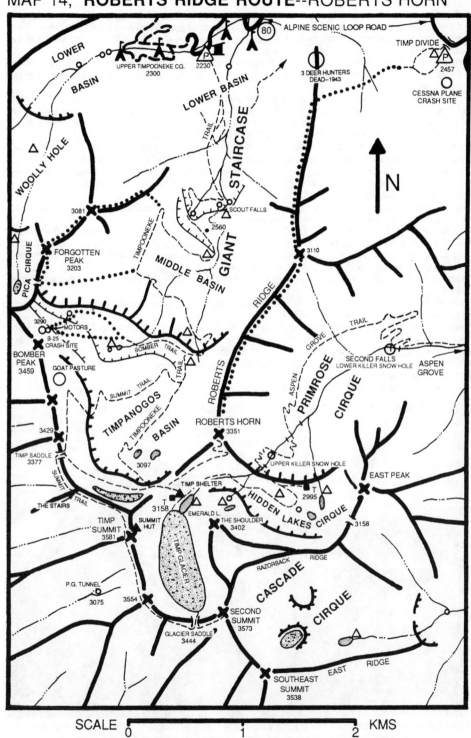

Peaks.

From the summit of Roberts Horn you can return the same way, or you can walk down to the lake and shelter and take the easier Aspen Grove Trail down to Aspen Grove and the Alpine Scenic Loop Road. Then you can either walk or hitch hike back to your car. If you're with a group, then one car could be left at Aspen Grove for the return trip.

Distance and Time Needed The distance from the trailhead to the summit of the Horn is about 6 or 7 kms. It should take most people 3 to 4 hours for the one-way trip. The author made the summit in 2 hrs. 13 min.

The fastest way down would be along the Aspen Grove Trail. For most that's another 2 hours or so. The author went down this trail, then hitched a ride to his car at the pass. The total time for the round-trip was 5 hrs. and 45 min. In summer there's lots of traffic on the Loop Road, especially on weekends and drivers seem willing to pick up (hitch) hikers if they have room.

Best Time The Roberts Ridge Route can be climbed in summer type conditions anytime between about June 1 until mid-October. But if you decide to return via the Aspen Grove Trail, you will find lots of snow in the upper basins in early June. If you do it before or after the summer heat, then you will feel better about wearing long pants, which will get you through some of the minor bushwhacking areas near the beginning of this climb.

Main Attractions An unusual route nobody ever climbs(with the possible exception of a few deer hunters), and some great views of the higher peaks of Timpanogos.

Elevations Timp Divide Trailhead, 2457 meters; Roberts Horn, 3351, Aspen Grove, 2109 meters.

Water There is no water at the trailhead or anywhere along the ridge, so take some with you. If it's early or late in the season, then you may find some snow, but never any water. The closest water would be in the streams and spring near Emerald Lake.

Boots or Shoes One could do this climb in running shoes, but light weight hiking shoes or boots would be best.

Campsites At or near the trailhead, or at Emerald Lake. There are no really good campsites on the ridge, because there's no water anywhere.

Winter Climbing This is not a good route to take in winter, mainly because the Alpine Scenic Loop Road is closed from about early November until about June 1 each year. To get to the Timp Divide in winter time, you'd have to use skis or snowshoes for about 7 kms from the Aspen Grove side, or about 8 kms from the area around Mutual Dell. If you had access to a snowmobile, that would make the climb a lot shorter and easier.

If you are determined to make this climb in winter, you may have a tough time getting up to the

From the summit of Roberts Horn looking south at Razorback Ridge. The Shoulder, Second Summit and the Timp Glacier are to the right. Hidden Lakes Cirque is in the lower left.

ridge top because of steepness and possible avalanche danger. Once on the lower northern end of Roberts Ridge, one could expect some soft snow, but as you emerge from the trees near timber line, you could expect to find harder wind-blown snow. The dead trees you see at the eastern base of the ridge west of the trailhead, are old quakies put on the ground by an avalanche sliding off the face.

From the summit of Timpanogos looking down on Emerald Lake and Roberts Horn to the upper left.

Roberts Horn as seen from the Hidden Lakes Cirque in winter.

History of Provo Canyon

Obviously the first explorers in Provo Canyon were the Indians. When the Dominguez and Escalante Expedition came through Utah Valley in 1776, they met natives who called themselves *Timpanogotzis* people(probably Ute Indians). The expedition called the valley *Nuestra Señora De La Merced of the Timpanogotzis*. The expedition spent several days in the valley exploring around and found Indian settlements on each of the 4 major streams. The largest settlement was on the largest river which they called the Rio San Antonio de Padua(Provo River). The location of the many settlements along the river bottoms indicated Provo Canyon was a major travel route for these Native Americans.

There were other Indian tribes in the area as well, including the Shoshone, whose hunting grounds were mostly to the north; the Goshutes, lived to the west; and the Piutes, who stayed to the south of Utah Valley. The Utes wandered around what is now Utah Valley and regions to the east.

In the early 1800's came the mountain men. Four important names were Jedidiah Smith, Jim Bridger, Etienne Provost and William H. Ashley. Provost, according to some historians, was the first white man to travel through the canyon which now bears his name. That was in 1824. There is no evidence, but some writers have claimed Ashley once had a trading post on Utah Lake in about 1825. Smith was in the valley in 1825, and Bridger's exploration of the region was instrumental in Brigham Young's decision to come to Utah. The first government explorer to traverse the canyon was John C. Fremont in 1845. After he passed through the canyon, he pioneered the Hastings Cut-off Route to California.

During the early days of the Mormon settlements in Utah, about all the Indians in Utah Valley were from the Ute Tribe. When the Mormons first arrived in the Provo area in 1849, they found Utes camped along the lower Provo River and in the canyon. Because the settlers had to go into the canyon to get lumber for building homes, they intruded on the Ute's hunting and camping grounds, which was the cause for several clashes.

According to Eugene E. Campbell's unpublished short history on Provo Canyon, *in 1853, Ft. Supply, near Ft. Bridger was built by the Mormons, and a road through Provo Canyon was advocated because of the feed available for the horses and cattle. A start was made, but it was not completed until 1858.* This replaced the old Indian trail on the north side of the river. Campbell goes on to say, *In the early 1850's the government became interested in exploring a transcontinental railroad route and one of the possible passes through the Wasatch for such a route was Provo Canyon.* The report on the route was favorable, but Weber Canyon won out for the first transcontinental railroad route.

Quoting again from Campbell's History of Provo Canyon. *The practice in Utah during the early pioneer period concerning roads, was for the legislature to empower private persons to build roads on which the owners were then entitled to collect toll. In 1855 the legislature authorized William Wall, Evan M. Green, Thomas S. Williams, and Aaron Johnson to build a toll road from the mouth of Provo Canyon through the canyon, through Kamas Prairie, and over the best route leading into the main wagon road between Utah and the States.*

The construction of the road, however, was delayed. During 1857 and 1858, the Mormons were occupied with problems resulting from the approach of the Federal Army. Brigham Young, feeling that the Mormons should avoid a confrontation with the Federal Army by moving south of Salt Lake Valley instigated a move to Utah County by all northern Utah Mormons. Provo City became the temporary headquarters of the church. Brigham Young, apparently decided that all the surplus manpower around Provo ought to be put to work and one obvious project was the completion of the Provo Canyon road. Brigham Young in two successive nights at the Provo Bowery organized the Provo Canyon Road Company with Feramorz Little as superintendent and W. G. Mills as clerk. Thus the Provo Canyon Road Company came into existence on June 6 and 7, 1858, [and it was completed later that summer.]

In those early years the road was very rough, narrow, and winding. In many places it was between 15 and 50 meters above the river and mostly on the north side. Although the road was privately owned, the Mormon bishops of Provo were required to keep it up just like the public roads. In some cases the workers may have been paid from tolls collected. At one time a toll gate for the canyon road was located on a hill near the present-day settlement of Springdell. Later on, there was a toll gate further up canyon just below Vivian Park at the ranch of Billy Ferguson.

The Provo Canyon Road Company's lease on the right-of-way expired in 1887 and small sums of money were paid to stockholders for their investment. At that time the road became public and

PROVO CANYON RECREATION AND HISTORIC SITES THEN AND NOW

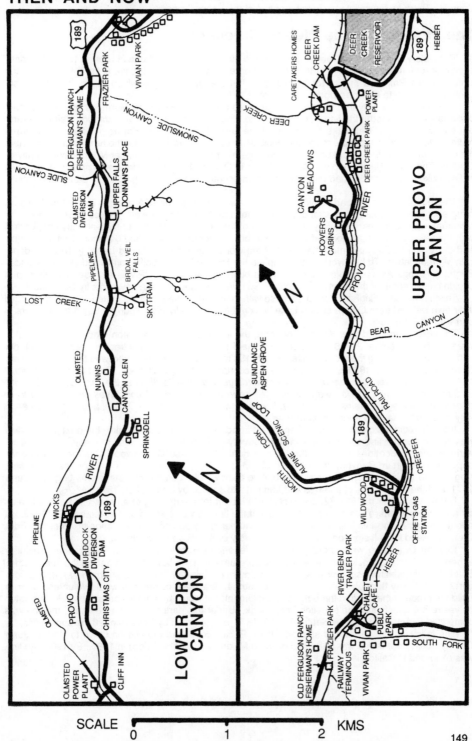

SCALE 0 1 2 KMS

became county property. Over the years the road developed into a major highway link.

In 1896, the Denver and Rio Grande Western Railroad surveyed a route for a rail line through Provo Canyon. This was the initial step in the creation of the Heber Creeper.

The History of the Heber Creeper

The history of the Heber Creeper goes back to the arrival of the railroad in Utah in 1869. The date everyone remembers is May 10, 1869. On that date at Promontory Point, the Central Pacific and the Union Pacific Railways met. Not long before that the Union Pacific which came from the east, completed its line to as far as Ogden, on March 8, 1869.

Even before the arrival of the railway there was a battle between the Mormons and the railroad builders as to what route the line would take. The Mormons wanted it to come through Salt Lake City, but the route west of Salt Lake and south of the Great Salt Lake was not as good as the northern route. After the railway people made the decision to use the northern route, the next battle was where the main hub for the line would be; in Corinne, a gentile hangout, or in the larger Mormon community of Ogden. The Union Pacific hub was finally placed in Ogden. But since Ogden was north of the capital of Salt Lake City it was decided to run a branch line south to service the majority of Utah's population.

The thought of the railroad coming to the state was met with mixed feelings. The railroads would bring economic prosperity, but a lot of non-Mormons and outsiders as well. As you might expect, the Mormons wanted to keep as many *gentiles* out of the state as possible. In the end they cooperated with the railway companies to build the system, but the agreement reached between Brigham Young and the Union Pacific stipulated that most of the work of grading and laying tracks in Utah be done with Mormon labor. To hire workers to complete the line the Union Pacific contracted Mormons under Brigham Young. As it turned out, the Mormons built the line, but the UP was strapped for funds, and couldn't make some of the payments in cash. So it was decided to make payments in rolling stock.

This set well with Brigham Young because with their own workers and the materials they could build their own railroad from Ogden to Salt Lake, which they eventually did. Young paid off the workers in part with tithing credits.

To make a long and interesting story short, the first rails running between Ogden and Salt Lake were laid on September 22, 1869. Seventy men laid 1 1/2 kms(one mile) of track a day during October and November. During the month of December, 150 men worked on the project and the last spike was driven on January 10, 1870, in Salt Lake City. According to Arrington's book, *Great Basin Kingdom,* it states; *freight houses, passenger and freight landings and other facilities at the Utah Central Depots in Salt Lake City and Ogden were completed soon afterward, and locomotives were placed in to operation. Two regular trains ran daily each way between Salt Lake and Ogden, and a third ran each way on Wednesdays, Saturdays, and Sundays.*

After the completion of the Utah Central Railroad from Ogden to Salt Lake, the next logical step was to run another line south to take in Utah County and points south; also to create spur lines to various mining locations such as the granite quarries in Little Cottonwood Canyon, the copper deposits in Bingham Canyon, and the gold diggings in Upper American Fork Canyon, etc. The first stage of the Utah Southern Railroad was built to Sandy. Work on the first stage was begun in June 1871, and the first 20 kms of line was laid and put into service by September, 1871.

During the winter of 1871-72, contracts were let out for the grading of an extension of the line as far as Lehi, in northern Utah Valley. This part of the line was completed on September, 23, 1872. At about the same time this line was being built, another line was under construction in American Fork Canyon. Read the full story on this under the *History of American Fork Canyon.*

Beyond Lehi there were more political and economic problems. Union Pacific was providing expertise and rolling stock, but the Mormons were providing the labor for the part of the line south of Salt Lake City, which was then called the Utah Southern Railway. Since the Mormons wanted to be a part of the railway through their country, it was agreed that each community would volunteer labor to build the grade of the railroad through each settlement, but would be paid in company stock. Arrington delves rather deeply into the situation in his book. Under this partnership or agreement, the line was completed to American Fork by September 23, 1873, and to Provo by November 28 the same year.

The following fall and winter season, Union Pacific continued the line on down to York in Juab County. Still later the line was extended down to Milford, and west to Frisco in 1880. By 1903, the line was extended to California.

The Heber Creeper steam engine ready for its journey into Provo Canyon.

Heber Creeper Steam Railway Station village complex in Heber.

The Denver & Rio Grande Western Railroad first began construction of a line in Utah beginning in about 1880. That line was run west out of Grand Junction, Colorado, across the base of the Book Cliffs to Green River, then northwest to Price, and finally up Price Canyon to Soldier Summit and down Spanish Fork Canyon to intersect the Utah Southern at Springville. It was completed on March 30, 1883.

Much later in history the **Heber Creeper** was begun. In 1898, the Denver and Rio Grande Western Railroad extended a line from Provo, into Provo Canyon to as far as Upper Falls, just beyond Bridal Veil. It was primarily an excursion or recreation railway line, as there were no mines or any other reason for it to be in Provo Canyon.

The next big step toward completing this line was in 1899. That's when the **Utah Eastern Railway Company,** headquartered in Salt Lake City, opened a line from Upper Falls to the town of Heber. The grading for the line began on March 20, 1899, the laying of tracks began on April 24, 1899, and construction ended on September 22, 1899. It was described in the local Heber newspaper known as the *Wasatch Wave.* Here is how they reported the event.

RAILROAD COMPLETED FRIDAY, SEPTEMBER 29, 1899.

The Provo Canyon branch of the Rio Grande Western Railroad which connects Heber City with Provo is now completed and ready for business. The length of the road is 25.8 miles[41 kms]. There are seven stations on the line between Provo and Heber. Their names and their distances from Provo are as follows: Smoot, one mile[1.6 kms]; Crahurst, six miles[10 kms]; Nunns, nine miles[14.5 kms]; Falls, ten miles[16 kms]; Forks[Vivian Park], twelve miles[19 kms]; Wallsburg, eighteen miles[29 kms]; Charleston, twenty-one miles[34 kms]. None of these station will have an agent. E. W. Sullivan has been appointed agent at Heber. He comes well recommended, having been in the employ of the company for a number of years.

Elsewhere in this issue will be found the time table showing the arrival and departure of trains. This schedule is very satisfactory indeed. The trains connect at Provo with the fast-continental trains both east and west without any of those long, tiresome waits. If you have business in Salt lake you can take the 6:40 am train--arrive in the City 10:00 o'clock; returning you can leave Salt Lake at 5 o'clock pm and reach Heber at 8:05. This gives you seven hours in the metropolis, and the whole of the business day in the city which is from 10 o'clock to 5. On the other hand our Salt Lake friends can leave there at 8 am, reach Heber at 11:10 am, spend 3 1/2 hours in Heber and leave at 2:20, arriving in Salt Lake at 5:35 in the evening.

In the book on Wasatch County history entitled, *How Beautiful Upon the Mountains,* it states; *The*

Inside one of the railway cars of the Heber Creeper.

community leaders were sufficiently moved by the significance of the occasion that they planned a special railroad holiday on Friday, October 6, 1899 and invited people from all over the state to attend.

The railroad company set up a special train of seven cars which arrived in Heber at 3 pm, carrying many state dignitaries, including Governor J. T. Hammond, Provo City officials and some 400 persons.

Residents of Heber and Wasatch County along with the Heber Brass Band met the train and its passengers at the depot and proceeded to the court house yard where a special platform had been erected.

Here a special program began with an address of welcome by Abram Hatch, stake president[a Mormon church leader]. Mayor Jones of Provo made a brief response and each of the state officials present spoke for a few minutes. These included Gov. Hammond, James Chipman, state treasurer; Morgan Richards, Jr., J.J. Thomas, secretary of the state board of equalization and U.S. Senator Reed Smoot. Numerous railway officials and officers of Provo City were also honored. Music was furnished by quartets from Heber and Provo and by the Heber Brass Band.

After the program the large crowd adjourned to Heber Social Hall where they were served free food between 4 and 7 pm. A dance in Turner's Hall during the evening concluded the festivities. The special train left Heber shortly after 10 pm and arrived in Provo at 12:30 am.

Another comment quoted directly from the *Wasatch Wave* stated; *All seemed to enjoy themselves during the afternoon and evening, and we believe the visitors went home feeling that they had been well treated by the people of Heber and having a somewhat warmer feeling toward us than they formerly had.*

The Wasatch County history book goes on to mention something about one of the new businesses which sprung up in the Heber Valley. *The coming of the railroad gave rise to a number of related businesses, including "hack" service. Frank Carlile of the Heber Livery Stable was one of the most reliable drivers of the time. He met all the trains leaving town or arriving. Often his hack was so loaded with townspeople, traveling salesmen or other travelers that two or three had to stand on the step at the rear of the buggy. His reputation was for reliability, and people knew they could always catch their train if they rode with Frank Carlile.*

On August 1, 1908, the entire line from Provo to Heber was consolidated into the Denver & Rio Grande Western Railway Company. Utah Eastern Railroad engineers had planned to run the line from Heber over the Wolf Creek Pass to the east into the Uinta Basin and on to Colorado, but those plans never materialized.

In the early years of the Provo Canyon railway, which eventually became known as the Heber Creeper, there was both passenger service and freight hauling, but gradually things changed. In the

Passengers boarding one of the cars at the Heber Creeper Station.

early years of the Annual Timp Hike one of the normal ways to reach the mountain was via the train from Provo. People also used the train to reach the Bridal Veil Falls and Vivian Park area.

However, throughout the years, the building of more and better highways, the advancements in truck transportation and the convenience of automobile travel cut into the railway's business. In the 20 to 30 years before it was sold by the Denver and Rio Grande Western Railroad, traffic slowed to a trickle and was all but nonexistent.

In 1969, the Denver and Rio Grande Western Railroad Company sold the railway, which included both the tracks and right-of-way, to the Utah Department of Transportation(UDOT). According to Lowe Ashston, the present owner of the Heber Creeper line, UDOT didn't really want the railway or tracks, but the right-of-way instead. This right-of-way included much more land than did the present highway through Provo Canyon. They apparently had some big plans for the route through the canyon which included putting most of the length of Provo River in a pipeline, and constructing a completely new 4-lane freeway-type highway in addition to the present road. This was the beginning of the uproar over UDOT's Provo Canyon Highway plan.

The next thing to happen was that two committees were formed, one from Utah County, the other from Wasatch County, which were in opposition to UDOT's plan. Out of this came one committee which wanted to save the canyon and begin a scenic steam engine railway instead. This Railway Committee went to the Utah State Legislature urging them to put a hault to UDOT's plan and for help with a plan to form a scenic railway with the old Heber Creeper tracks.

The state legislature apparently overruled UDOT on the matter. As it turned out, the freeway plans for Provo Canyon were scuttled and Utah Parks and Recreation was given the rights to the old Heber Creeper line from Bridal Veil Falls to the depot in Heber. This was the beginning of the present-day Heber Creeper.

One member of the Railroad Committee was Heber business man and owner of Ashton Lumber Company, Lowe Ashton. He became one of the point men for the project because during the 1969 sale of the D & RGW right-of-way, he bought the railway station site. With the train station in private hands, the Wasatch Mountain Scenic Railway Company was started. The steam powered train made its first run in July of 1970 and has been operating ever since. In 1972, the company adopted the name Heber Creeper as it official patented logo.

For various reasons, in 1980 the Wasatch Mtn. Scenic Railway Co. was taken over by a non-profit organization by the name of Timpanogos Preservation Society. While the TPS was running the Heber Creeper, it obtained a number of historic structures from the Sons of the Utah Pioneers which were previously located in Corinne, Utah, along with some rolling stock and locomotives. They also

The Heber Creeper chugging toward Mt. Timpanogos in the background.

received an economic development grant for the railroad's development. During this period of time the ridership slacked off and the society went into receivership in 1983, because they did not meet the requirements of being a non-profit operation.

When this happened, Ashton again gained control and was given a two year lease. In July of 1983, the name of the company was changed to the Deer Creek Scenic Railroad. In 1984, the Timpanogos Preservation Society filed for bankruptcy. Today the company or rather small corporation, which is called the New London Railroad and Village, is still running the Heber Creeper and doing rather well.

From 1970 until about 1983, the train ran in the summer months only, and to as far as Bridal Veil Falls. In 1983, high water and spring flooding of the Provo River caused some damage to the line between Vivian Park and Bridal Veil Falls, so after that time the train went only to as far as Vivian Park. In 1986-87, the steam-driven train began year-round service for the first time. Recently the Heber Creeper has begun a *ride and dine service* in cooperation with the Homestead Resort of Midway.

Here is an approximate train schedule. The summer schedule usually begins the week of Memorial Day at the end of May with trains running daily to Vivian Park(half way through Provo Canyon), until about the first week of October. During the summer season there are two runs a day, each lasting about 3 1/2 hours, round-trip.

October is a slack month, so they shut down the line for repairs and maintenance service, then re-open it in November making only one run a day and only to the Deer Creek Reservoir Dam and back. The winter schedule continues until about May 1. They then shut it down again for repairs and maintenance. May is another slow month, because there is no skiing at Park City and many of the winter-time riders are skiers. About half the riders are out of staters, and many come by way of Park City. The above schedule will change for sure, so it's best to call 654-2900 in Heber, 531-6022 in Salt Lake, or 649-9521 in Park City, before you make the drive to the Heber Valley.

When you get to Heber, drive to the center of town and turn west at the sign stating, *Wasatch Mtn. Visitor Center and Historic Steam Train,* which is at the only signal light in town on 100 South. Head due west about one km until you cross the only set of tracks. On your right will be the station, several old locomotives on display, and a small western style town with a number of small shops selling tourist items and food.

This 1924 foto shows the giant snowslide which roared down the mountain at Bridal Veil Falls killing two workmen(Mr. Robert Curtis foto).

Provo Canyon Resorts, Picnic Sites & Summer Home Sites.

If you were driving up Provo Canyon earlier this century, the first business or stopping place you would come to would have been the **Cliff Inn.** It was a Shell gas station located right where the east end of 800 North of Orem meets the main highway running into the canyon from Provo. It was just across the road from the Hale Steam Power Plant. This service station was built by Y.M. Offret back in about 1920, but he never owned the place. It was owned by Shell Oil Co., who leased it to Offret and others. Later, Offret was offered a job at Wildwood in 1929, so he moved there to run another gas station until he died in 1967.

Part of the facility was dug into the limestone cliff, thus the name Cliff Inn. The Offret family actually had their bedrooms under ground. Inside, was a small store with pinball machines, punch boards, slot machines, a snack bar and lunch counter. They did some cooking for a simple menu. To one side of the station, Offret built a small miniature model of Hoover Dam, complete with water, as a promotion. In later years, the cliff began to crumble, so the place was taken down some time in the 1950's.

Up-stream around a couple of bends from the mouth of the canyon and just down-stream from the present-day Murdock Diversion Dam, was a gas station and bar called **Christmas City.** It's still listed on some of the 1950's USGS maps. In March 1938, a man by the name of Mel Close bought about 16 hectares(40 acres) there along the river bottom from a man named Butler. In the summer of 1938 he built a small hamburger stand which the family called **Whimpy's Inn.** Mel's son, Wayne Close, operated the stand that summer when he was 15 years old. Wayne, who is the source of this information, slept in a tent behind the stand.

In 1939, Mel Close began building a gas station, restaurant, bar and dance hall all under one roof. The place was called Christmas City. The gas station end of the business was part of the Gilmore Oil Company, owned in part by Mel Close and others. At one time this small outfit had about half a dozen stations in northern Utah. Behind this *beer joint* as some called it, was a small two room cabin where members of the Close family lived part time. Some of the trees they planted are still there today. The place had kind of a bad reputation, partly because Mel used to operate slot machines in the bar, and the police would occasionally raid the place and close it down.

The Close family never did actually run Christmas City, instead they leased it out to others. A couple by the name of Harry and Benny managed it for several years during World War II. In February, 1946, Elden Price bought the place. As it turned out, Christmas City burned to the ground in the

A May 1932 foto of the Cliff Inn at the lower end of Provo Canyon(Bertha McKean Offret foto)

1950's. After that nothing was ever built on the site, and later on the property was bought by Provo City which is the present land

About 2 kms up-canyon from the Olmsted Power Plant is a place that used to be called **Wicks** or **Wick's Place.** Today there are six homes or cottages on the north side of the road and another home and very large log cabin restaurant on the south side against the cliffs. The story behind this place comes by way of Carol Bartlett Hoover. Wick was her father.

It all started in Wyoming when two Bartlett brothers purchased a ranch near Saratoga. During the Depression, the two families couldn't make enough money off the land to survive, so they flipped a coin. Willis Earl(Wick) Bartlett lost, so he moved out of Wyoming and settled in Provo Canyon. Wick was a nick name given to him in his younger years, a name that stayed with him all his life. People called him and the location Wicks and his daughter states that everyone thought it was their family's last name.

At first the Bartlett family lived in the rear of a gas station owned by Utah Oil Company. The station was on the south side of the road, where the big log restaurant is today. In June 1932, Wick told Utah Oil he wanted to either buy the station or build another one across the highway. He ended up buying it. Wick's Place not only served gas, but it also was a small store and restaurant, with a dance hall on the west side. Later he purchased the homes across the road from the Utoco station and converted some of the cabins into a small resort-type motel. On the west side of the gas station-restaurant, was a shaded picnic site. Just east of the station was a small zoo of sorts, with half a dozen cages. Carol remembers one bear, a monkey and a porcupine.

In the mid-1950's, Wick retired and sold the business to Ken and Hazel Craven. For many years Wick and his wife Maud continued to live in the home across the highway north of the station while managing the cabins. But after nearly 40 years in the canyon, disaster struck. Wick was hit by a car as he walked across the highway and was killed. That was in November of 1971. When he died, she never went back to her home to live.

Springdell was formed in 1904 after several years in which the land was used only as a campground and recreational area. A group of men obtained a 99 year lease from the government allowing them to settle the meadow area permanently. There were 13 families originally involved. These men formed a corporation and would own and operate the land as joint-stockholders. At the end of the 99 year period the land would then convert into the private ownership of all property owners.

Some of the stockholders built homes or cabins immediately, while others waited and built later. Over the years, the cabins got larger and better, and because it's so close to the valley, some are now full sized homes and are lived in year-round. Originally, the place was called Springdell Resort Co., but today the company name is Springdell Inc.

Just above Springdell is **Canyon Glen Picnic Grounds.** It is presently owned and operated by Utah County, but it was different in the good old days. In 1909, the Cañon Glen Park Company purchased land in that area from DeWitt C. Flanagon. Little has been found of the situation in those early days, but according to several former canyon residents, in the 1930's the site had a small store which sold candy and sandwiches, and had pinball machines supplied by Christmas City owner Mel Close. There was also picnic and camping sites on both sides of the river and a baseball diamond.

Christmas City gas station and beer joint in 1939. Cascade Peak in the background(Wayne Close foto).

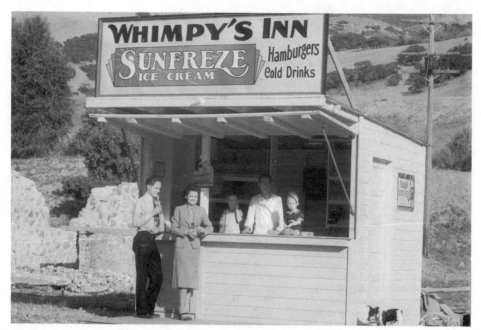

Whimpy's Inn lasted only one summer--1938. The next year Christmas City was built in its place(Wayne Close foto).

Wicks gas station as it looked in 1934. A dance hall was built on a year or two later(Carol Bartlett Hoover foto).

Whoever operated it also had ponies for rent during the summer season. This situation existed until after World War II, then Provo City tore the store down and made it a day-time picnic park only.

Even before the railroad got started in Provo Canyon(1899), there was some big-time development in the area. This was the hydroelectric power station known simply as **Nunns.** It's located about one km below Bridal Veil Falls. Eugene Campbell covers this subject in this Provo Canyon History.

About 1894, Lucien L. Nunn and P. N. Nunn began looking for further hydroelectric developments. In 1897 Nunn's Telluride Company contracted with Mercur mine and mill owner, S. L. Delamar to bring 500 horsepower of electricity to Delamar's Golden Gate Mill. The Telluride Company thus began development of a sixteen-foot[5 meter] dam on the Provo River and a thirty-two mile[51 km], high power transmission line from the dam to Mercur[in the Oquirrh Mtns.]. The hydro-electric plant was named Nunns, in honor of the two brothers who provided the genius behind the Telluride Company. This 32 mile[51 km] line was hailed as the first long distance, high transmission of electricity in the world, and Mercur was the first city to have its main street lighted electrically.

Later in 1904, after completion of a waterway through tunnels and flumes to the mouth of the canyon, a permanent generating plant was finished. The new plant at Olmsted was a model plant and served as the center of instruction for the Telluride Company and its employees. The Olmsted plant converted the water power under a 350 foot[107 meter] head and had a 9650 horsepower generator capacity. Later, the Utah Power and Light Company became the successor to the Telluride Company of the Nunns.

Utah Power and Light came into existence in September of 1912, and shortly thereafter purchased both the Nunns and Olmsted Power Stations. This Telluride Power Company was the same outfit which built a similar power station at the mouth of Battle Creek Canyon east of Pleasant Grove.

At one time there were about half a dozen cottages surrounding the Nunns plant where company employees lived even after the power station was shut down. In March of 1984, Utah Power & Light sold the Nunns property to Utah County. That year the county began to develop the site as a county park. Later in summer of 1984, Dave Eagar moved into the only home left at the site to be caretaker. The old original Nunns Power Station building is still there, but in early 1980's the roof caved in, and on June 6, 1985, while workmen were trying to make repairs, it caught on fire. All that's standing are the stone walls. This tumbled-down building is now on the national register of historic sites. Surrounding the power plant site today is what is known as the Nunns Picnic Grounds, one of 4 county-run picnic sites in Provo Canyon.

Between 1904 and 1912, the **Olmsted Hydroelectric Plant** was the center of the Telluride Institute, which was a practical training ground in which to develop worthy and bright young men in the field of electricity. The institute was nick-named the *School of the Pinheads*. The founders of this facility were the two brothers, Lucien L. and Paul N. Nunn. Many of the old timers in the UP&L organization today received some of their initial training there.

In recent years the government agency building the Central Utah Project decided they had a better use for the pipe which brings water from the Upper Falls area to the Olmsted Hydroelectric Station. So they condemned the pipe, and have been using it ever since to transport drinking water to the high benches and tanks around Utah Valley instead. It seems they could use the water both for making hydroelectricity and for drinking, but they would then have to pump it back up-hill to various city tanks. So as of 1989, the Olmsted plant was shut down--likely for good, but the case was in court as this book goes to press. Regardless of the future, the facilities at Olmsted are still impressive and are still being used today by UP&L for training purposes.

Just south of the Olmsted plant is the **Hale Steam Power Plant.** It was built in 1936 as a backup to hydroelectricity. It was originally named the Orem Plant until it was enlarged in 1950. In the early 1980's, it was shut down for a couple of reasons. First, the railway tracks were torn up leading to the plant and coal could only be delivered by truck, which made it much more costly to operate. Second, there were some problems with the EPA and the air pollution standards which the Hale Plant could not meet.

About half a km up Provo Canyon from the old Nunns Power Station is **Bridal Veil Falls.** The first time the place was mentioned by any white man was in the dairy of John C. Fremont. On one of his trips through Provo Canyon, which was before the Mormons arrived in Utah, he called these waterfalls *Beautiful Cascades*.

The falls are actually on the north face of Cascade Peak, directly across the river and highway from the mouth of Lost Creek. Bridal Veil is made up of two falls, upper and lower. If you combine the two, it's a drop of 185 meters. Not far above the falls are several large springs. This is the beginning of Bridal Veil Creek. The parking lot at the base of the falls is at 1561 meters, while the springs above are about 1950 meters elevation.

The big gray wall where the falls are located is known as the Bridal Veil Member of the Oquirrh

Formation. All of the upper parts of both Timp and Cascade Peaks are made up of the Oquirrh, which consists of alternating bands of mostly limestone and quartzite. The Bridal Veil Member is the lowest part of this formation and is made up almost entirely of limestone. This member makes up the lower half of the big cliffs which are seen on the north and west face of Cascade Peak. As measured in the vicinity of the falls, the Bridal Veil Member has been found to be 380 meters thick.

Bridal Veil Falls has long been a landmark in Provo Canyon and a favorite destination for tourists and day-trippers from Utah Valley. It became especially popular when the railroad made it through the canyon in 1899 and more so when a good highway was built. The canyon road was first paved to as far as Bridal Veil Falls in 1927. At the same time as the paving, a new bridge was built across the river about half a km down-stream or west of the Bridal Veil Falls parking lot. The original wood and stone bridge crossed the river about where the west end of the parking lot is today. On the south side of the river, you can still see some of the remains of that original old bridge foundation.

In the middle part of the 20th century, Rue L. Clegg, a former state senator from Provo, got interested in the site and began to make plans to promote the falls. It was thought that a cable car of some kind would be a good beginning.

In the spring of 1961, Clegg realized a boyhood dream when construction began on a Skytram from the highway to the cliffs above the falls. He hired a Swiss company to design and build the Bauchman Reversible Tram. The Swiss contracted the actual building of the system to a company in Italy, as later owners found out.

The general contractor for the project was Witt Construction of Provo. They built the lower terminal and prepared the site for the specialists. They then contracted the Utah Crane and Rigging Company out of Salt Lake to actually put up the lines and tram itself. Although the tram was Swiss built, they

Billy Dominguez rides the Skytram with the small bulldozer to the top of Bridal Veil Falls. He was killed later when this same caterpillar rolled off the cliff with him on it(Ray Crandall foto).

never did send engineers over to help in the construction.

Ray Crandall of Springville worked for Rue Clegg during the construction period. He remembers some of the problems they had in putting the thing together. The biggest headache was when they made the very first trial run. Everything went well until the first tram car reached the top. Instead of sliding into the dock like it should have, it bumped up against the cliff face below the deck. They then had to move the cables and extend the landing deck out a meter or two, so the car would dock properly.

At a later date, word must have leaked out that they were having problems, because a Swiss born immigrant by the name of Paul Hunziker arrived on the scene. He heard about the situation while working at the Mammoth Ski Resort in California. He had some expertise on the subject, and was hired by Utah Crane to help finish the project. After working at the site for more than a year, the tram was finally opened in 1962.

The Skytram is said to be the steepest in the world, with an average angle of 45 degree. The steepest part is right at the top which is 66 degrees. The cable itself is 534 meters long, and has a vertical rise from bottom to top of 374 meters. Each of the two tram cars holds 6 passengers, and makes the ascent at 8 kms per hour. It is powered by a 45 horse power direct current electric motor, with a 40 horse power Volkswagon industrial engine as a backup. The bottom of the lift is at about 1561 meters, while the top is 1935 meters altitude.

Not long after the Skytram was in operation, the second phase of construction began. This was the building of a restaurant at the upper terminal. Some of the preliminary work began in the fall of 1962. The tram was used part-time that fall to take tourists up, but was also used to take all materials for the construction up as well. Sand, gravel, lumber, machinery, tools, everything went up via the tram, including a very small caterpillar. To get it up, they removed one tram car, and tied the cat on in its place.

Not long after the caterpillar was taken up, a terrible accident occurred. The following information comes from the Provo Daily Herald for December 18, 1962. It states, *tractor operator Billy Dominguez, 23, Orem, was killed instantly shortly before 10 a.m. today when the small bulldozer he was operating at the top of the cliffs of Bridal Veil Falls plunged over the rim.*

An eye witness, Byron Prestwich, 23, Orem, said Mr. Dominguez had been scooping up dirt with the cat and dumping it over the rim. He was backing up the cat and apparently miscalculated distance.

The Skyride aerial tramway, important Utah County tourist attraction with a perfect safety record since it began operation over a year ago, was not in operation at the time and was in no way involved in the accident.

Bridal Falls in winter is even more interesting than in summer.

Mr. Dominguez was an employee of the Swiss-American Cable Way Co., which has contract for excavation for a restaurant and dance hall at the top of the falls.

Horrified witnesses saw the caterpillar tractor hurtle downward from the rim to a point below the falls, some 1600 feet[500 meters?] from the rim. Five men were working with him on the rim at the time. The area of operation is about 25 by 40 feet[8 by 12 meters].

Things shut down for awhile, then in the spring and summer of 1963, the dance hall and restaurant were finally finished. Not long after that, Rue Clegg and his wife Margret went to Mexico for a warm vacation. During that trip, Clegg died of a heart attack. Margret then ran the business for two or three years before selling it to Alpine Engineering. Still later, brothers David and Steve Grow bought the company in 1974 and the Grow families have run the operation ever since.

At Bridal Veil Falls Resort today, you will find a gift and curio shop featuring handicrafts by local artisans in the same building as the lower terminal of the Skytram. Nearby are several tables and a snack bar in an old railway caboose, which was built in 1942 and used for over 43 years by the Union Pacific Railroad. There is a large paved parking lot, and a foot bridge you can use to reach the other side of the river. You can take one trail which runs to a small duck and fish pond below the falls, and another trail running about 500 meters to near the base of the falls themselves. All the lower terminal facilities are on private land, but part of the upper lodge and terminal is on Forest Service land.

At the upper terminal called the Rocky Top Lodge, the original full-service restaurant was closed in 1968. However, during the summer season there are still public dances at the upper terminal on Saturday nights. It can also be reserved by various groups for private meetings. There are also two short trails; one heading to an overlook of Utah Valley, the other to the creek and forest to the east of the falls. Both trails have interesting views of the canyon and are worth the time to walk.

The Bridal Veil Falls Resort is open from about May 15 to October 15 each year. Opening and closing dates can change, so you might call ahead at 225-4461, if you want to ride the tram. This world's steepest Skytram does not operate in rainy or windy conditions for safety reasons.

Extending west from the base of the falls on the south side of the Provo River, is a very long and narrow park. It's called **Bridal Veil Falls Park.** It's about half a km long and ends at the highway where a parking lot is situated. The land is owned by Provo City, but they lease it to Dave Grow and the Scenic Canyon Preservation Society for $1 a year. The money for improvements and maintenance has been provided by a Provo River Trail Committee and the Bridal Veil Falls Resort Company.

About a km above Bridal Veil Falls and right where the small stream from **Upper Falls** comes down to the Provo River, is where Lyman L. Donnan set up a homestead late in the 1800's, probably in

The top of the Skytram with the lower slopes of Timp on the right in background.

Fisherman's Home as it appeared in the winter of 1936(Bertha McKean Offret foto).

The same Fisherman's Home during the flood of July 1938(Bertha McKean Offret fotos).

1899. In 1904 he officially got title to the 65 hectares(160 acres) of river-front land. He lived there and slowly developed a small resort called **Donnan's Place** or **Upper Falls Resort**. It was a small lodge or inn with a store and restaurant and about 10 small summer cabins to rent for the night, a weekend, or a week. The place became famous for trout dinners.

Here is what a June, 1923 ad in the Provo Daily Herald had to say: *UPPER FALLS RESORT--Provo Canyon. Furnished Bungalow and Board, $3 per day, $15 per week. Tents with screen wire kitchenette, $5 to $7 per week. Trout Dinners and Spring Fry Dinners our Specialties DONNAN'S PLACE.* The site of the resort was located not far below the present-day Olmsted Diversion Dam. The last entry for either Lyman or Dolly Donnan in the county court records was October, 1944. At that time they sold all of their property to Provo City. Today Provo City still owns the land, but the county runs Upper Falls as a day-use only picnic park.

Another little waystation along the scenic Provo Canyon Highway was **Fisherman's Home.** It was a small store and restaurant, which catered to fishermen, picnickers and especially beer drinkers. In was first built after about 1933 by Billy Williams. He lived across the road in the small cabin which is presently on the north side of the road. Fisherman's Home was built near the river just after F.D. Roosevelt came to office and Prohibition ended. The local people referred to it as another *beer joint.*

The site of this tavern was in the general area as the old Ferguson Ranch, which was also apparently the home of the "Toll Gate Keeper" on the old Provo Canyon Road at one time. It's also where a giant snowslide came down in February, 1897, which killed Billy Ferguson and wiped out his home. Read more details on that event in the chapter *Tragedies on Mt. Timpanogos.*

In the summer of 1938, the Fisherman's Home was severly damaged by the flooding of the Provo River. A thunder storm on Wednesday, July 13, 1938, brought mud, rocks and trees down out of Snowslide Canyon blocking the river. For a short period of time a lake developed behind the dam and many homes were flooded in Vivian Park. The same storm also stranded campers in Provo Canyon and made another small lake at Wicks. Much later in time this area was owned by Leon Frazier. Today the Frazier family has built a summer-time resting place called *Frazier Park* in the same general location. In summer, someone operates a small store and fruit stand there.

The next significant location or landmark going up-canyon is at the lower end of the South Fork of Provo River and at what is known today as **Vivian Park.** According to Eugene Campbell's History of

Provo Canyon, *small homes and cabins have marked the area since before the turn of the century. Their number and permanency was very slight however. After the first World War the area began to grow and develop steadily. The area has been owned, prior to 1943, by several different families. The Slick family was one of the early owners and it is reported that it is from a young daughter, Vivian Slick, that the area received its name. Some other early owners were the Jim Poulton and Parley Hafen families. The area was originally homesteaded by William Ferguson, who at one time operated a toll gate on the early road through the canyon[see above].*

During the years of the First World War, some of the early owners started building and developing the area. One such owner was the Associated Investment Company of Salt Lake City. They ran an ad in the Provo Post(a forerunner of the Herald) on July 18, 1916 which states among other things, *Home Sweet Home In The Good Old Summer Time At VIVIAN PARK, in the Heart of Provo Canyon.* Apparently in the beginning, it was a camping and picknicking area, but then the investment company began selling lots.

The ad goes on to say, *VIVIAN PARK is equipped to furnish the ideal comforts of summer with its naturally attractive location, which includes fishing, boating, hiking, swimming, camping, dancing and a dozen other summer sports.....26 camping tents; 10 bungalows; spacious dining room accommodations; store; dancing hall; daily mail service; railroad facilities; electric lights; telephones; swings for the children and an abundance of shade are some of the features....VIVIAN PARK offers you the opportunity of acquiring a permanent summer home at "ground floor prices".* Throughout the 1910's, 1920's and 1930's, there were more advertisements in the Provo paper promoting dances being held at Vivian Park. World War II brought among other things gas rationing, which put a damper on cars cruising the canyon, so things changed at that time.

In later years, *the Vivian Park Home Owners Association was incorporated on September 6, 1943, and the incorporation is to last for 100 years. The incorporated town or community was to be governed by a Board of Directors. The board holds annual meetings.*

In addition to Vivian Park, several summer homes and some ranch homes have been built further up South Fork. Provo City has acquired 1001 acres[405 hectares] for future recreational developments in the Big Spring, Bunnel's Fork and Shingle Mill Canyons of South Fork(Campbell).

Today at Vivian Park there are the small cabin-type homes, some of which are lived in on a year-round basis. There is also a small county owned and operated picnic site, with a covered ramada and a duck pond. Next to the park is where the Heber Creeper terminates its down-canyon run in summer-time.

Right on the highway and where the South Fork road crosses the Provo River is the **Chalet Cafe**, a long-time land mark in the canyon built in about 1937 by Grover Purvance and John Carter. Just across the highway from the Chalet is the River Bend Trailer Park. Down canyon less than a km from the Chalet is the small recreation site now called Frazier Park.

About one km up-canyon or to the east of the Chalet Cafe, is where the North Fork Creek enters Provo Canyon. This is where you turn off Highway 189 onto the Alpine Scenic Loop Road toward Sundance and Aspen Grove. At that junction is another small, mostly summer home-type community called **Wildwood.**

This settlement began with a small ranch owned by George I. Taylor, which was purchased by a group of 14 citizens who formed what was known as Wildwood Resort Company in June of 1906. The

Y. M. Offret's gas station at Wildwood in 1941(Bertha McKean Offret foto).

Y. M. Offret's little children's train at Wildwood in 1945(Bertha McKean Offret foto).

various families involved drew lots to determine the location of individual cabin sites. Part of the area was laid out for cabins, while the area nearest the highway was set aside for recreation such as tennis and softball. In the first couple of years, the various families set up tents, some with wooden floors. Then slowly the cabins were built.

Much later in time, there was a service station built next to the highway ran by a Frenchman named Y. M. Offret. He was the caretaker of Wildwood who lived in the stone house near the community entrance. He came to Wildwood in 1929, after spending some time leasing the Cliff Inn service station at the mouth of the canyon.

Soon after arriving at Wildwood, Offret built a service station and store. Over a period of years he built a number of other improvements to the place. He had a small childrens railroad that ran in and around the lower part of Wildwood, and he had a perpetual motion water wheel and tap which never ran out of water. These frustrated many passersby. The small store was run by his wife. Offret lived at Wildwood for 38 years until his death in 1967. After that the Wildwood Association members decided to tear down the service station and store a year or two after his death.

In the beginning, the road up North Fork went right up the middle of Wildwood, but as the crowds going to the Timp Hike got bigger, the association of cabin owners asked the county to build the road on the other side of the creek, which is about where it is today. Today, many of the cabin owners are descendents of the original members.

Perhaps the largest community in the canyon is what is now called **Sundance.** It has an interesting history as told by a 75 year-old son of one of the original homesteaders to the area, Justin C. Stewart. Much of the following information comes from a book by Stewart, which as of the winter of 1989, had yet to be published. The Sundance Resort people are reportedly in the process of publishing his book titled, *A History of Sundance Utah.*

In the summer of 1899, the same year the railway was completed through Provo Canyon, the area just east of Timp was first surveyed. The government surveyor was Andrew Jackson Stewart Jr., and his two sons, John R. Stewart(Justin's father), and Scott P. Stewart. The young men were 20 and 22 years of age. After seeing the beauty of the **North Fork,** these two fellows vowed they would homestead the area after the public survey was completed.

In the year 1900, these two young brothers got all their family involved(aunts, uncles and in-laws) and ended up homesteading 1416 hectares(3500 acres) in the area where the Sundance Ski Resort and ski runs, all the summer homes and Aspen Grove are now located. Under the Homestead Act, each person was allowed only 160 acres, or a quarter section(one section is one square mile, or 640 acres--259 hectares). But with the help of relatives, they got it all. As things worked out, the two brothers put together what they called the *North Fork Investment Company,* which combined all of the homesteaded land. In short, it was a family affair.

In the beginning, all of the family members involved ended up building and making improvements on each quarter section as the Homestead Act specified. Most of them built a small wooden platform, with a tent on top, which satisfied the requirements of the act. They also built a road-of-sorts to the area. Justin Stewart says it wasn't really a road, but an old sheep trail which was also used to drag logs down the V-shaped canyon to Wildwood and to a sawmill in Provo Canyon. As time went on, the family built 13 simple bridges over the small stream between Wildwood and **Stewart Flat**(which is where Sundance Ski Resort is located today).

By the beginning of 1920, the County Road Commission was petitioned by members of the Stewart family and BYU's Eugene L.(Timp) Roberts(the original Timp Hike organizer) to built a road from Wildwood to Aspen Grove. The commission acted by appropriating $5000 for an 8 km road running from the Provo Canyon highway at Wildwood to Aspen Grove. The contractor was Isaac Wadley of Pleasant Grove. The road bed Wadley built was almost in the same place as the present road alignment of today. Between Wildwood and Stewart Flat they reduced the number of bridges from 13 to 8, and made it good enough for automobiles to reach Aspen Grove. This first rough road was completed in the summer of 1920(according to some Provo Daily Herald accounts of the Timp Hike of 1920) and about 50 cars made it up to Aspen Grove for the Timp Hike.

In 1921, Scott P. Stewart and John R. Stewart, donated 10 acres(4 hectares) of land at Aspen Grove to BYU for the creation of a summer school campus.

Several years later the road was completely rebuilt. This time it was the U.S. Bureau of Public Roads which did the work between 1929 and 1933. That construction put the road in the same location as it is today. In 1933, the road was oiled for the first time, and in 1937 was paved all the way from Provo Canyon to Aspen Grove. In 1921 the road over the top from Aspen Grove to the head of American Fork Canyon was rebuilt and made good enough for average cars, but it wasn't a real good road for several more years. Years later and after much improvement, it was given the name **Alpine Scenic Loop.**

Throughout the early years the North Fork area was used only during the summer months. The cabins were not built for the cold weather and the road was closed by snow. During this time, there were some interesting events as discussed by Justin C. Stewart in his soon-to-be-published book on Sundance.

Stewart mentions the family's attempts at summer farming. It was first tried at what they called Middle Field. This place is located between the two major switchbacks between Sundance and Aspen Grove, and on the southwest side of the road(today it's a horse pasture). Sometime during World War I, a Mrs. Thurber planted and grew potatoes in Middle Field, and they won first prize in the Dry Land Potato category at the Utah State Fair.

John Stewart Jr. held part of what the family called the Big Field, which is the largest open area within North Fork. The Big Field is located about one km north, northwest of the ski resort and 500

The old Timp Haven Ski Resort in about 1954. Lunch stand on the right(Ray Stewart foto).

meters north of Middle Field. It can't be seen from the road. In the 1880's and 1890's, this was a favorite place for sheepmen to take their flocks. The Stewarts remember it as being totally over-grazed and nothing but dust when they first homesteaded the place. However, in about 1931 John decided he would try raising potatoes. He bought a small tractor and tilled 10 to 15 acres(4 to 6 hectares) of the Big Field. His first crop of Dry Land Potatoes won first prize in the Utah State Fair.

After the first road was completed to Aspen Grove and when the BYU summer school was in operation, Scott P. Stewart and his wife Myrtle Maiben, opened a small store in his cabin which was very near the summer school and where the lower parking lot to the Theater-in-the-Pines is now located. The store first bagan to operate in about 1922 and was open only during the summer when the school was operating. After the huge avalanche of 1936 wiped out the cabin, the little store was moved to another relative's cabin, and it remained open until about the mid-1950's when the lady who operated it died. This was Mrs. John R.(Ester) Stewart, who used to do a good business each year when the Annual Timp Hike was on. She also hired young students to carry food and drinks up the mountain to sell at Emerald Lake during the annual hike in the 1930's.

In the summer of 1938, the North Fork Investment Company permitted a saw mill to be set up at Stewart Flat, which was very near where the ski resort is now located(it was at the Meadow, about 200 meters to the northwest of Redford's present film editing building). The operator was allowed to work only one season and cut those trees which John R. Stewart had marked. Many of the trees cut were on the present-day ski slopes to the south.

Rather late in the history of North Fork, Raymond R. Stewart, began a small ski resort named **Timp Haven.** According to Stewart's account, a group called the Timp Mountain Club, had persuaded a Mr. I. E. Daniels to open a ski area in Hobble Creek Canyon east of Springville in the early 1940's. Daniels had put together a truck body with a series of pulleys which served as power for a rope tow. The experiment in Hobble Creek failed, but later Stewart bought the equipment and took it to the area of the MIA Lodge(now called the Timp Lodge) part way up the slope from the present-day lower terminal of the Sundance ski lifts. A small area was cleared and an attempt was made to operate the ski tow in the winter of 1944-45, but it was a failure.

During the next summer, the equipment was overhauled and rebuilt and in the winter of 1945-46 they tried it again. They occasional had trouble getting up the snowy road above Wildwood and even more difficulties getting from the end of the plowed road to the rope tow site. Getting gasoline to the tow was a chore and since they only operated the equipment on weekends, they had to lug the batteries up and down each week to keep them charged. Junior Bounous and Frank Hirst were prominent men who helped with the project.

Sundance Ski Resort with Cascade Cirque and surrounding peaks in the background.

During the summer of 1946, Stewart hired Stan Roberts of Provo to bulldoze another clearing down-slope near the present-day lower terminals, and all the rope tow equipment was moved down-hill. Four hundred meters of new rope was purchased and made into one long strand. This gave the resort a 200 meter-long rope tow. Stewart bought two old cabins and put them in place at what was known as Stewart Flat. One housed the rope tow and equipment; the other was made into a lunch stand operated by his wife Ava. Provo City installed lights for night skiing and organized a ski school for the next season. BYU also started skiing classes which helped promote skiing and kept the Raymond R. Stewart family alive. They considered the winter of 1946-47 a success, by their standards.

In the summer of 1947, the rope tow was moved to the west about 100 meters, and a new cable tow was installed in its place. This opened up new country to skiers. In 1953 there was a merger between Raymond R. Stewart, brother S. Paul, and Junior Bounous. They bought a used chair lift which had been used in the Park City area, and installed it at Timp Haven. In 1957, a new Poma lift from France was bought and installed further up the slopes near Dry Lake. The lower terminal was later wiped out by a snowslide in 1963. In 1960, S. Paul Stewart took over the ski resort and ran it alone. In 1965, the resort's first all-electric double chair lift was installed--another big leap forward. This was called the Mandan lift and it's still operating today. In 1969, a second double chair lift was installed. This is what they call the Navajo. Over the years the resort gradually grew into what it is today.

In the 1950's, a water pipeline was laid from Aspen Grove Spring to the vicinity of Stewart Flats and the Timp Haven Ski Resort. A bit later, the Stewart Family Company began selling lots to the public. One of the later buyers of a two-acre lot was Charles Robert Redford and wife Lola Van Wagenen of Provo, on July 29(recorded on August 1), 1965. The Redford's first cabin was right next to the road, and after the movie *Butch Cassidy and the Sundance Kid* came out in the late 1960's, it became necessary for him to grudgingly put up a chain-link fence for privacy sake.

In the late 1960's, Redford made the movie *Jeremiah Johnson,* much of which was filmed in the Sundance and North Fork area. Because of his movie successes, he suddenly acquired a small fortune which needed to be invested. Negotiations took place and on August 5, 1968, there were two purchases recorded in the Utah County court house. One purchase for about half the property was in the area north of the ski resort. Redford himself bought this part, which was most of the holdings of the Stewart Canyon Corporation and which amounted to about 477 hectares(1179 acres). It was 6 separate Stewart families who sold the property.

The second half of the sale involved the Timp Haven Ski Resort itself belonging to S. Paul Stewart Enterprises. This part was officially bought by the Wildwood Development Corporation. Redford had 4

The rustic front to the small store at Sundance.

partners in this half of the deal. They were Stanley Collins, Hans Estin, Robert M. Gottschalk and the Coudert Brothers. This purchase involved most of the present ski areas of the resort which included about 900 hectares(over 2200 acres). With this acquisition and the release of the movie, *Butch Cassidy and the Sundance Kid* not long afterwards, the name of the entire area was changed to **Sundance.**

In recent years and with Redford's financial investments, Sundance has grown into a major ski resort. The original 1377 hectares(3379 acres) has grown into about 2400 hectares(6000 acres), according to Terry Minger, president of the Sundance Institute. But there's a lot more there today than just skiing. Sundance is the home of the Sundance Institute, founded by Robert Redford in 1980, which helps create new film making in the United States. The Institute also sponsors the annual United States Film Festival at Park City and operates the Sundance Summer Theatre, which has performances at a mountain-side amphitheatre from Mondays through Saturdays and from June through early September.

In one of the buildings west of the ski lifts are facilities for editing films. The movie, *Milagro Bean Field War* was edited there. Sundance is also the home of the Institute for Resource Management, an organization dedicated to preserving America's natural resources.

Right at the bottom of the ski lifts is a building housing a small general store which sells gifts, souvenir items, books and hand crafts. Next to it in the same building is the Tree Room Restaurant and Grill for dining. There's another building for skiers near the parking lot which houses a ski rental & repair shop and a cafeteria. Over the years, the resort has built a number of rustic cabins and cottages uphill and to the west of the resort, which are used for accommodating tourists and guests of the Institute.

Beyond Sundance and about 4 kms up the North Fork to the northwest and along the Alpine Scenic Loop Road is **Aspen Grove.** It involves both a public picnic site and campground, plus the BYU Aspen Grove Alumni Association Camp. This is not a permanent settlement, but the road to the site is cleared of snow, and there are some activities there on Saturdays during winter months. It started out as the beginning point for hikers going up the mountain on the Annual Timp Hike, but later evolved into a BYU summer school. Eugene E. Campbell discussed it in his unpublished *History of Provo Canyon.* He states:

The first intimation of an Alpine Summer School came in a report of [BYU] President Harris to the Executive Committee at a session held August 15, 1921, in which he stated that the North Fork Investment Company had proffered to the University a tract of land in the North Fork of Provo Canyon, adjoining Aspen Grove, for camping and other such purposes as the school might wish to make of it.

Ski trail grooming machines at Sundance. The east peaks of Timp in the background.

President Harris had always felt that Brigham Young University should avail itself of the natural educational resources of the mountains surrounding Provo, and under his promptings the offer was accepted. J. William Knight was appointed to represent the committee in making a selection of the tract. A selection of ten acres[4 hectares] adjacent to Aspen Grove was made and a deed therefore executed by the investment company. The personnel of the company was as follows: John R. Stewart and family, Scott P. Stewart and family, Joseph Nelson and family, Rose Young Stewart and Melissa R. Stewart, all of Provo.

It was on July 3, 1922, when BYU finalized plans to create an Alpine Summer School at Aspen Grove. The first summer it was held was in 1922. At that time they used army tents for both students and faculty, because they had no permanent buildings. After two successful summers, it became necessary to purchase more land. These summer school sessions continued through World War II, but afterwards the summer school changed its headquarters to the Provo Campus. Some of the classes taught after the war were geology, geography, botany, zoology and art.

The summer school continued until 1963. At that time it was decided to alter the situation and create a new program. The property was turned over to the BYU Alumni Association which began new recreation oriented facilities. In recent years the association has built two lodges, a large recreation and dining hall, cabins, a swimming pool, basketball and tennis court, and baseball diamond. The facilities are open full-time during the summer months, and part-time in winter when snow is deep enough for snowshoeing, cross-country skiing and snowmobiling. In winter the lodge is open on Saturdays only and they rent out skis and snowshoes and groom several trails in the area.

Back now to Provo Canyon. Further east in what the author calls Upper Provo Canyon, was a place called **Hoover's** or **Hoover's Cabins.** This was on land originally owned by a Wilford D. Wright back in 1885. On January 8, 1896, about 130 hectares(320 acres) was bought by a John W. Hoover. Hoover was a cattle and sheep rancher in the early days. Hoover's original home was on the highway near a spring, but the ranch itself was up on some flats to the north just over a hill. In the late 1930's, the family built several cabins which housed some of the men who worked on the Deer Creek Dam. Later, each of the sons bought their home sites and rented the cabins. As time went on, one of the sons named Jean, bought most of the original spread. Today, all of the ranch except the cabins on the highway, is owned by a development company under the name of Canyon Meadows.

In the canyon bottom just below Deer Creek Dam is a group of summer homes which is called **Deer Creek Park.** The river bottom land was originally bought from the state in 1909 by John McEwan

In front of one of the lodges at Aspen Grove. This complex is now run by the BYU Alumni Association.

and Edwin Van Wagenen. Later in time, the Rub Weeks family owned a large parcel of land in the area, and it was Weeks who started to develop the park and sell lots. In the years when the dam was being built(late 1930's), Weeks opened another *beer joint*, but it didn't stay open long. Today there are 18 different lots, each with a summer cabin. One of the owners has developed a small private campground. You can see this area from the highway just before you arrive on the dam.

Just below the dam and to the north of the highway are several homes along the lower end of Deer Creek. These are homes of the men and families who maintain the hydroelectric plant below Deer Creek Dam.

In the far eastern end of Provo Canyon, is **Deer Creek Reservoir.** Construction began on the dam in 1938 and was completed in 1941. This project provides water for irrigation as well as drinking water for Salt Lake City, Provo, Orem, Pleasant Grove, Lindon, American Fork and Lehi. In 1958, a hydroelectric power station was completed which generates 4950 kilowatts of power.

Mt. Timpanogos as seen from the Wallsburg Valley south of Heber(telefoto lens).

History of American Fork Canyon

Much of the following information comes from a thesis by Gary Vern Keetch written at BYU. It's titled, *The Changing Impact of Man in American Fork Canyon.* Also used was *Early History of American Fork,* by George F. Shelley, and an unpublished paper presented to the D.U.P. by Alma Kirk in 1923. It was in the Pleasant Grove paper on January 18, 1987, titled *Old Canyon Railroad Was Thought Impossible.* Another information source is entitled *Pleasant Grove Ranger District-- Information Handbook.* This is an excellent source.

The human history of American Fork Canyon began with the Indians, who had been in the canyon for thousands of years. About the only evidence of these early peoples has been found in a cave about 8 kms up the canyon. In that small cave archaeologists found arrowheads, spear points, scrapers, metates and manos; as well as beads and ropes and cords made from animal and vegetable matter. The people who lived there inhabited the region before the white men arrived on the continent and are believed to be from Shoshone stock.

At the time of the arrival of the first white men, which was the Dominguez and Escalante Expedition, the valley was full of Indians, camped mostly along the 4 major stream courses. That expedition traveled as far north as Provo, but they could see the groves of cottonwood trees along the American Fork River from afar and named it *Rio de Santa Ana.* The expedition learned from the local people the highest mountain there was called *Timpanois,* the lake was called *Timpanogo,* and the people themselves were called *Timpanogotzis.*

In the early 1800's, there were both Indians and trappers in the valley and canyon. Some of the first trappers or mountain men had names like Provost, Ashley, Smith, Bridger and Fremont. When the Mormon pioneers came to the valley in 1849, the Indians in the area were Utes, but there were also Goshutes, Piutes and Shoshoni at times.

Provo was settled in 1849, followed by American Fork in the fall of 1850. After that Lehi, Pleasant Grove and Alpine were put on the map. All these settlements were placed near canyons and mountain streams for obvious reasons.

One of the first reasons for the white settlers to go into American Fork Canyon was to cut timber for home construction. From 1850 until about 1870, the only way into the canyon was along a rough logging road. It was easier to drag out logs than haul out cut lumber, so the first sawmills were built in the towns. Later the mills themselves were built in the canyon or side canyons. They cut mostly spruce and Douglas fir which were on the lower slopes.

Throughout the years **sawmills** were located at the mouth of Burned Canyon(just east Timp Cave); at the present site of Mutual Dell in the South Fork; at Holman Flat in the North Fork of American Fork Canyon and another one further up the North Fork at the site of Forest City. In about 1890, the sawmill in Burned Canyon caught fire and set the countryside a blaze. The fire spread south and around onto the face of Timpanogos, and east as far as Mill Canyon and Aspen Grove. This particular fire burned for 9 months and was finally put out by winter snow.

One of the early industries in American Fork Canyon was the **milling of flour.** In Shelley's book it states, *In 1852, Lorenzo H. Hatch and Nathan Packer built the first real flour mill in Utah County at the mouth of American Fork Canyon. This pioneer mill was destroyed by the fire after doing only a very little grinding, but it was soon rebuilt and was known for many years as "Packers Mill".* It was operated by running water.

Grazing was an early and important use for the canyon by valley residents. There was some grazing in the canyon as early as the 1850's but between 1880 and 1900 the canyon was very much denuded by heavy concentrations of livestock, mostly sheep. Keetch mentions that someone estimated all the sheepmen of American Fork alone owned up to 150,000 head, many of which were in the canyon and on Mt. Timpanogos during the summer months. All or most of the big floods which have roared down the canyon can be credited to the overgrazing by these early stockmen. Read more on overgrazing under the chapter, *Livestock Grazing, Erosion and Terracing on Mt. Timpanogos.*

An interesting historic site in the middle part of the canyon was a place called **Dance Hall Cave.** According to Eldon Johnson of Pleasant Grove and the late Tom Walker of American Fork, dances were held in this natural cave as far back as the 1870's and up until the early part of the 20th century. During the 1870's, most of the people who used the cave were miners from Forest City, located in the upper end of American Fork Canyon near the mines. They would ride the train down the canyon for a night of fun and dancing.

In a Pleasant Grove Review article dated August 27, 1987, Walker stated that as *a boy he remembered a rock wall across the front of Dance Hall Cave to help level up the floor. This made it large enough for three sets of square dancers to use it at one time. Places were chipped out of the sides of the cave by hand for two musicians to sit while they played for the dancers. Music was provided by a fiddler and Mark Richins playing the accordion. Richins was also hired to play nightly for George Tyng at the mines.*

Clyde Burke, who has since passed away, told Walker his grandfather set up a refreshment stand in the smaller of the two caves which led to its eventual name of the "Beer Cave". Walker said that the life of the cave as a dance hall was short lived, and by the turn of the century had fallen into disrepair.

This site is located about 700 meters east or above the Timpanogos Cave visitor center on the right or south side of the road and across the river. Stop 100 to 200 meters beyond the bridge where you cross the creek for the first time above the cave parking lot. Then hop across the American Fork Creek and look for trails heading up-slope to the south. About 100 meters uphill is Dance Hall Cave and about another 100 meters to the west is the smaller Beer Cave. Both can be seen from the road, but you'll have to look for a wide place in the road to park.

The upper northeast end of the **North Fork** is not exactly under the shadow of Timp, but its mining history is closely linked to that of the lower American Fork Canyon. The discovery of silver, lead, and some gold in the area of Mineral Basin(directly south of Alta and Brighton, on the American Fork side) in 1870 filled the canyons with prospectors. According to George F. Shelley, the American Fork Mining District was organized July 21, 1870, with headquarters at what is known as **Mineral Basin.** The first mining claim was the Sunbeam Lode. Most of the ore bodies in the region were discovered between 1870 and 1905. More on mining below.

The history of transportation in American Fork Canyon is perhaps the most interesting part of the canyon's history. As previously mentioned, there was a very rough logging road up the canyon beginning after about 1851. However, when mining first got started in 1870, the ore wagons couldn't make it up or down the canyon on that rough track. It was up to the miners to build the first real road into the canyon. It went all the way from American Fork to Mineral Basin.

Keetch talks about the road this way. *The road took a great deal of maintenance to keep it open, so the users built a fence across the mouth of the canyon, put up a gate and charged fifty cents a wagon to travel the canyon. The money went to the caretaker of the road and it was his job to keep the road in good repair.* With increased mining activity in the canyon it became necessary to build a railroad to get the ore out.

The **American Fork Canyon Railroad,** like nearly all early railroads in Utah, was sponsored by the mining interests. During the late 1860's and early 1870's prospecting and opening of mining

Beer Cave in the middle part of American Fork Canyon.

properties were taking place in the Bingham, Cottonwood, and American Fork Districts. Railroad connections were made to all of these sections by 1872.

The Utah Central Railroad was finished from Ogden to Salt Lake in 1870. It was then extended from Salt Lake south to Draper later the same year. From Draper, spurs were built to the Bingham and Cottonwood mining properties. Rich ore had been found in the American Fork Canyon district at this time and the Utah Southern Railroad was urged to continue its construction south as rapidly as possible to make connections at American Fork. The difficulties of grading and making cuts around the Point of the Mountain at Jordan Narrows held construction up for more than a year so that the railroad in American Fork Canyon was finished before the Utah Southern reached American Fork. Connection was made with this railroad at Lehi in 1872. The next year American Fork became the terminus and the American Fork Canyon Railroad built its switch yards there.

Since the narrow gauge American Fork Canyon Railroad was completed before the Utah Southern reached Utah County, it was necessary to transport the first engine and rolling stock overland from the terminus at Draper, a distance of 40 kms. Mr. Jacob Foutz and Hensen Walker of Pleasant Grove had contracted to do the work. A rather ingenious method was employed. Three teams of oxen furnished the pulling power. Three lengths of track were made and were laid down, the engine was pulled to the end of them, then two lengths were taken up and laid down again in front, and the process repeated. It took seven days to transport the engine from Draper to Lehi.

It was generally considered an impossible feat to build a railroad through the steep, narrow and rugged canyon, and several interesting bets were made that the enterprise would never be completed. Mayor Wilkes was given charge of the construction and a surveyor by the name of Fox staked the grade. The work was done by day labor, the wages being $2.75 per ten hour day. The laborers were

The American Fork Canyon Railroad at Hanging Rock.
This foto was taken in about 1872.

MINING AREAS IN UPPER AMERICAN FORK CANYON

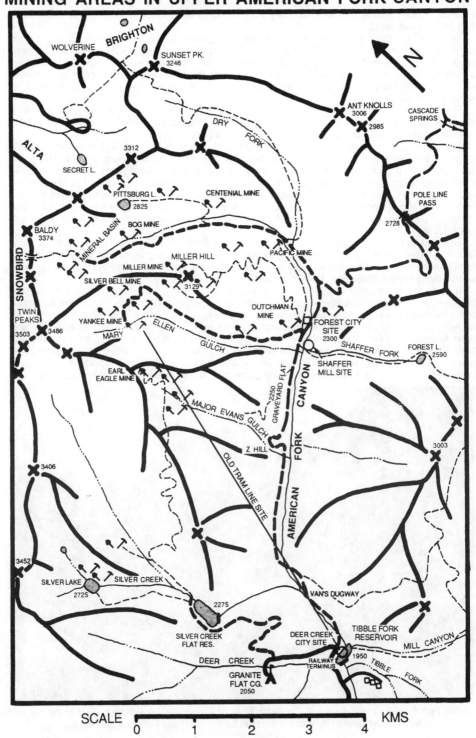

SCALE

0 1 2 3 4 KMS

under the direct charge of a boss by the name of General LeDuke, a Frenchman. Horses and scrapers were not available or at least not used in the construction of the grade, all work being done by hand. Picks, shovels, and wheelbarrows were the tools used. Where blasting was necessary, black powder was used.

The road-bed from Lehi to American Fork, across Highland Bench, and through American Fork Canyon to Deer Creek Flat(where Tibble Fork Reservoir is today) totaled 28 kms. The last 19 kms of this distance represented canyon construction. It was the original intention of the Aspinwall Company to build the railroad to the mines in Mineral Basin, but upon reaching Deer Creek, steeper grades were encountered and **Deer Creek Flat** became the terminus of the railway. The tracks stopped there on November 26, 1872.

The upper part of the railway project was supervised by a Major Evans, an engineer. He felt a railway could be built anywhere if only he had the money. Much of the grade for the upper end of the railroad was completed, but it proved too costly, so plans were scrapped.

The first engine used was of an early type and entirely too small for the job. It was one of the old upright boiler types and burned wood for fuel. Upon testing, it was found this engine could only pull a very small load up the steep grade in the canyon, so it was used to transport passengers and mail. All empties and freight were pulled up the tracks by horses and mules most of the time. Loads of lumber, poles, ties and ore from the mines returned to American Fork by gravity, checked by several men on each section of cars who handled the brakes. From 1876 to 1878 a larger engine was brought in to pull all trains. This was one of the newer coal burning engines used because at about that time the first coal fields in the region were developed.

The cost for the entire project is estimated to have reached $13,000 per km with a total cost near $240,000. The owners tried everything they could to make it a paying venture. For two years they advertised heavily to get tourists to come and ride the train and see American Fork Canyon scenery, but that didn't pay the bills and in 1878, the tracks were torn up and the iron sold.

Now to the mining history itself. The promising ore in the area was discovered by men of Johnson's Army, but the Civil War interrupted further exploration. According to Keetch, *the first major find in the canyon was the Miller Mine found in 1870[by Jacob and William Miller], The mine was sold the following year to the Aspinwall Company, from the east.....The principal owners were General Lloyd Aspinwall and Mr. Howland of New York, L. A. Hopkins of Chicago, and Mr. Baskin of Salt Lake City. Between 1871 and 1973, two million dollars worth of silver, lead, gold and copper were taken from the ground.* The discovery of this mine was the one which caused the mining boom in the canyon.

In 1871 and 1872, the Pittsburg and Wild Dutchman Mines were discovered and opened. The

Tibble Fork Reservoir and dam, with the North Peak of Timp in the background. This is the site of the former Deer Creek City and the terminal for the American Fork Canyon Railway.

Pittsburg was mined until 1909. The Wild Dutchman Mine was soon sold to the Omaha Smelting and Refining Company of Nebraska, and worked until 1917.

In 1872, a tramway was built to connect Miller Mine with its smelter at Shaffer's Fork, a distance of about 3 kms. This helped in transporting the ore from the high mine down to the smelter, which was located on the road. Sometime later another tram was extended down to Deer Creek Flat.

The Aspinwall Company built 25 charcoal kilns in the area as well. Fifteen were built at the **Sultana Smelter** and 10 at Deer Creek City, which was the end of the railroad and where Tibble Fork Reservoir is today. These kilns had the typical beehive look and held up to 25 cords of wood each. They ran almost continuously from 1872 until 1877, making charcoal for the Sultana Smelter and for the Salt Lake smelters.

During the time of the mining boom which was from about 1872 until 1876 or 77, two small communities developed in the canyon. One was at Deer Creek Flat, called **Deer Creek City;** the other was at **Dutchman Flat** further up canyon and just above where Mary Ellen Gulch and Shaffer Fork enter the upper American Fork Canyon. This upper community was called **Forest City,** and for several years it had a population of 150 to 300 people.

Forest City housed the miners, Sultana Smelter workers, the teamsters and people engaged in the retail trades. The town had a small school and a lady school teacher from Salt Lake. A man named Worth Nash operated a sawmill and kept a small herd of dairy cows and supplied the camp with fresh milk and butter. Frank Birk operated a saloon and according to Keetch, *got much richer than most of the miners.* There was never a doctor in town, so those who got sick had to go down to American Fork either by train or the rough road to find one.

In the winter of 1872-73, an epidemic struck the town. Today, in the area of Graveyard Flat is a sign stating: *Grave Yard Flat--During the winter of 1872 a Diptheria Epidemic swept the small mining town of Forest City that was adjacent to here. Eleven children who perished were buried at this site. Later additional children plus some mining fatalities were laid to rest in this flat. Approximately sixteen graves are here.* The graveyard is just below town.

At Deer Creek City and the terminus of the railroad, another small town developed. This community grew around the railway and charcoal kilns workers and lumberjacks. It had hotels, saloons, stores, homes and a large boarding house, a mining district office, a cemetery, the charcoal kilns and one lime kiln to provide lime for the Sultana Smelter at Forest City. When the boom was on the population reached an estimated several hundred at one time.

The American Fork mines proved pockety. Older mines were worked out and newer ones failed to materialize. The smelter could not be kept busy. In fact, the whole project; mines, smelter and

From Tibble Fork Reservoir a telefoto lens views the north slopes of North Peak. The North Ridge is in the middle, with the snow gully of the northeast face to the left. Northwest Ridge is on the right.

railroad, showed heavy losses. In 1878, all was abandoned and the railroad was removed. The rails and rolling stock were sold to other railroad interests at Springville and the roadbed was used as a wagon road.

From 1872 to 1876 all traffic in the canyon went over the railroad, but the cash charged for all services and the scarcity of money caused considerable friction. In 1876, a wagon toll road was projected and started. When the railroad discontinued, a great portion of the grade was used by this new road. Not until 1906 was the road through American Fork Canyon made a public road, maintained by the county.

From 1880 to 1905 the mining of ore in Mineral Basin was quite slow. A number of people searched the area, but it wasn't until 1905 that more rich ore bodies were found. In that year George Tyng secured a lease from the Aspinwall Company in another location on Miller Hill and another good vein was uncovered.

Keetch covered the history of Tyng like this. *For the next few years Miller Hill activity boomed. Mr. Tyng built a large boarding house for his miners and none but the best cooks were employed. This boarding house became the talk of the area and people traveled into the canyon just to stay at the Tyng house. Forty teams were kept busy hauling ore and supplies and 30 men were employed in a shift.*

At the height of the prosperity Mr. Tyng was killed in a snowslide. He had stepped from his cabin to one of the outbuildings and while he was there a slide passed over the building. According to the story, no great amount of property damage was done but a nail in one of the roof boards had been driven into Mr. Tyng's skull.

The body was hauled by sleigh to American Fork and embalmed. However, on opening the will it was found that he requested to be buried just below the boarding house on the brow of the hill. So eight teams of horses left American Fork and traveled the difficult road back to the mine, where the deep snow was cleared off the hill and a grave dug by the miners.

Today, high on a grassy slope stands a white picket fence around the grave of Mr. Tyng. The fence was originally put there by the family but over the years it fell apart. In 1965, the U. S. Forest Service placed a new picket fence around the grave of this early miner.

According to George F. Shelley's book, it was in 1897 the American Fork City council was petitioned to bring electricity to the town. About two years later, on June 6, 1899, the Garff Brothers began building a **hydroelectric power plant** at the mouth of American Fork Canyon. To make the venture cost effective, Pleasant Grove and Lehi were included. Each town put $6000 into the operation.

The Lower American Fork Hydroelectric Power Station in the early 1900's.
It was removed in 1956.

The electric project involved building a wooden dam about half way up the canyon, near what is today the Hanging Rock Picnic Site. An updated dam is still there today next to the road. A wooden pipeline was also constructed along the north side of the canyon wall. This pipeline took water to a point high above the mouth of the canyon. Immediately below was the power plant itself. This initial system was finished in early 1901. This plant became known as **American Fork Power Plant No. 1,** or the Lower Plant.

A few years later in 1907, a second plant was built about half way between the wooden dam and the Lower Plant. This was known as the **Upper American Fork Power Plant** or No. 2 Plant. This plant is still there day, but the lower one is gone. Right at the mouth of the canyon where the two highways meet, look to the north and you can still see remnants of the lower plant and the penstock's location.

In 1912, the Utah County Light & Power Company sold its interest to the Knight Consolidated Power Company. Later the same year, Utah Power & Light absorbed it into its own system. This was in the same time frame as when the Battle Creek, Nunns and Olmsted Hydroelectric Power Stations were sold by L.L. Nunn and the Telluride Power Company to UP&L. The Lower Plant had an old wooden flume and some ancient dynamos, so it became uneconomical to operate. It was dismantled in 1956, but the No. 2 Plant was renovated in 1954 and is still operating.

Throughout the years, recreation has been popular in American Fork Canyon. People would go the canyon, usually on weekend camping trips to fish or hunt, or just to picnic. As roads improved, more people went to the canyon. Much of the area of Mt. Timpanogos was first made into the Uintah Forest Reserve on February 22, 1897, but in those early days the Forest Service wasn't out building campgrounds.

It appears the first real effort to make campgrounds and other facilities in the canyon came in about 1921, when Forest crews built the Timpooneke Trail. Before that time the first guard station was built in South Fork, but in 1934, the one seen there today, was built by the CCC crews. In 1921 and 1922, the first trail to Timp Cave was built, opening up that area. In 1921, the Alpine Scenic Loop Road was upgraded to accommodated common cars, but it was rebuilt in the early 1930's, and totally paved in a few years later. This road's construction marked the beginning of summer time recreation in the canyon. Today there are about 8 campgrounds and one picnic site in American Fork Canyon area below Tibble Fork Reservoir.

The north slopes of North Peak, seen from Tibble Fork Reservoir.

Geology and Glaciation on Mt. Timpanogos

For the most part Mt. Timpanogos is made up of limestone rocks which originated at the bottom of Pennsylvanian and Mississippian Age seas. The age of most of the rocks making up the mass of this mountain is from about 335 to 270 million years old. The age of the various rock formations is shown on the Geology Time Table. Below is a discussion on the various formations making up the mountain. The oldest rocks are at the bottom of American Fork Canyon; the youngest are at the summit of Timp.

There are 5 basic types of rocks making up the mountain, ranging from the quartzites of the lower parts of American Fork Canyon to the limestones and quartzites of the summit ridge. The 5 rock types are: sandstone, quartzite, shale, limestone and dolomite. Below is a description of the rock types and where they are found on the mountain.

Sandstone Thick beds of sandstone were originally part of a sandy desert, perhaps like what we find today in the Sahara or other dry sandy places. The sand comes from the weathering of still older rocks of various kinds. After an area had accumulated so much sand, it was then involved in crustal movements of the earth which lowered the region to below sea level. At that time, other sediments from higher nearby locations were deposited on top and after millions of years it was compacted and the individual grains of sand became cemented together. At a much later time, the crustal movements again raised the land and erosion exposed various layers. At that point in time the sand particles are known as sandstone. This is basically how the great sandstone beds of southern Utah and the Colorado Plateau were formed.

In the region of the Timp Massif, what little sandstone there is has been sandwiched in between layers of dolomite and limestone in the Humbug and Ophir Formations. These very thin beds were likely formed in desert areas which were not extensive in size. All these minor beds of sandstone are found in the walls of American Fork Canyon.

Quartzite These rocks were originally beds of sand, then at a later time developed into sandstone. Sandstone beds which are then buried under many other layers or deposits, are subject to great pressures. One result of pressure is heat, and heat causes the sandstone to re-crystalize into a new rock called quartzite. Quartzite is a hard rock which comes in many varieties and colors depending on composition of the original sandstone and how much heat and pressure it was subjected to.

The main bulk of the upper part of Mt. Timpanogos is about half quartzite. Quartzite beds are sandwiched in between different layers of limestone or dolomite. The limestones and dolomites are dark gray in color, whereas the quartzite is a light brown. As you eat your lunch at Emerald Lake, look west at the big cliffs making up the eastern face of the summit ridge. The grays are the limestones and the lighter sandy colored strata are the quartzite layers of the Oquirrh Formation. The very summit of Timp is quartzite, below which is a gray band of limestone, then more quartzite and gray limestone. All the higher peaks are about half limestone, half quartzite, all of which make up the main body of the Oquirrh Formation

Shale This is one of the softer rocks in existence. It erodes very easily and always forms a bench or slope and never a cliff, as does sandstone or limestone. Shale is formed when silt and mud are deposited at the bottom of a lake or sea, usually in a freshwater environment. The Mississippi River Delta will someday be a great thick layer of shale or siltstone, depending on how much it's compacted.

Most of the shale on Mt. Timpanogos is part of the Ophir and Manning Canyon Shale Formations. You can see the Ophir Formation as you walk the trail to the Timp Cave. The presence of the Manning Canyon Shale has created the big semi-level area between Mahogany Mtn. and the main part of Timp.

Limestone All limestones in the world were formed the same way, at the bottom of ancient seas or oceans. Over a long period of time, sea animals, especially those with shells, die and settle to the bottom. In time these sediments add up to enormous deposits. Then as the earth's crust is pushed up and buckled, the limestone beds can end up above sea level. When this happens the land is then subjected to erosion which starts a new cycle all over again.

About half of the main body of Mt. Timpanogos is made up of limestone. Most of the rest is

GEOLOGY TIME TABLE--MT. TIMPANOGOS AREA

SYSTEM OR PERIOD	AGE (MILLIONS OF YEARS)	FORMATIONS ON MT. TIMPANOGOS
PENNSYLVANIAN	270	OQUIRRH FORMATION
		BRIDAL VEIL LIMESTONE
MISSISSIPPIAN	325	MANNING CANYON SHALE
		GREAT BLUE LIMESTONE
		HUMBUG FORMATION
		DESERET LIMESTONE
		GARDISON LIMESTONE
		FITCHVILLE DOLOMITE
DOVONIAN	350	UNCONFORMITY--MISSING ROCKS
SILURIAN	400	EITHER NO ROCKS WERE DEPOSITED OR ALL FORMER ROCK FORMATIONS WERE ERODED AWAY
ORDOVICIAN	440	
CAMBRIAN	500	MAXFIELD LIMESTONE
		OPHIR FORMATION
		TINTIC QUARTZITE
PRECAMBRIAN	600	MUTUAL FORMATION

quartzite, with smaller amounts of dolomite, sandstone and shale. The top half of the mountain is a mixture of the limestone and quartzite and is part of the Oquirrh Formation, while just below that is a solid band of limestone called the Bridal Veil Limestone Member(of the lower Oquirrh). This is seen on both sides of Provo Canyon at Bridal Veil Falls. All limestones will have some kind of marine fossils which are sea shells of various kinds and coral.

Dolomite This rock was formed exactly the same way limestone is formed, at the bottom of oceans or seas. The only difference is the amount of magnesium carbonate in the rock. If the rock is made up almost entirely of calcium carbonate, then it's ordinary limestone. But if there is a certain amount of magnesium carbonate replacing the calcium, then it's classified as a dolomite rock.

On Timp, there is some dolomite in the Humbug, Deseret, Gardison, Fitchville and Maxfield Formations. The ordinary person can't tell the difference between the limestones and dolomites. The difference is mainly in the mineral content.

List of Formations on Timp

Below is a list of all the formations making up Mt. Timpanogos. It starts at the bottom of American Fork Canyon with the oldest rocks, and ends at the summit, which has the youngest formations.

Mutual Formation Type Location--In the area of Big and Little Cottonwood Canyons, southeast of Salt Lake City. These mostly quartzite rocks are best seen along the bottom of the trail to the Timp Cave. The USGS report on the geology of Mt. Timpanogos states the Mutual Formation is made up of *rusty to red-purple quartzite, grit, and conglomerate with minor red-purple or greenish shale.* These are the oldest rocks in the immediate area, dating back to Precambrian times and a little over 600 million years old.

Tintic Quartzite Type Location--Tintic Canyon, in the East Tintic Mountains near Eureka, Utah. This is quartzite rock found only in the bottom part of American Fork Canyon. The best place to see this one is along the lower part of the trail running up to the Timp Cave. It consists of *medium to coarse-grained white or pale pinkish quartzite, and is pebbly and locally purplish near the base.* These are some of the oldest rocks in the area, and in the Cambrian period, which date from 600 up to about 570 million years ago.

Ophir Formation Type Location--In the Oquirrh Mountains near the old mining town of Ophir. These too are very old rocks, dating from the middle Cambrian Period, or from about 570 to 550 million years ago. They are best seen along the walls of American Fork Canyon and along the trail to Timp Cave. This formation is divided into three members. The *Upper member: blocky brown calcareous[limy] sandstone. Middle member: massive wavy-bedded gray limestone. Lower member: olive-green shale.*

Maxfield Limestone Type Location--It's seen at the Maxfield Mine near Alta, southeast of Salt Lake City. These along with all the older rocks in the region of Mt. Timpanogos, are found only in the lower walls of American Fork Canyon. You can see this one along the trail leading to Timp Cave. Buy the little self-guide booklet *Along the way to the Caves* at the Timp Cave visitor center before you begin that hike. It explains a little about the rocks and the vegetation along that trail. The Maxfield is another formation from the middle part of the Cambrian period, perhaps 550 to 525 million years old, or thereabouts. Its rocks are described as *thin to thick-bedded gray mottled magnesian limestone and dolomite. Oolitic or pisolitic, near the base.*

Fitchville Dolomite Type Location--Fitchville Ridge, in the East Tintic Mountains near Eureka, Utah. At the contact point between the Maxfield Limestone and the Fitchville Dolomite is an **unconformity;** that is, a missing gap in the geologic time table. This means there were either no new rocks formed or deposited, or that they were there at one time and later eroded away. The missing gap is from the upper Cambrian, or roughly 525 to 500 million years ago, down to the lower or older Mississippian period, or about 350 million years ago. There is roughly 150 million years of the geologic time table missing. The Fitchville Dolomite Formation is in the lower Mississippian period, and younger than 350 million years old.

These rocks are exposed in the walls of American Fork Canyon. The best place to see them is along the trail to Timp Cave. Baker and Crittenden describe this formation as having two distinct

GEOLOGY CROSS SECTION--MT. TIMPANOGOS

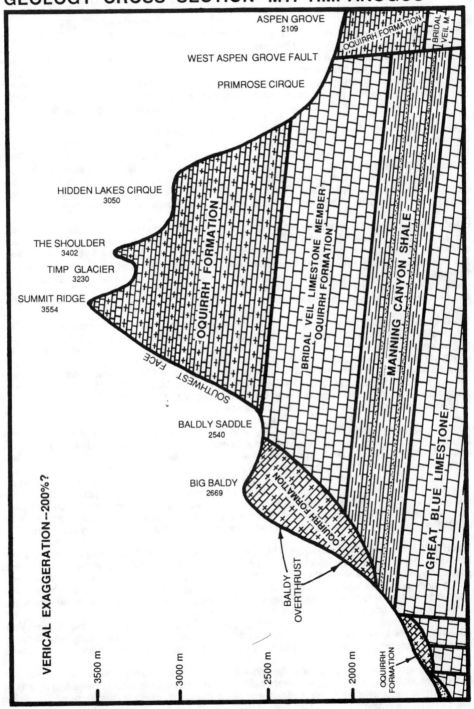

ASPEN GROVE
2109

WEST ASPEN GROVE FAULT

PRIMROSE CIRQUE

HIDDEN LAKES CIRQUE
3050

THE SHOULDER
3402

TIMP GLACIER
3230

SUMMIT RIDGE
3554

BALDLY SADDLE
2540

BIG BALDY
2669

SOUTHWEST FACE

OQUIRRH FORMATION

BRIDAL VEIL LIMESTONE MEMBER
OQUIRRH FORMATION

MANNING CANYON SHALE

GREAT BLUE LIMESTONE

BRIDAL VEIL M.

OQUIRRH FORMATION

OQUIRRH FORMATION

BALDY OVERTHRUST

OQUIRRH FORMATION

VERICAL EXAGGERATION--200%?

3500 m

3000 m

2500 m

2000 m

members. *Upper part: massive dark-gray dolomite, thin white beds at top. Lower part: medium-bedded pale-gray vuggy dolomite.*

Gardison Limestone Type Location--The East Tintic Mountains near Eureka, Utah. The Gardison Limestone Formation is seen in about the middle part of the wall of American Fork Canyon. You can see these beds as you walk the trail to Timp Cave. This formation is mostly limestone, but of the three members, the upper and lower parts are made up of dolomite. The Gardison is found in the lower Mississippian strata, which is roughly 345 million years of age. The USGS describes these beds this way. *Upper part: massive gray to black course-grained cherty dolomite. Middle part: thin-bedded fine grained fossiliferous limestone. Lower part: dark gray coarse-grained crossbedded dolomite.*

Deseret Limestone Type Location--The East Tintic Mountains near Eureka, Utah. The Deseret Limestone Formation is made up mostly of limestone, but with some beds of dolomite. This is the formation where the Timp Cave is located, about half way up the wall of American Fork Canyon. Read more about the cave under Map 10. The Deseret is found in the lower Mississippian rocks, but near the middle of that time period. These beds were formed at the bottom of an ancient sea somewhere around 340 or 335 million years ago. The formation has been described this way. *Massive dark to light-gray cherty dolomite. Thin-bedded platy-weathering fossiliferous limestone as base.*

Humbug Formation Type Location--Named for exposures near the Humbug Tunnels, southeast of Eureka in the East Tintic Mountains. The Humbug Formation is made up of beds of dolomite and sandstone, one of the few formations on Timp with sandstone beds. This is the first formation above the Deseret Limestone, where Timp Cave is located. It's found in the upper walls of American Fork Canyon. It is located in the upper or younger part of the Mississippian period or about 335 million years old. This formation is *thick to thin-bedded, fine to coarse-grained, dark to light-gray dolomite, interbedded with tawny-weathering sandstone.*

Great Blue Limestone Type Location--From many locations in the Oquirrh Mountains, west of Salt Lake Valley. This massive limestone formation is one of the thickest in the area of Mt. Timpanogos. As you approach the mouth of American Fork Canyon it forms all the walls you can see at that point, especially those walls on the south side of the lower canyon. Also, the entire Mahogany Mountain Massif is made up of this limestone. It's also seen in the lower end of Dry Canyon where the blue-gray cliffs form a kind of gate or narrows. See Map 6 on Dry Canyon. This formation is located in the upper Mississippian period, and is approximately 330 million years old. The Great Blue is *thin-bedded dark-gray limestone and shaly limestone. Black shale at base.*

Manning Canyon Shale Type Location--In Soldier Canyon, 5 kms southeast of Stockton in the Oquirrh Mountains. The Manning Canyon Shale Formation is made up mostly of shale, but with a few thin beds of limestone and sandstone. It has one of the characteristics shared by all shales, that is, it forms a bench. This formation forms the bench around the west and north sides of Mt. Timpanogos. It is the formation which has created the big flat region called Sagebrush Flat between Mahogany Mountain and the main summit region of Timp. The Timpooneke Road runs along the bench formed by this group of rocks. The age of the Manning Canyon Shale has been determined to be on the border line between Mississippian and Pennsylvanian time periods. In other words, these rocks are about 325 million years old. It is *black shale and shaly limestone, [with thin beds of sugary sandstone].*

Oquirrh Formation Type Location--This one is the dominate formation found in the Oquirrh Mountains west of the Salt Lake Valley. The entire bulk of Mt. Timpanogos above the inclined or titled plain of Sagebrush Flat is made of this formation. It has an upper and lower member, and for the most part is made up of alternating beds of limestone and quartzite. One of the best places to see these alternating beds is at Emerald Lake. From the Timp Shelter, look to the west and at the face of the summit ridge. The gray bands are limestone, the light browns are quartzite.

The lower member is made up almost entirely of limestone and called the **Bridal Veil Limestone.** The best place to see it is on both sides of Provo Canyon, on both Timp and Cascade Peak(the mountain on which Bridal Veil Falls originates from). The type location for this one is obviously Bridal Veil Falls.

In this region, the Oquirrh is entirely within the lower Pennsylvanian time period, or roughly between about 315-320 to 275 million years old. This formation is described as consisting of *gray to tan quartzitic sandstone units, interbedded with black limestone, which is fossiliferous. The Bridal Veil Limestone member consists of medium to dark-gray, thin to thick-bedded limestone with nodules and thin modular beds of black chert in the upper part and with some interbedded dark-gray to black shale and a few beds of quartzite, with abundant fossils.*

Pleistocene and Recent Glaciation on Mt. Timpanogos

Dates cannot be set exactly, but most geologists believe the last great ice age in North American and Utah ended about 12,000 to 10,000 years ago. At about that time, there was a rapid melting of glaciers the world over. The **Pleistocene Epoch** ended 10,000 years ago, which marked the beginning of what geologists call the **Recent** time period.

On Mt. Timpanogos there is evidence of both Pleistocene and Recent glaciation. Pleistocene glacial till or deposits can be found on the north and east sides of the mountain. These deposits are in the form of unsorted rocks of various sizes mixed with sand and gravel. Other evidence of glaciation are valleys which are rounded or "U" shaped indicating they were scoured by moving ice. Some valleys such as lower American Fork Canyon have a "V" shape, meaning it was eroded by running water. In the upper basins, you can see exposed bedrock with scratches put there by rocks captured in moving ice. Also in the upper basins you can see rounded mounds of rock and rubble which are either terminal or lateral moraines of former cirque glaciers.

One large Pleistocene glacier moved down the mountain to the north from the Timpanogos Basin and the Pica and Woolly Hole Cirques. Part of that ice sheet moved down into the upper part of Bear Canyon, while another tongue moved down to about where the lower end of the Altamont Campground is today. This ice mass was apparently connected to the east side glacier system in the area of the Timp Divide.

On the east side, there were two major rivers of ice moving downhill to the east. One ice mass began where the present-day glacier is and joined ice from the Hidden Lakes Cirque. It slid over the edge of the upper basins and filled the Primrose Cirque, then flowed southeast as far as Stewart Flat, which is where the lower ski lifts are now located at Sundance. A second major flow started in the Big Provo Hole and Cascade Cirque and flowed downhill to the east. Lower down and in the Sundance area, this large glacier merged with the one from the Primrose Cirque. We know the glaciers stopped at about the bottom of the present-day ski lifts, because the North Fork Canyon below Sundance is "V" shaped and rugged. That part has never been scoured by moving ice.

Three circular glacier moraines inside Cascade Cirque, as seen from the top of Razorback Ridge.

To the north of Aspen Grove is another area covered by glacial till or deposits, although it must be very shallow. This is the high area between the North Fork of Provo Canyon and American Fork Canyon. Apparently there was lots of ice originating on the east slopes of Roberts Ridge that flowed east. This formed a connecting ice link between the north and east side glacier systems.

In addition to the two great flows just mentioned, there was a smaller ice field that flowed north from the north face of North Peak and down what locals call the Rock Slide. It stopped about half way between the Timpooneke Road and the bottom of American Fork Canyon in the Rock Canyon drainage.

On the southwest face of the Mt. Timpanogos there were never any real glaciers, but the upper parts of the mountain appear to have held small *névé* (perpetual snow) *fields*. They probably looked something like the present-day Timp Glacier. The largest of these névé fields was located in the upper regions of Dry Canyon.

After the great ice sheets of North American and the state of Utah melted away, there has been many intermittent mini-ice ages, but none to rival those of the distant past. During the Recent time period on Timp, the only glaciation has been in the upper basins, but today these are down to almost nothing. The largest ice sheet on the mountain is what we all call the Timp Glacier. Actually, this is not a true glacier for several reasons. One, it moves downhill very little if at all. Second, it is almost devoid of crevasses, although on the upper slopes next to the head and side walls, there are some small openings commonly called *bergschrunds*. These crevasses open up next to the rock wall as the ice mass slowly drifts downhill creating an opening. The bergschrunds on the Timp Glacier are small and harmless.

There are several other locations on the mountain where some perpetual ice or snow lingers the year-round. The largest is at the bottom of the north face of the main summit of Timpanogos. You will walk on part of this in early to mid-summer as you pass between Emerald Lake and the Timp Saddle. In the late summer or early fall, some of this small icefield survives by being tucked away in the shadows of the summit.

Another small icefield is located in the Cascade Cirque above and west of Sundance. It forms partly because it's shadowed in the afternoons and because it gets some of its snow from avalanches coming off the northeast face of the Southeast Summit. This one even has a recently-made lateral and terminal moraine which is very distinct when viewed up close or from one of the summits or Razorback Ridge.

On the north end of the mountain are two very small patches of ice, which appear to be there on a year-round basis. However, after several seasons of below average precipitation, these two will likely

Looking down on small glacier moraines in Cascade Cirque from the top of the Second Summit.

disappear by September. One is in the Pica Cirque, up against the bottom of the the north face of Bomber Peak. It too has a very small circular moraine on three sides. The other is in a deep gully or couloir running down the northeast face of the North Peak.

Emerald Lake with the Timp Glacier in the background. This is typical of high mountain cirque lakes.

From the top of Roberts Horn, you have a good view of the glacier and Emerald Lake. It was the last big surge of the glacier which created the lake.

Livestock Grazing, Erosion and Terracing on Timpanogos

Grazing of sheep and cattle on the slopes and in the canyons surrounding Mt. Timpanogos, began in the early 1850's not long after the first Mormon settlers arrived in Utah Valley. Over the years, the herds gradually increased in numbers. At first the herds stayed close to home, but as the white man finally conquered the various Indian groups, they went further afield. In winter, some of the livestock was sent out in the west deserts to graze, but in the summer months they were taken to the mountains. For the people of Alpine, American Fork, Lehi and Pleasant Grove, Timp was their first choice for summer range.

Keetch, in this thesis on American Fork Canyon, mentions that someone estimated all the sheep men of American Fork alone owned up to 150,000 head of sheep, many of which were in A.F. Canyon and on Timp for the summer months. In those early years it was *free-for-all grazing*. There were no rules set, because no one was authorized to do so. All over America, the land was being settled and used. Many people describe it as being over-used or abused in those early days. But since land was plentiful, why worry?

But some people began to worry as early as the 1880's, and by February 22, 1897, Congress passed a bill establishing Forest Reserves in America. One of these was the Uintah Forest Reserve, which in the beginning was mostly in the Uinta Mountains. There was a great national debate on the issue *preservation vs. free use*.

Another important date was February 1, 1905. That's when the Forest Reserves were transferred from the Department of Interior to the Department of Agriculture. In the early years, Gifford Pinchot became America's first Forest Service chief. At about that time and in some places, a system of permits for grazing was begun.

Still another important date was March 4, 1907; that's when the name was changed from Forest Reserves to National Forests. As far as grazing on Timp is concerned, this also appears to be the first year grazing took place under a permit system.

Up to 1907, Mt. Timpanogos was grazed at will and those who got to a spring or pasture first, had it for the entire summer. Things went well until the 1880's and 1890's, then there were so many different herds on the mountain it began to deteriorate. Grazing herds were placed on slopes just as the snow left and before the grass had a chance to grow. It was in the last 20 years of the 19th Century when the real abuse of Timp began. That's when the range was terribly depleted and erosion and floods began to take place.

According to the thesis by Keetch he states; *Summer thunderstorms are quite common in the American Fork Canyon and have been directly responsible for six summer floods. [While throughout the years many floods occur, the] major floods occurred in 1890, 1921, 1951, 1952, 1953 and 1965.* In another Forest Service document entitled, *A history of Destruction and Restoration* by Rodney Greeno, it states; *the first major flood of record in eastern Utah County destroyed seven bridges in American Fork Canyon on August 19, 1869. No major floods were reported from 1869 to 1880, but there were many damaging floods during the 1880's and 1890's.* During the 20th Century there has been much flooding and destruction on or near Mt. Timpanogos. Everyone seems to agree these floods were caused by the overgrazing in the early years. Road building and timber cutting would be two additional reasons for flooding.

According to the research by Keetch, *it appears that 1907 was the first year permits were issued[for A. F. Canyon], at which time the records indicate there were 4500 cattle and horses, and 23,100 head of sheep permitted for 1907.* As you can imagine, there were conflicts between the free-roaming stockmen and the Forest Service bureaucrats. Of course, everyone knew something had to be done, and slowly but surely the permit system was accepted by all.

Quoting again from Greeno's document; *Despite the grazing restrictions and reductions which the Forest Service enacted in 1907 and years following, overgrazing continued to plague the Uinta National Forest until the 1960's. The problem was recognized in the 1920's and 1930's, but no extensive remedial action was taken until the 1950's. While sheep had been seen as the main culprits in overgrazing until the 1930's, cattle became the principal object of concern as sheep allotments were converted to cattle allotments with the general decline of the sheep industry after the*

Depression.

Locally, one of the first movements toward allowing fewer livestock on Timp, was began by Fred Buss in 1923. He was a professor of geography and geology at BYU. He reported that grazing on Mt. Timpanogos had left the southern cirques barren allowing floodwaters to cut deep gullies. He wrote a letter to the Forest Supervisor asking that sheep be completely removed from Timp.

A few years later, in 1931 and 1932, the Forest Service made studies of the watershed along the Wasatch Front, and *found serious vegetal depletion from overgrazing and accelerated erosion on Box Elder Peak[just north of Timp's North Peak], upper American Fork Canyon and Mt. Timpanogos.*

After much debate over the issue between what we now call environmentalists and the livestock industry, there was a gradual change of attitude. One reason for the change on the part of the stockmen were some drastic floods in the early 1950's down American Fork Canyon. Further studies of the situation were carried out by the Forest Service in 1953, which linked the floods directly to overgrazing. Finally in 1957, Clarence Thornock, the Supervisor of the Uinta National Forest, began a concerted effort to reduce grazing all over the forest.

After the grazing permits were greatly reduced or curtailed completely, the next step was to devote time and money to watershed restoration projects. In the 1930's there were some feeble attempts at range rehabilitation which included artificial seeding, fencing and dispersed livestock, but those CCC projects were of little consequence.

Finally in 1958, plans were drawn up for the American Fork--Dry Creek Restoration Projects. *North Utah Valley municipalities, soil conservation districts, and stockmen sought funding for a watershed rehabilitation project in the American Fork--Dry Creek area under the Watershed Protection and Flood Prevention Act of 1954. They prepared a work plan and applied for federal assistance in 1958. From 1959 to 1971, contour trenches were constructed, ranges were artificially seeded, gully plugs were installed, and reservoirs were created at an estimated cost of $4,000,000(Greeno).*

The area included all of the American Fork Canyon drainage, the canyons east of Alpine on Box Elder Peak, and along the west face of Mt. Timpanogos(another project was to terrace the mountain slopes east of Provo). The flood control reservoirs were at the mouths of various canyons including Dry, Battle Creek and Grove Creek. The trenching or terracing on Timpanogos took place at the head of Dry Canyon, between Big and Little Baldy, and to a much lesser extent at the head of Battle Creek. There's also terracing at the head of Grove Creek Canyon near Grove Creek Spring, around Chris Fisher Flat and in the area of Sagebrush Flat.

The man who got the contract for most of the trenching for the project was Wes Walker of Pleasant Grove. He is still the owner of the Walker Construction Company. He has told the author the project

Looking down on Big Baldy and the terraces from half way up the southwest face of Timp.

189

of terracing actually began in about 1959 at the head of Rock Canyon east of Provo. From there they went to the other sites in the project area. By about 1962 all the trenching or terracing was completed and re-seeding began.

Perhaps the best place to see the terracing up close on Mt. Timpanogos is to walk up Dry Canyon,

A fall scene. Looking at the upper Cascade Cirque from the Sundance area.

Geologic explanation for the springs at Cascade Springs nature trail.

then climb up on the face of the mountain a ways where you can look down on the slopes just south of Big Baldy. In the years since the trenching took place and where artificial seeding was done, not one terrace has been found to have been breached. In short, even though there are still many visible scars on the mountain tops, the restoration project appears to have been a success. Back in 1966, the project won the honor of *Watershed of the Year* as the outstanding project of its kind in the nation.

Cascade Springs & Cascade Springs Scenic Drive

If you're out for just a weekend drive along the Alpine Scenic Loop, and aren't interested in doing any mountaineering, you might consider taking the short drive to Cascade Springs. This road begins about 200 meters downhill and to the south of the Timp Divide, which is the high point along the loop road. A sign points out the paved road running east to Cascade Springs, a distance of about 10 kms. This road was first upgraded and graveled beginning in the late 1960's, but paving wasn't finished until September 15, 1971.

The **Cascade Springs Scenic Drive** runs downhill as it zig zags to the east ending at an area with a number of very large springs. From near the end of the paved road, you can turn off onto one of three rough dirt roads and drive in the direction of Deer Creek Dam to the south, or into the Heber Valley.

Cascade Springs has a large volume, something like 26 million liters(7 millions gallons) per day. Here's the reason why there's so much water at just this location. The springs are located in an area covered by glacial moraines and outwash which are about one million years old. This glacial deposit overlies the Park City Limestone. Water from snow melting high above seeps down through the glacial deposits and the Park City Formation, but when the Tintic Quartzite is exposed at the surface, all the water is forced out at these springs. There are 2 thrust faults in the area as well, which help force the water to the surface in this location.

Cascade Springs has been a gathering place for a long time. Indians used it long before the white men discovered the west. Sometime in the early history of the Heber Valley, pioneers from both Heber and Midway built a small sawmill not far below the springs, and used the swift flowing water to power it. The sawmill was abandoned when the timber ran out. Later, in the 1880's and 1890's and for many years afterwards, sheep and cattle invaded the region and overgrazed it to the point of making large gullies along the hillsides.

At the end of the paved road is a large parking lot with restrooms, and a picnic site with running water. At the west side of the parking lot is a little lookout and a map showing the trail system which winds its way up to the west. At first the trail crosses a small stream which is called Provo Deer Creek(this stream meets the Provo River just below Deer Creek Dam). Just beyond that, the dirt trail turns into a raised board-walk as it crosses over a series of shallow ponds. These ponds were created by the deposition of travertine from the water flowing from the main source which are about 250 meters uphill to the northwest. The travertine is dissolved by the water as it seeps through the limestone beds above, then it's left as deposits when the water reaches the atmosphere.

In this lower area, there appear to be no springs, but the different ponds are separated by little rims of travertine, that look something like the *bath tub rings* around some of the hot springs in Yellowstone Park. There are fish in these ponds which hide in the bright green moss, cattails and watercress. Fishing is not allowed in this immediate area.

From the lower ponds, the trail splits. One branch goes up the south side and another heads up along the north side of the moderately large stream making a loop trail around the little basin where all the water originates. Take either one and you will automatically make the loop hike and return back to the starting point. While there are many springs in the region, this has to be one of the largest in the state.

Going to Cascade Springs is an excellent outing for the whole family and well worth the trip. The road is paved all the way from the Alpine Scenic Loop, and it should be open as long as the loop road is. This road should be open from about June 1 until the first part of November, but each year is different. October is an excellent time to visit the place with all the fall colors. From these springs you can just barely see the top part of Timp in the background.

Small bridge over the creek at Cascade Springs.

The lower part of the Cascade Springs natural area, and the small ponds built by travertine deposits.

Rocky Mountain Goats in Utah and on Mt. Timpanogos

When the Mormon pioneers first came to Utah there were no Rocky Mountain Goats in the state, according to most researchers. But there have been conflicting reports about their existence in the northern Wasatch and Uinta Mountains from that time period. It's likely they were not in the state at that time. However, there is evidence that goats did inhabit some regions of the state in prehistoric times, such as near the end of the last glacier age. About 12,000 to 10,000 years ago, there were mammoths and ground sloths in the state as well. The dung from these two animals has been found in southern Utah sandstone caves in recent years and other dung in the same studies indicate goats may have been in the same area.

Even though these animals likely left the area hundreds of years ago, there are several areas in the state which are prime habitat for Rocky Mtn. Goats. Some of these areas are: all the higher peaks in the northern Wasatch Mountains; most areas of the Uinta Mountains; and in the La Sal, Deep Creek and Tushar Mountains.

In the 1960's, the Utah Division of Wildlife Resources contacted several states about the possibility of a goat transplant to this state. As it turned out, the state of Washington had a surplus of goats in the northern Cascades. So in 1967, the state of Washington trapped 6 animals, 4 female(nannies) and 2 males(billies), and they were trucked to Utah. The release site was on the north side of Little Cottonwood Canyon and at the foot of Twin Peaks.

Quoting now from a Utah DWR information sheet. It states, *only sporadic sightings of these goat were reported until the early 1970's when goats were observed in the Coalpit and Hogum Fork area of Little Cottonwood Canyon. Soon after that, goats were observed wintering on the south side of Little Cottonwood Canyon near its mouth. The largest concentration of goats seems to be wintering in the Coalpit Gulch-Bells Canyon area and moving to adjacent higher elevations to summer. During the summer of 1981, the goat population in that area was estimated to be about 60 animals.*

During July, 1981, 10 head of goats were obtained from Olympic National Park and put onto Mt. Timpanogos. They explored and used much of the mountain during the summer and fall seasons and then moved to the south end for the winter. It was later found that one of these first animals on Mt. Timpanogos was killed by an avalanche. An additional 10 head of goats were received from Olympic National Park during June of 1982. These animals, 3 males, 4 females and 3 kids, were put on Mt. Olympus in the Neffs Canyon area.

During July, 1986, six Rocky Mountain Goats(5 female and 1 yearling male) were captured using a net gun and helicopter in the Lone Peak area and moved to the Tushar Range of south central Utah just to the east of Beaver. In September of the same year, a mature male goat was tranquilized on Mt. Timpanogos and moved to the Tushar Range to increase the probability of successful breeding in December. All seven animals were released in the Mount Holly area but soon scattered throughout the available habitat.

During June 1987, eight Rocky Mountain Goats(6 female and 2 male) were captured using a net gun and helicopter in the Lone Peak area and moved to the Bald Mountain area in the western portion of the Uinta Mountain range.

On June 25, 1988, nine goats(3 billies and 6 nannies) were captured near Port Angeles, Washington, in Olympic National Park, and transported by truck to Beaver, Utah. They were transported by Utah Wildlife personnel after they were told by Washington state officials of the impending trapping date. This particular road trip took 20-plus hours, non-stop. As soon as they arrived in Utah they were quickly released into the Tushar Range east of Beaver, to supplement the original 7 head first introduced there in 1986.

Later in 1988, an additional 16 goats(10 billies and 6 nannies) were taken out of Olympic National Park and released in the Bald Mountain area of the Uinta Mountains. A total of 33 goats were transplanted in the summer of 1988 to two separate sites.

Utah's first Rocky Mountain Goat hunting season was held in September, 1981. The Board of Big Game Control authorized one permit for a mature goat in the area between American Fork and Little Cottonwood Canyons. A mature male goat was taken in the area of Box Elder Peak[due north of North Peak and Timp Cave]. Since 1981 there has been a goat hunt each year, but each year the number of permits has risen in accordance to the population. In 1986 and 1987, four permits were issued. See the table below.

Yearly Summary of Utah's Rocky Mountain Goat Hunt

Year	Permit Applications	Permits Sold	Harvest Male	Female	% Succ.
1981	214	1	1	0	100
1982	170	1	0	1	100
1983	228	3	3	0	100
1984	258	4	2	1	75
1985	217	3	3	0	100
1986	241	4	2	2	100
1987	287	4	3	1	100
1988	389	4	3	1	100

The Timpanogos Herd

Since the 10 Rocky Mountain Goats from Olympic National Park were first introduced onto Mt. Timpanogos in 1981, there has been a dramatic increase in their numbers. The Utah DWR has not kept an accurate record of the number of goats on Timp in part due to the rugged terrain, but in 1988 they estimated the herd had increased to about 50 head. The Board of Big Game Control has authorized one hunting permit for a mature goat for the fall of 1989 and plans are being made to move some goats to the Provo Peak area during the summer of 1989.

The author's experience with the goats came in the summer of 1988. Of all the hikes and climbs he did during the late winter, spring, summer and fall of that year, he ran into the goats on 4 occasions. In each case they were in the same general area. He saw some larger animals, presumably billies, on the top of Bomber Peak and the summit ridge extending south to the first peak north of the Timp Saddle, and he saw a small herd of nannies and kids on the first bench down on the east side of the summit ridge not far north of the Timp Saddle on two separate trips. See Map 13 for a look at what the author calls Goat Pasture. On a fourth trip, he spotted several head on the steep North Face of Bomber Peak, as he viewed it from the top of Forgotten Peak.

On one trip to the top of Bomber Peak, the author got within about 15 meters of several goats, presumably billies. They didn't seem anxious to run, but instead held their ground. They did tend to begin to wander off upon closer inspection. A telefoto lens captured some good close-up fotos. On two occasions, the author found a herd of nannies and kids(13 and 17 goats) on the same bench level as the B-25 crash site, but closer to the Timp summit trail. In each case the animals seemed curious, but did not run. They did however, begin to move away as the author got to within about 12 to 14 meters. The young kids were found to be playful and fun to watch.

One hiker who had seen goats on the mountain reported seeing one on the steep north face of the Timp Summit. Another man saw several on the cliffs and crags on the east face of Southwest Peak, which is one of several jagged summits making up the South Peaks around the Big Provo Hole. Several people said they saw nannies and kids in the area around Emerald Lake during early summer hikes. Still another story came from a fellow who came upon a large billy lying on the trail not far from the summit of Timp. The billy refused to move off, so the hiker had to go around to get to the summit.

From the testimonies of the people the author spoke to, it appears these goats have some of the same characteristics as our domestic goats. This means a little stubbornness, some fearlessness and high intelligence. Perhaps there are two reasons why these goats don't run when you approach. First, they were likely rather tame and hadn't been hunted when they arrived on Timp from Olympic National Park; and second, this herd has not yet been hunted. All hunts for the goats thus far have been in areas north of American Fork Canyon and in the Lone Peak area. It's also likely there are some goats which attempt to hide in more inaccessible corners of the mountain and which are less likely to be tame.

Rocky Mountain Goats in some ways eat the same type of food as deer. Basically they are browse eaters, just like deer, but like our domestic goats they will eat anything. In the high meadows of Mt. Timpanogos, there seems to be only grass, flowers and a few other small shrubs. In winter, the goats head down to the lower slopes to the south and southwest, where they eat shrubs and browse of various kinds.

If you'd like to fotograph the goats, it's best to head for the mountain starting about the end of June and the first part of July. During this time you will likely see some nannies and kids in the Hidden

Lakes Cirque, near Emerald Lake and around the Timpanogos Basin. Use a telefoto lens if you have one. Look up on the face of the cliffs and on the tiny ledges for the billies, and in the basins for the nannies and kids. When late summer comes, look for goats around the remaining snowbanks. During the hottest time of year they seem to congregate on top of snowdrifts to cool off. The author remembers many of the goats had their mouths open and tongues hanging out on hot days.

From a distance, the male and female goats look almost identical, at least to the un-trained observer. But the billies are much larger than nannies, some weighing as much as 135 kgs(300 lbs.). They both have a white coat of fur or wool, which they shed in the early summer. Both male and female have black horns, but the horns of the male are a little thicker, and have a slightly tighter curve near the upper end.

Billy goat standing on top of Bomber Peak.

Rocky Mountain Goats look for snowbanks to cool off on during the middle of summer.

Tragedies on Mt. Timpanogos

Over the years there have been a number of people perish on the slopes of Mt. Timpanogos. Some have died from plane crashes, others from falls over cliffs or through snow bridges above one of the streams, several have frozen to death while deer hunting and there have been 3 girls believed murdered at Aspen Grove and in American Fork Canyon.

In researching the different events discussed below, the author first asked various people in the valley, especially some of the old-timers living in Pleasant Grove, if they could remember when anyone had died on the mountain. After that the next step was to go to newspaper microfilm files and try and locate the event. Sometimes it was necessary to make many telefone calls to get a closer date for the event. A year and a month was enough, but it's hard to remember such things, unless a tragedy occurred to friends or was connected to some special occasion.

Another very helpful source was the self-published diary of Utah County Sheriff Mack Holley, who served in the area from 1960 until 1985. From his diary, many important events were discovered. In some cases he gave details, but in other cases it was necessary to go to the newspaper files to fill in the blanks. Most of what is below are quotations from the Provo Daily Herald or its predecessor.

It's very possible some deaths have occurred on the mountain which are not discussed here. If any readers have knowledge of any accidental deaths on the mountain which are not listed below, please contact the author.

Man Hangs Himself with his own Belt in Battle Creek Canyon at what is now Hangman's Spring.

The author has never been able to track down enough information about this story to make it solid. Many people in Pleasant Grove seem to know of someone going up Battle Creek Canyon and hanging himself, but no dates or positive names have been found. One report said it was a guy named Harriman, someone else stated it was a Walker. No one is sure of when the event occurred, but it seems to have been before the 20th century. The event allegedly happened at a place now called Hangman's Spring, which is very near the beginning of the Curly Spring Trail as it leaves Battle Creek.

Snowslide Covers Ranch, Buries One Man--February 19, 1897.

Throughout the years there have been many snowslides in Provo Canyon. The place most often hit is the Bridal Veil Falls area. At that point, slides from both Lost Creek Canyon on the south face of Timp, and from Cascade Peak above the falls, often cover the highway, Provo River and the rail line. Another place big slides come down is at the mouth of Slide Canyon, about a km and a half down stream from Vivian Park. That's where the Olmsted Diversion Dam is presently located. The third place prone to avalanches is Snowslide Canyon, located on the northeast corner of Cascade Peak about 500 meters below Vivian Park. This is about where Frazier Park is located today, and where the old ranch belonging to Billy Ferguson was situated. In the early morning hours of February 19, 1897, a big slide came down Snowslide Canyon(south side of the canyon wall) and buried the ranch belonging to William W. Ferguson. Below is some of what was in the Daily Herald for Saturday, February 20, 1897.

The mangled and crushed body of William W. Ferguson was yesterday found entombed in eight feet[2 1/2 meters] of snow, in a portion of his cabin which had been swept away by a snowslide, by a crowd of workmen of the Power dam[Nunns power station]. He had retired for the night and it is thought was quietly sleeping when the calamity came.....

The slide must have happened during the night or early in the morning. No one has been found who heard the noise caused by the slide, and the first knowledge of it was yesterday forenoon when the power plant people noticed that the river was dammed off. Wm. Slick and others proceeded up the canyon to ascertain the location of the blockade. The men were horror-stricken at the sight presented at the Ferguson place where snow was banked up across the canyon, in places as high as fifty feet[15 meters].....On the east side of the mountain of snow everything was flooded; the rock work of the house was flooded, in fact it was a heart-rendering sight.

A man on horseback was dispatched to the city to notify the sons of the unfortunate man, while the rest set themselves to work with a will. Before the rescuing party from Provo reached the scene, the power dam people had, through hard work, picking, digging and cutting, reached the room in which

Ferguson slept. The unfortunate man was found lying on his bed, which was all broken down, on his back. A rafter which had fallen from the roof of the wrecked house, lay across the right side of his head.

Here's a story from the July 22, 1983 edition of the Daily Herald, which had recounted the event. *One more story: William Jonathan Clegg and Henry McMullin, brothers-in-law of Heber City, hauled a load of wood to Provo and sold it on Feb. 18, 1897. Returning to Heber, they stopped at Ferguson's for dinner and rest. They were tempted by Billy's invitation to stay overnight, but decided to press on and camp at Deer Creek. They learned the next day what their fate would have been had they accepted the invitation.*

In the same general area where the Ferguson Ranch was located, is presently a small RV and picnic site called Frazier Park. This is about half a km west or down-canyon from the Chalet Cafe at Vivian Park.

Giant Snowslide Kills 2 in Provo Canyon--March 28-29, 1924.

An article in the Daily Herald on July 22, 1983, brought back to life the events of a big snowslide disaster of 1924 in Provo Canyon. That full page story had fotos by Robert E. Curtis, showing men with shovels, a clam-shell crane, and several locomotives working to clear the snowslide away from the tracks and highway at the bottom of Bridal Veil Falls.

The first slide occurred on Friday, March 28. It came roaring down Lost Creek Canyon on the south slopes of Mt. Timpanogos and buried the highway, railway line and the Provo River. The next morning the D&RGW organized a large work crew to open the canyon to traffic.

A 75-man crew of the D&RGW Railroad was working to clear trackage from the previous day's slide when the avalanche of Saturday, thundered down from the cliffs above Bridal Veil Falls to the south. News accounts said watchguards saw the snow coming and fired their guns. With the warning, 30 men scrambled to safety. Fortyfive others were hit by the snow and debris. All dug out or were rescued except the two. Mark Hyslop's body was found April 1; Don Allred's four or five days later.

One man who wanted to be hired to work on the slide, but who missed the train on that Saturday morning, was Doren D. Boyden of Provo. He saw the slide later, and recalled seeing trees cutoff like a hedge and the remains of a team of horses which were killed.

Ohio Man Dies of Heart Attack on Timpanogos Trail--Saturday, July 17, 1937.

This death was the first ever on the Annual Timp Hike. Later in time two more would die from accidents, but this was from a heart attack. Here's part of what the Sunday Herald for July 18, 1937 had to say. *Wendell Pfouts, 53, Ohio School Teacher Succumbs to Heart Attack While Returning From Summit. Tragedy marred the twenty-sixth annual Timpanogos hike Saturday, as the life of Wendell Pfouts, 53-year-old Reliance, Ohio, school teacher, was snuffed out by a heart attack shortly after 10 a.m. on the trail near the glacier.*

Pfouts, a strapping fellow of 225 pounds[102 kgs], was returning with his brother, Dr. L. D. Pfouts of Payson, from the summit when suddenly he collapsed on the trail. James Blake of Vineyard, one of the first to reach him, said he saw him lying on the snow-covered trail, about 200 feet[60 meters] from the top of the glacier.

Dr. Pfouts, who was following but a few rods behind, ran to his brother's aid. With accompanying Boy Scouts artificial respiration was attempted, but all efforts failed to revive him. He was breathing faintly as Dr. Pfouts reached him, but shortly after Dr. Grant Y. Anderson of Pleasant Grove arrived and pronounced him dead. The doctor indicated death must have been instantaneous.

Blake and a nephew, George Blake, son of S. H. Blake of Vineyard, helped to bring Pfouts down to the edge of the snow, on the side of Emerald Lake. Runners were dispatched to get horses from the forest ranger to carry out the Ohioan, and inform Acting Sheriff Walter Durrant and County Attorney Arnold C. Roylance.....Owning to transportation difficulties, the body could not be brought down until late last night.

Three Deer Hunters Perish on Mt. Timpanogos--Tuesday, October 19, 1943.

The first we hear about these deer hunting deaths was in the newspaper of Wednesday, October 20. It states: *Two lives and probably a third today had been claimed by Utah county's deer hunting tragedy in which four hunters, two from Provo and two from Pleasant Grove, were trapped high in the Timpanogos mountains by heavy storms Monday night[October 18].*

Only one of four thinly-clad hunters who were caught by the sudden storm had been rescued alive.

He is Bill Hunter, 25, of Pleasant Grove, brought down by the posse Tuesday evening. Hunter was reported in "good" condition at the American Fork hospital.

One of the bodies was identified as that of Owen Ash, 31, of Pleasant Grove. The other was that of Ronald Malcon, 31, of Provo. The bodies were found on a ledge and had been pretty well swept of snow by the wind. The snow ranges in depth up to hip-deep, it was reported.

Hunter was found late yesterday with his severely frozen arms wrapped around a tree. He was found after weakly answering calls by searchers. He collapsed after being sighted.

In the Thursday, October 21 Daily Herald it states: The search continued today for the body of Merland Remington, 32, of Provo, one of three deer hunters trapped by heavy sudden storms late Monday high in the Timpanogos mountains off American Fork canyon.....

Bill Hunter, 25, Pleasant Grove, the lone survivor of the hunting tragedy, who was found by searchers late Tuesday.......told Deputy Durrant how the four stranded men tried desperately without success to build a fire in the ledges where they spent Monday night. Wet matches and fuel hampered their efforts. They burned their ration books, and finally, with the last match, tried to light a $10 bill.

Friday, October 22, 1943. Funeral services were being arranged today for A. Merland Remington, 32, of Provo, employee of the Pacific States Cast Iron Pipe company,.....Mr. Remington's body was found Thursday afternoon following an intensive search by friends, soldiers, and officers. The body was located in the snow not far from where two companions......were likewise frozen. Worker at the pipe plant turned out en mass to help find the body of Mt. Remington, their fellow worker.

One Girl Killed On Timp Hike--Saturday, July 17, 1954

In the Sunday Daily Herald of July 18, 1954, there appeared a story about the death of a hiker on Timp. Here are some excerpts. The 43rd annual Timpanogos Hike ended in tragedy Saturday, with a 19-year-old girl dead from a huge rock which struck her in the head as it crashed down in an avalanche from a ledge above the glacier. She was Vera Mecham, daughter of Mr. and Mrs. Lynn Mecham, 662 W. 1st N., who was making the hike in company with her sister and brother-in-law Mr. and Mrs. Van Washburn of Provo.

Witnesses said the rock, one of several which crashed down through a group of hikers, struck the girl in the back of the head. She never regained consciousness and died perhaps two hours later.....The accident occurred between 11;30 a.m. and noon.....The girl was carried from the point on the glacier where she was hit, to Emerald Lake at the foot of the glacier. She died there before help could reach her.

The girl's body was brought by horseback from Emerald Lake down to Aspen Grove, where an ambulance took it to Provo. Deputy Sheriff Harold Hansen said there was no evidence that the avalanche was started directly by hikers. No one appeared to be in the vicinity of the source of the avalanche at the time it started.

It was the first accidental death in the 43-year history of the Timpanogos Hike, according to the best memory of forest rangers long familiar with the event. Several years ago[1937] a hiker died on the mountain from a heart attack.

B-25 Bomber Crashes on Mt. Timpanogos and Kills all Five--Wednesday, March 9, 1955.

This story is explained in full under Map 13, the Timpooneke Trail.

Cessna 172 Crashes, Kills one Man, Another Survives--Saturday, October 7, 1961.

This plane wreck on the back side of Timp happened in the fall of the year during a snowstorm. The pilot, Joel T. Honey of Needles, California, was on his way to see his son Bruce who was a student at BYU. The plane took off from Needles late in the morning with two men on board and had a scheduled re-fueling stop in Delta, Utah. But the weather was bad, so Honey radioed Delta at 1:22 pm saying he was above the clouds and would continue on to Provo. At 1:53 pm, he made contact with the Salt Lake Airport asking for directional assistance. A few moments later the plane disappeared from radar southeast of Salt Lake.

Because of bad weather, nothing was done on Sunday the 8th, but some search planes went out on Monday, but to no avail. It was still bad weather, but the Jeep Patrol and Sheriff's Posse did get out. The search was all over Utah County, but they concentrated their efforts in the Mt. Timpanogos area. In the Daily Herald for Tuesday, October 10, it stated: BULLETIN--A Civil Air Patrol pilot from Dugway sighted wreckage of an airplane at the 9050 foot [2760 meter]-level on the northeast slopes of Mt. Timpanogos about 2 pm today.

Quoting now from Sheriff Mack Holley's Diary. *The white colored plane, covered with an additional layer of white snow was impossible to see from the air. An airforce helicopter from Hill Air Base, one of the many search planes used in the search, spotted a place where several trees appeared to have been sheared down. At the time of the spotting it was almost dark. Circling the area, they dropped a lighted flashlight to the snow covered ground, radioed the information to our search party on the ground, and flew back to Hill Air Base.*

It had been five days since the emergency locater transmitter had been picked up from the downed plane and the missing pilot and his passenger from California had been identified. We knew that if they had survived the crash, they couldn't last much longer. The ground search people began the ascent to the supposed crash site. In the dark, it seemed impossible to find the spot, but the group pushed on using maps and compasses to chart the way. It was probably a distance of about three miles[5 kms] from where the vehicles had been left, but it seemed much longer. Suddenly one of the search group spotted what appeared to be a dim light. On reaching the spot, it was found that the flashlight dropped from the airforce helicopter was shining up through the snow, where it had buried itself. A search of the surrounding area soon located the crashed plane. Mr. Honey, still alive, was found inside the fuselage of the plane. His passenger was dead. Miraculously, Mr. Honey had been able to stay alive, despite being badly broken up, by reaching the snow for water, and eating some candy he had in his pocket. How he stayed alive in the cold no one knows. He was a heavy man, over two hundred pound[90 kgs]. Carrying him out on a stretcher was no easy task. A path through the snow had been tramped by the searchers, but carrying the stretcher with three men on each side, straddling the beaten path, made it tough going all the way out.....A horse was used to bring out the body of the passenger, who must have been killed instantly.

In addition to this version, here is part of what was printed in the Daily Herald on Thursday, October 12, 1961. *Condition of Joel T. Honey, 52, despite a fractured dislocated hip, broken jaw, broken ankle, lack of food and exposure was described by his physician as remarkably good. His companion, William Royal, about 45, was killed instantly, a piece of metal from the plane piercing his head.*

Just before midnight[Wednesday], they found the Cessna, its fuselage pretty well intact, although wing tips were chewed up, down in aspens which rose to 20 and 30 feet[6 to 9 meters] above it. Joel's son Bruce had been with search parties ever since the plane went down and here are some of the things he told Bruce, who in turn told a Herald reporter.

Saturday afternoon he encountered extreme turbulence, and a "blank spot" on his omnirange

Scattered parts of the B-25 wreckage. These parts will be visible only late in summer and in the fall season when most of the mountain snows have melted.

One of the motors of the B-25 with the main summits of Timp in the background.

receiver. *Directly over the omni directional guide atop mountains west of Utah Lake an aircraft's home needle can't point to direction--just as the compass has no direction over the north pole. But the California pilot felt he was not over the Utah Lake Mountains......He saw a hole in the clouds and dropped down, Often pilots caught in Timp's violent down drafts have been able to pull out towards Deer Creek or Provo Canyon--but the Cessna was sucked down.*

The pilot saw the mountain looming dead ahead. There was not even time to put on full flaps. He pulled back on his stick, stalled in, and made a skilled crash-landing in trees.....He[Honey] estimated he was unconscious for 45 minutes following the crash. When he came to, his companion was dead. The entire instrument panel was smashed, and he could not radio for help. The mountain was enshrouded in a heavy snow storm with gale winds. He was cold and in pain, his hip out of its socket and splintered; his jaw broken in three places. His food was a few grapes.

He managed to crawl into the plane's baggage compartment, and donned three pairs of pants, a coat and a blanket. As the weather broke, and planes searched over head, he tried to signal them. He twice crawled out of the plane, setting fire to wings of the plane with gasoline. He shredded his blanket, and using ice balls for weight, threw them over the limbs of trees above him. When a plane circled at night, he blinked his flashlight at it.

Mr. Honey told his son he kept bumping the plane--which must have been painful in his injured condition, hoping to dislodge some snow from the wings and make it more visible. Several times land parties were very close to him.....

Mr. Honey,....was in full possession of his faculties, when rescuers reached him.....It was 1:30 am[Thursday, October 12] this morning as they began moving down.....About 3:45 am, they reached the loop road two miles[3 kms] below where an American Fork ambulance was waiting. At 4:30 am, he was admitted in Utah Valley Hospital, and into surgery for his hip at 9 am. And a fairly happy ending to a dramatic rescue effort.

Boy Killed on Timp Hike--Saturday, July 18, 1964.

This story comes from the July 19, 1964 edition of the Provo Daily Herald. *Approximately 2400 hikers reached the sun-drenched, wind-swept summit of Mount Timpanogos Saturday--but the death of a nine-year-old Orem boy turned the day into tragedy*

Paul Alan Neilson, son of Mr. and Mrs. Kirk Neilson of 466 E. 1834 S., Orem, suffered fatal injuries when he fell and rolled an estimated 300 feet[100 meters] down the east slope from the summit of the mountain. The child was brought back up the sheer cliffs to the top by a litter and ropes and rushed to the Utah Valley Hospital by helicopter. He was then taken to Salt Lake by Helicopter to Fort Douglas where the craft landed, and was rushed by ambulance to the Salt Lake LDS Hospital. He was pronounced dead on arrival.....

The boy's father was on the summit with him. In company with Bob Smith, Provo, and George Cunningham, Orem, of the Utah County Jeep Patrol, he descended the mountain by ropes to the child, who had stopped rolling just a few feet short of another 1000-foot[300 meter] cliff. The three brought the child back to the top, where a helicopter, which had been waiting at Emerald Lake, hovered just long enough to strap the litter on. The helicopter then descended to Emerald Lake......The child died of severe head injuries, including bad lacerations and skull fractures.

Just how the tragedy occurred could not definitely be ascertained. Two stories were current, one that a dog nudged him or frightened him as he stood near the edge just east of the summit house; the other that a gust of wind might have overbalanced him. Heavy gusts were blowing at the time. Where the boy went over, observers said it was about a 10-foot[3 meter] sheer drop, then a steep slide or roll to where he stopped.....The boy fell shortly after 9 a.m. By the time he was pulled back up the sheer cliffs by ropes in a litter and then taken to Emerald Lake and from there to Provo, it was nearly 1 p.m.

Two Killed, 5 Injured on Timp Haven Ski Lift Accident, Thursday, July 14, 1966.

On Friday, July 15, 1966, the Daily Herald states: Tragedy fell with a blanket of gloom on a gay and carefree summer camping outing of a group of LDS girls from Edgemont Thursday afternoon, leaving two dead and injuring five. Killed when they fell an estimated 40 feet[12 meters], according to investigating officers, from chairs on the Timp Haven ski lift in the North Fork of Provo Canyon were Mrs. Sherman(Lucile) Peterson, 49, of 526 E. 2825 N., Provo, and Susan Carroll, 13, daughter to Mr. and Mrs. Cecil Carroll, 531 E. 2950 N., Provo.

Susan was killed instantly when she apparently landed on her head but Mrs. Peterson lived for about two hours before she died, despite the valiant efforts of a team of five doctors.....Sheriff Ralph Chapple, in charge of the rescue operations and probe of the accident, said early investigation indicated one chair on the lift jammed against the pulleys at the top of one of the highest towers. The occupants of the chair were spilled out to the ground an estimated 40 feet[12 meters] below,.....the sheriff said there was a possibility the chair involved may have been swinging at the time it become jammed.

The jamming of the chair caused the lift to come to an abrupt halt which evidently "bounced" several other girls out of nearby chairs. A couple of girls who did not fall apparently became panic stricken and jumped. A number of the occupants of others chairs had to be lowered to the ground with ropes.

The tragedy occurred about three-fourths of a mile[1 km] above the bottom terminal of the ski lift, and the force of the chairs jamming moved the base of the giant tower about eight inches[20 cms].

Ray Crandall of Springville, one of the workers who built the Bridal Veil Falls Skytram, was also involved in the repair of the Timp Haven ski lift. He stated the problem was how the ski lift was designed. It was built to take uphill passengers only. The chairs on the cable were supposed to make the return run without passengers and without weight. This particular accident occurred as the passengers were on the downhill ride to the base of the mountain. Because of the design, the cable became disengaged from the pulleys, then failed to re-engage; thus the jamming of the chair against the ski lift support tower. Crandall and Paul Hunziker were hired to made modifications, so a similar accident would never happen again, but even so, the lift has apparently never been used during the summertime since.

Boy Falls to his Death Near Elk Point--Sunday, June 15, 1969.

The Sunday Daily Herald of June 22, 1969 carried this story. It appeared the boy fell and died Sunday, June 15, 1969. The body of Rickie Smith, 16-year-old son of Dr. and Mrs. J. Lowrey Smith, Murray, was found Saturday[June 21] around 11:45 a.m. near the top of Elk Point, a jutting peak east of Mt. Timpanogos[on the east slope of East Peak].

Finding the body culminated a week-long search that started when the boy was reported missing last Sunday night by his parents. Young Smith had left the family cabin just before noon to hike up Elk Point. When he did not return Sunday evening, his parents called the Utah County Sheriff's office.

The body was found by a group of eight veteran climbers who had been dropped on the peak of the mountain by helicopter. The group was surveying the peak and was about to divide and search down the mountain but before the climbers had hiked 100 yards[90 meters] they saw the body lying face down at the foot of a shale-covered area. The clothing of the boy blended with the terrain at that point according to Mack Holley, chief deputy for the Utah County Sheriff's Office. He said that many persons had passed near the body, but just had not been in the right spot.

The mountaineers had radio equipment and promptly notified the sheriff's office on the ground. The helicopter was flown to the spot and picked up the body, which was taken to the Jenkins Mortuary and then transferred to the University of Utah Medical Center for an autopsy. The autopsy was waived later, but an external examination indicated the boy had died from a fall.

The body was found almost at the top of Elk Point, at an elevation of 10,500 feet[3200 meters]. Holley said no one knew if the boy was climbing up or down, but it appeared that he had slid down the shale patch to the point where he was found. Holley said nothing had been touched in his pack and he had a full canteen, which further indicated that the boy died Sunday night.

Two Girls Murdered by Jim Winkle at Aspen Grove--Sunday, August 20, 1972

This story was first covered in the Daily Herald on Tuesday, August 22, 1972, and for several days afterwards. But the full story is best told by Mack Holley in his self-published book entitled, From the Journal of Sheriff Mack Holley.

On August 22, 1972, the bodies of Lillian Anderson, 16, [of Provo], and her sister-in-law, Kimberly Anderson, 17, [of Orem], were found under the floor of an old shack at the Dividend Mine, just inside Utah County, near Eureka. Autopsies revealed that both had been raped and shot with a 22 pistol.

Further investigation showed that Jim[Walter] Winkle, [31 years of age], recently released from the Utah State Hospital, had been with them, the husband, and a boyfriend on an early morning hike up Mount Timpanogos, above Aspen Grove [on Sunday, August 20]. The girls had become too exhausted to continue the hike. Shortly after, Jim, who was about 6 ft. 4[193 cms], and 240 lbs.[110 kgs], decided he also was too tired to continue.

Back at the car, Jim met the girls, where the rapes and the murders took place. Each girl was shot with a small revolver, which Jim had carried with him, unknown to the others. Because he had been such a friendly, innocent appearing person, these newly found friends had not suspected his potentially violent nature.

On the basis of Jim's disappearance, and other physical evidence we had accumulated, we got a warrant of arrest for him and put out a wanted broadcast. He traveled to Colorado after the murders, then caught a ride back to Salt Lake City within a few days, where he was arrested and held for us.

I had known Jim Winkle for many years, since the time he was about nine years old. He was always very large for his age, very friendly, and retarded. He had been a source of concern for neighbors, who suspected him of all kinds of mischief.

After shooting two horses, in a situation that appeared to have sexual connotation, he was committed to the state hospital, where he spent many years as a resident. He was finally released, a short time before the incident for which he was now arrested.

Jim confessed the murders to me. He had raped and killed both of them at Aspen Grove, then drove to the hotel in Provo, where he had been living, with both bodies in the car. He went to his room, changed clothes, and then drove to the place near Eureka, where he deposited the bodies under the floor of the old shack.

His confession was challenged by the defense attorneys. They claimed that it had been given because of his acquaintance with me, and that it shouldn't be considered as being voluntarily given. It was accepted by the court, however, and he was sentenced to prison for life. The appeal process finally took the case to the United States Supreme Court, where the conviction was upheld. Jim's life term wasn't long. He died in prison of a brain tumor, on July 6, 1976.

Murdered Girl's Body Found in American Fork Canyon--November 27, 1974. Another Ted Bundy Job?

This story comes from the November 27 issue of the Provo Daily Herald, and for several days afterwards. Sgt. Owen Quarnberg said the Body found Wednesday by hikers just east of the Timpanogos Cave Monument was that of Laura Ann Aime, 17, of Salem. The daughter of Mr. and Mrs. James Aime.

Miss Aime died of multiple blows to the head and strangulation, and she had been raped, according to the Utah Medical Examiner's office. The body was found nude, part-way down an embankment, just off the American Fork Canyon road, the sheriff's office said. The manner in which Miss Aime died parallels that of the murder of Melissa Smith, 17, of Midvale.

This murder went unsolved for many years, but privately law officers believed the killer was Ted

Bundy. Bundy was eventually put to death in a Florida electric chair on January 24, 1989, for the rape and murder of a 12 year old Florida girl. In the Wednesday edition of the Herald for January 25, 1989, some statements went like this, *Ted Bundy neither confirmed nor denied involvement in the 1974 death of Laura Aime of Salem during his interview with a Salt Lake County detective.....Bundy was specifically asked about Laura Aime, but he declined to comment.....During his talks with Couch and investigators from other agencies, Bundy "admitted in a general way connection with eight homicides in Utah".* Later another investigator said, *I'm almost sure Bundy was responsible for Laura Aime's death.*

BYU Student Falls to his Death from Cliff Near Timp Cave--Sunday, May 11, 1975

This hiking death was reported by the Daily Herald on May 12, 1975. *Van D. Bush, 26, of 362 N. 600 W., Provo, died Sunday afternoon in a 150-foot[50 meters] fall in American Fork Canyon near Timpanogos Cave. He and his wife, Lorraine, accompanied by the Don E. Liston family of American Fork went into the canyon about 1 p.m. for an outing. Mr. Bush went for a hike alone and tried to climb a cliff. He was about 150 feet[50 meters] up when he fell.*

Donnie Liston, 15, saw Mr. Bush fall and told her father, who summoned help. Mr. Bush was up the mountain about one-half mile[700 meters], according to the Utah County Sheriff's Office. Deputy Sheriffs Gail Peters and Merlin Hill, assisted by three Parks and Recreation men, and six American Fork ambulance and police officers brought Mr. Bush down with ropes and a litter basket. He was pronounced dead on arrival at American Fork Hospital.

Two Timp Hikers Die Falling into the Same Snow Hole--Sunday and Monday, June 8 & 9, 1980.

The Tuesday, June 10, 1980 edition of the Provo Daily Herald ran the following article. This Killer Snow Hole was the lower one shown on the hiking maps about a km above Aspen Grove. *In an almost astronomical coincidence, two hikers, each 26 and having the same first name of Richard, fell to their deaths in separate and unrelated climbing deaths Sunday and Monday. Utah County Sheriff's Sgt. Jerry Scott said Richard Weaver of Orem and Dr. Richard Lambert of Portland, Ore., both fell into the same 75-foot[23 meter]-deep crevasse on the backside of Mt. Timpanogos. Lambert had disappeared Sunday.*

Scott said both men were hiking off the main trail near the lower falls of Aspen Trail when the hiking accidents occurred. "There is no doubt that if the two men had stayed on the trail this would not have happened. It has to be a million-to-one chance that both men would have fallen into the same hole".

Scott said Weaver died about noon Monday when he apparently saw Lambert's tracks across a snowfield and followed them. The trail, according to Scott, was across a large snowfield covered by cracks and crevices in the ice. "They were only a little ways off the main trail but at this time of the year hikers should be warned of the danger of leaving the main path with so many uncertainties."

Sheriff Quarnberg said rescuers went to the crevasse, a deep crack in the mountain side which is still partially covered by winter snowpack, in an effort to find Weaver. When rescuers found a body at the bottom of the crevasse at 3:30 p.m. Monday, they assumed it was Weaver. "But when the body was taken out, it was discovered it was the body of Dr. Lambert." Rescue crews went back into the crevasse and found Weaver's body at 3:54 p.m.

Jerry Scott has told the author the sheriff's office and search and rescue groups around the valley have gone up the mountain on several occasions and blown up and made more visible the big snow bridge located on the lowest falls on the Aspen Grove Trail. This is about one km up from Aspen Grove and at the second of the two falls located there. Three hikers in the 1980's have been killed in the same location. For hikers, the trick to staying alive is to stay away from waterfalls while walking up the Aspen Grove Trail during late spring or early summer.

Brazilian Student Falls to his Death near Aspen Grove Trail--Friday, October 31, 1980.

In the Sunday edition of the Provo Daily Herald for November 2, 1980, is a story of a Brazilian boy who died falling from a cliff on the east side of Timp. *Utah County Sheriff's officers Saturday[November 1] located the body of a 24-year-old hiker who fell to his death while descending Mt. Timpanogos with five friends.*

Killed in the fall was Milton Amoral DoSantos, 24, of Saõ Paulo, Brazil, who was living in Provo at 138 S. 300 W. No.2. The Sheriff's Department was notified of the accident Friday at 7:15 p.m. by two of the hikers, Ken Salt and Marcos Gomez, both of Provo, who hiked down to the nearest telephone.

They told officers their companion had fallen and the party had been unable to locate him because of darkness.

Officers hiked the mountain with warm clothing for the party, but were not able to locate DoSanto's body until daylight. The accident took place above the three-mile[5 km] marker on the Aspen Grove side of Mt. Timpanogos.

Another Hiker Falls to his Death and "Killer Hole" Dynamited on Timp-- Sunday, May 23, 1982.

Still another tragic story is told in the Tuesday, May 25, 1982 edition of the Provo Daily Herald. This was the third death in two years of a hiker who fell through a thin snow bridge along the normal route up the mountain and near the Aspen Grove Trail. This accident occurred at the lower Killer Snow Hole, which is about one km above Aspen Grove.

Utah County Sheriff's deputies today were hoping to dynamite a hazardous portion of the Aspen Trail behind Mt. Timpanogos after a 29-year old Nephi man fell to his death Sunday. Sheriff Mack Holley identified the victim as Terrence Brown, 29 of Nephi. He was an employee of the U. S. Geological Survey, working out of Denver, Colo., when the accident occurred. But he was not working on any project when he began his climb Sunday.

Brown's hiking death occurred in the exact same area as two fatalities two years ago when two men died in separate hiking incidents about one mile[1 1/2 kms-actually closer to one km] up the Aspen Grove Trail. Brown first was reported missing Monday morning when a fellow worker told the Sheriff's Department about the man not being seen since 7 a.m. Sunday morning. All three died when they fell on the ice-covered trail and into a snow cavern about 60 feet[18 meters] deep.

So hazardous is the trail area that explosives experts from the sheriff's department, led by Sgt. Jerry Scott, planned to dynamite the trail and several fragile ice bridges to remove some of the extreme danger. Just after the man was reported missing, the sheriff's department received a phone call from the Pleasant Grove Ranger District, telling about a truck left unattended with a dog, in the parking lot of Aspen Grove.

A party of three searchers--Lt. Owen Quarnberg, Deputy George Cunningham and Brown's co-worker--hiked the trail and found the body about noon. The victim was lying face down in some water. The body had a large gash on the back of the head, apparently from hitting some rocks in the fall. After making positive identification, the rescuers hiked back and called an additional six men from the jeep patrol to help carry the body down the mountain.

Holley cautioned hikers to stay off the high mountain trails along the Wasatch Front since hazardous snow conditions still exist. "It can be very deceiving. While some trails look good and firm with the snow they are not. In this case, water from a waterfall had eaten away at the snow and made small caverns under the trail".

Another Killer Hole Takes an Orem Youth--Saturday, July 3, 1982.

The fourth death from people falling through thin snow bridges in a two year period was reported in the Monday, July 5, 1982, edition of the Provo Daily Herald. This accident occurred just a short distance down from the lip of the upper basin called Hidden Lakes Cirque and near one of the upper-most waterfalls near the Aspen Grove Trail. The person who wrote this article made several mistakes. The author made corrections in parenthesis.

Utah County jeep posse and deputies recovered the body of a 14-year-old Orem youth Sunday off the Aspen[Grove] Trail after he fell 70 feet[21 meters] to his death late Saturday while hiking with some friends. A sheriff's dispatcher identified the victim as Mark Morgan[Gordon], 14, of 242 N. 400 W., Orem. He was hiking with five friends above Emerald Lake on the steep Aspen[Grove] Trail when he fell into an ice cavern.

The boy's death is the third[actually the fourth] on the Aspen[Grove] Trail in the past two months[two years]. Forest Service officials were forced to closed off the trail in late May when two[one] hikers lost their lives when they fell into the same ice cavern about a mile[1 1/2 kms] up the Aspen[Grove] Trail. After the second death[one death in May], sheriff's demolition experts, led by Sgt Jerry Scott, dynamited the cavern easing some of the hiking danger.

After the Orem youth fell to his death Saturday, his five hiking companions went down the mountain and notified authorities about 8 p.m. Saturday night. The Utah County Jeep posse and other rescuers climbed the trail and reached the accident location a few hours later. A Lifeflight helicopter was placed on alert in case the youth survived the fall into the 70-foot[21 meter] ice crevice. But a sheriff's deputy was lowered into the hole and confirmed the boy had died in the plunge.

Because of darkness, difficult terrain and deep water in the ice crevice, rescuers were forced to abandon recovery attempts Saturday. But by 1 p.m. Sunday, the body had been recovered and taken to the state medical examiner's office in Salt Lake City for an autopsy.

The location of this accident was much higher on the mountain than the previous site. On the hiking maps it's called the *Upper Killer Snow Hole*. The site is about 4 or 5 kms up the Aspen Grove Trail and just a short distance down from the lip of the upper basin. The hole was next to a cavern created by the stream coming out of Emerald Lake. The accident occurred because the hiker went straight down the mountain and near to the partially hidden waterfall rather than staying on the trail-- which at that time was snow-covered on that part of the mountain.

Orem Girl Killed in Fall from Ledges at the Bottom of the Big Provo Hole- -Monday, September 23, 1985.

This death happened during an Orem High School outing and was reported in the Daily Herald on September 24, 1985.

A quiet somber mood fills the halls at Orem High School today after a 17-year-old Orem High School coed was killed and another seriously injured Monday when they fell on Mt. Timpanogos. A Utah County Sheriff's spokesman said Tammy Witt, 17, was killed between 4 p.m. and 5:30 p.m. when she slipped and fell while hiking with other students.

Injured in a separate fall was Diana Bitter who was listed in serious condition at Utah Valley Regional Medical Center this morning. Orem High School Principal Berdean Jarman said the coeds were part of a group of about 50 students in an outdoor class. The sheriff's department identified the class as the Unified Study Group.

A sheriff's spokesman said Witt was apparently walking with part of the group and slipped on snow and started falling down the mountain. Jarman said students climbed up Aspen Grove trail and had circled into the Finger's area of the Provo Cirque where they were coming down a trail above the Stewart Falls.

The falls apparently occurred as the students slipped on snow and started falling down the mountain. Search and Rescue Team spokesman John L. Valentine said the accidents occurred in the Finger's area east and south of the Aspen Grove Trail[it occurred 300-400 meters south and above Stewart Falls].

The Utah County Sheriff's search and rescue unit was called to help rescue the victims, and helicopters were used for both the victims and to bring some other students off the mountain.

Orem Boy Scout Falls to his Death near Stewart Falls--Saturday, July 16, 1988

The last accidental death on Mt. Timpanogos before this book went to press, was a boy at Stewart Falls. It was featured in the Sunday Herald on July 17, 1988.

Kendall John Fletcher, 12, Orem, died Saturday, July 16, 1988 of injuries suffered in a fall near Stewart Falls in the north fork of Provo Canyon. A spokesman for the Utah County Sheriff's office reported the victim was camping with a group of Boy Scouts and two leaders when he and a friend went hiking alone at approximately 10 a.m. On his way back to the group, the boy lost his handhold while climbing across a rock wall. He fell 50 feet[15 meters] and then slid another 75 feet[23 meters].

Sheriff's reports indicate the boy died at the scene. His body was taken by Lifeflight to the Utah Valley Regional Medical Center.

Further Reading

A History of Sundance(manuscript copy-1987), Justin C. Stewart(to be published in 1989-90? by Sundance Institute?)

A Study of the Geology of The Timpanogos Caves, Kenneth C. Bullock, 1942, Geology Dept, BYU, Provo, Utah.

An Outline History of Provo Canyon, Eugene E. Campbell, unpublished manuscript, BYU Archives.

ATV Opportunity Guide, Uinta National Forest, Provo, Utah.

Cloudburst Floods in Eastern Utah County--A History of Destruction and Restoration, Rodney Greeno, Uinta National Forest, Provo, Utah.

Early History of American Fork, George F. Shelley, Published by American Fork City, 1945.

Eugene L.(Timp) Roberts--A study in Leadership, Gertrude Roberts Cash, 1959, Phys. Ed. Department, BYU.

From the Journal of Sheriff Mack Holley, Mack Holley, Self-Published, 1986, Spanish Fork, Utah.

Geology of Baldy Area, West Slope of Mount Timpanogos, Utah County, Utah, Ben L. Olsen, BYU Geology Dept., Provo, Utah, 1955.

Great Basin Kingdom, Leonard J. Arrington, University of Nebraska Press, Lincoln, 1968.

History of Wildwood, Maria Dixon Taylor, unpublished manuscript, BYU Archives.

How Beautiful Upon a Mountain--A Centennial History of Wasatch County, William J. Mortimer, Daughters of the Utah Pioneers, 1963.

Information on Cascade Springs, US Forest Service handout. **Information Handbook,** Uinta National Forest, Pleasant Grove.

L.L. Nunn: A Memoir, Stephen A. Bailey, Telluride Association--Ithaca, New York, 1933.

Memories That Live: Utah County Centennial History, Emma H. Huff and others, Daughters of the Utah Pioneers, 1947.

Mt. Timpanogos Wilderness, Implementation Plan, Uinta National Forest, Pleasant Grove, Utah.

Provo Daily Herald and Provo Post, various articles on the Annual Timp Hike and deaths on Timp from 1897 until 1989.

Recreation Residences in National Forests: American Fork Canyon, Utah--A Case Study, Douglas Gore, Thesis, Geography Dept, BYU, Provo, Utah, 1976.

Snowmobile Guide--American Fork Canyon, Pleasant Grove Ranger District, Uinta National Forest Publication.

Sundance, information brochure, Sundance, Utah.

The Changing Impact of Man in American Fork Canyon, Gary Vern Keetch, Thesis, BYU Geography Department, 1968.

The Timpanogos Cave Story, George V. Martin, Hawkes Publications, Salt Lake City, Utah, 1973.

The Timpanogos Trail(Thirteenth Annual Hike, July 18 and 19), BYU, 1924.

Timpanogos Shelter at Emerald Lake(Dedicatory Ceremonies on Saturday July 16, 1960), Uinta National Forest, Pleasant Grove, Utah.

Timpanogos Town(Story of Old Battle Creek and Pleasant Grove, Utah), Howard R. Driggs, self-published?

Timpanogos--Wonder Mountain, BYU Extension Division, Provo, Utah, July 1922.

Tri-County Railroad Development Economic Feasibility Study, James Webster Associates, 19 Exchange Place, Salt Lake City, Utah. Also at Mountainland Association of Governments, 2545 N. Canyon Road, Provo, Utah.

Uinta National Forest, Pleasant Grove Ranger District, Watershed Status Report, American Fork--Dry Creek PL 566 Project, Uinta National Forest, Provo, Utah.

Uinta National Forest(Map), USDA, Ogden, Utah.

Utah's First Forest's First 75 Years, Uinta National Forest, Provo, Utah, 1972.

Other Guide Books by the Author

Climbers and Hikers Guide to the World's Mountains(2nd Ed.), Kelsey, 800 pages, 377 maps, 380 fotos, waterproof cover, 14cm x 21cm(5 1/2" x 8" x 1 1/2"), ISBN 0-9605824-2-8.
(Sold out--3rd Ed. coming in 1990)
Utah Mountaineering Guide, and the Best Canyon Hikes(2nd Ed.), Kelsey, 192 pages, 105 fotos, ISBN 0-9605824-5-2. US $7.95 (Mail orders US $9.00).
Canyon Hiking Guide to the Colorado Plateau(2nd Printing), Kelsey, 256 pages, 117 hikes and maps, 130 fotos, ISBN 0-9605824-1-5. US $9.95 (Mail orders US $11.00).
Hiking Utah's San Rafael Swell, Kelsey, 144 pages, 30 mapped hikes, plus lots of history, 104 fotos, ISBN 0-9605824-4-4. US $7.95 (Mail orders US $9.00).
Hiking and Exploring Utah's Henry Mountains and Robbers Roost, Kelsey, 224 pages, 38 hikes or climbs, 163 fotos, including The Life and Legend of Butch Cassidy, ISBN 0-9605824-6-0. US $8.95 (Mail orders US $10.00).
Hiking and Exploring the Paria River, Kelsey, 208 pages, 30 different hikes from Bryce Canyon to Lee's Ferry, including the Story of John D. Lee, Mountain Meadows Massacre and Lee's Ferry, 155 fotos, ISBN 0-9605824-7-9. US $8.95(Mail Orders US $10,00).
Hiking and Exploring in the Great Basin National Park--A Guide to Nevada's Wheeler Peak, Mt. Moriah, and the Snake Range, Kelsey, 192 pages, 47 hikes or climbs, 125 fotos, ISBN 0-9605824-8-7. US $8.95(Mail Orders US $10.00).
Boater's Guide to Lake Powell: Featuring Hiking, Camping, Geology, History and Archaeology, Kelsey, 288 pages, 256 B+W fotos, ISBN 0-9605824-9-5. $10.95(Mail Orders $12.00).
China on Your Own, and The Hiking Guide to China's Nine Sacred Mountains(3rd and Revised Ed.), Jennings/Kelsey, 240 pages, 110 maps, 16 hikes or climbs, ISBN 0-9691363-1-5. US $9.95(Mail Orders US$11.00)(Please order this book from Milestone Publications, P.O. Box 35548, Station E, Vancouver, B.C., Canada, V6M 4G8).

Distributors for the Kelsey Publishing

Please write to one of these companies when ordering any of Mike Kelsey's guide books. The one which should carry all of his books is Wasatch Book Distribution in Salt Lake.

Primary Distributor
Wasatch Book Distribution, P.O. Box 1108, Salt Lake City, Utah, USA, 84110, Tele. 801-575-6735.

Alpenbooks, P.O. Box 27344, Seattle, Washington, 98125, Tele. 206-672-9316
Bookpeople, 2929 Fifth Street, Berkeley, California, 94710, Tele. 227-1516
Canyon Country Publications, P. O. Box 963, Moab, Utah, 84532, Tele. 801-259-6700
Gordon's Books, 2323 Delgany, Denver, Colorado, 80216, Tele. 303-296-1830
North Arizona News Company, 1709 East Street, Flagstaff, Arizona, 86001, Tele. 602-774-6171
Many Feathers, 2626 West, Indian School Road, Phoenix, Arizona, 85012, Tele. 602-266-1043
Nevada Publications, 4135 Badger Circle, Reno, Nevada, 89509, Tele. 702-747-0800
Pacific Pipeline, Inc., 19215 66th Avenue S., Kent, Washington, 98032-1171, Tele. 206-872-5523
Quality Books(Library Distributor), 918 Sherwood Drive, Lake Bluff, Illinois, 60044, Tele.
Mountain 'n Air Books, 3704 1/2 Foothill Blvd., La Crescenta, California, 91214, Tele. 818-957-5338
Recreational Equipment, Inc.(R.E.I.), P.O. Box C-88126, Seattle, Washington, 98188, Tele. 800-426-4840(or check at any of their local stores).

For the UK and Europe, and the rest of the world contact:
CORDEE, 3a De Montfort Street, Leicester, England, UK, LE1 7HD, Tele. 0533-54379

Olmsted penstocks above the old power plant at the mouth of Provo Canyon

A winter scene from the top of Roberts Horn. The Timp Glacier left, Timp Summit upper right.